Google This:

The New Media Driver's License®

Curating more than 600 great resources on Blogging for Business, Social Networking, Google Tools, Facebook, LinkedIn, Search Engine Marketing, Search Engine Optimization, Online Public Relations, Pinterest, Twitter, and much, much more . . .

Richard T. Cole
Michigan State University

Derek Mehraban
Ingenex Digital

Foreword by Michal Lorenc
Google, Inc.

RACOM
COMMUNICATIONS

Editor: Richard Hagle
Cover and interior design by Sans Serif, Inc., Saline, MI

Published by:
Racom Books/Racom Communications
150 N. Michigan Ave. Suite 2800
Chicago, IL 60601
312–494–0100/800–247–6553
www.racombooks.com

ISBN: 978–1–933199–43–6

Featuring Favorite Resource Lists from . . .

Ross Johnson
CEO, *3.7 Designs*

Nick Lucido
Digital Strategy Team Member, *Edelman PR*

Andrew Miller
CEO, *Your Search Advisor*

Katie Delahaye Paine
CEO, *KD Paine & Partners*

Steve Rubel
SVP and Director of Insights, *Edelman Digital*

David Meerman Scott
Author, *Real Time Marketing and PR*

Greg Verdino
Author, *microMARKETING:*
Get Big Results by Thinking and Acting Small

To get more detail on the resources in this book, follow our advice and Google the phrase
followed by (G).

To our students,
clients,
colleagues,
families, and
friends.

ACKNOWLEDGMENTS

The authors appreciate the help of our publisher, editor, and "inspirer," Rich Hagle, and of the authors of various postings we have curated and highlighted in this resource guide.

We also wish to thank the following MSU graduate students for research assistance on the Pinterest and Instragram sections: Barbara Firman, Samantha Goldberg, Xiaoxing Han, Tyler Hoover, Qi Liu, Sanghoon Lee, Caitlin McEvilly, Nicole Roofner, Adam Sheppard, Simin Shi, Melissa Ann Sitek, Xiaomeng (Serena) Wu.

CONTENTS

FOREWORD

Would TV's ultimate mad man, Don Draper, survive in the age of the Social Media?

Social Media—

- Where a mere "text link" can be more powerful than the 30 second TV Spot;
- Where a 140–character "tweet" can have higher reach and impact than a full-page ad in the nation's largest daily paper;
- Where potential consumers are connected, always; and,
- Where consumers are more than willing to chime in and express their opinions on any brand, product, or service they choose.

The pace of this technological innovation is breathtaking, and the seismic change in the marketing and PR landscape it is creating is . . . well . . . it's unprecedented.

New media has changed nearly everything. It has changed the way individuals and businesses communicate. It has changed the way we conduct transactions, interact with one another, learn (continuously) and are entertained.

And most importantly, and pertaining especially to this important book, social media has changed the way we market with, and to, one another.

So, who is leading this change? Is it the academic community or the innovators at Google? Well, as much as the academics or practitioners would like to think they are in charge, the real change in social media is driven by and, to a large extent, designed by the consumer.

And in no greater way is this consumer-driven change obvious than in the fact that the consumer is writing the new rules for when, how, and for what purpose companies are allowed to advertise to her or him. The consumer is in charge.

Just think about this simple question: Where does a marketer go to find the consumer today?

There she is on AOL, GeoCities, or TheGlobe. No wait. He's over there. He's on Friendster or MySpace or, more likely, Facebook. Now there she goes over to Google+, something that didn't even exist a few of years ago.

Does the consumer still IM and email, or have text messaging and online sharing and posting taken over?

Does he or she still tune in every Thursday night for "Must See TV," or has online access to video content changed the way all of us watch TV—and altered what advertising we see or don't see?

Is the consumer still online only while sitting at the desk using the 28.8 modem plugged into a Gateway desktop computer, or is the consumer on a tablet, or a phone, everywhere he or she goes, 24/7?

With nearly two billion online consumers around the globe, and more than three billion smart phones, when we talk about social media we are no longer talking about a niche discipline for geeks.

Google alone has one billion consumers. Facebook boasts three-quarters of a billion. Every minute there are more than two days' worth of new video content uploaded to YouTube. Online consumption continues to grow, and it is central to our lives. Some people even believe that online access is a human right.

Simply put, social media and online marketing and public relations needs to be more than an add-on. It needs to be the cornerstone of any company's overall business strategy.

With such a head-spinning pace of innovation, coupled with unprecedented access to data and the ability to "measure" nearly everything, it's no wonder advertising and PR are still struggling. There is a seismic shift underfoot to overcome the imbalance between all disciplines using social media. The best evidence of this imbalance may be the fact that companies are changing their ad and PR agencies more frequently than ever, and that the average tenure of a Fortune 1000 chief marketing officer (CMO) is measured in fish fly years—the shortest of any of the "C-level executives."

Companies large and small not only want to learn, better understand, and leverage the new media, but increasingly they recognize they need to change. Yet so many are struggling to find the right resources and the right talent to help them do so.

I've heard that story time and again, all over the world, while meeting with companies and speaking at various events during my many years at AOL and now Google. I've heard that story from students and scores of executives as they struggle to figure out the world of the advertising industry. They notice that change is all round them, and they even recognize they are part of that change, but they want to understand it. And most of all, they want to take advantage of it.

Yet, despite the change going on all around us, the traditional way that advertising, marketing, and PR have been taught at U.S. universities hasn't seemed to change that much over the years.

Professor Richard Cole and my marketing colleague Derek Mehraban share my passion for new technology, especially in the way it empowers consumers, and in how it opens up great new opportunities for conversation-based promoting, selling, and relationship building. After all, imagine knowing not only your potential consumers' demographic characteristics (how boring), but also his or her likes and dislikes, moods, location, and, perhaps, intent.

Almost "all of a sudden" we are able to connect with our consumer at the "Moment of Relevance": What can I wear? Where can we eat? What should we drive? This almost entirely new concept is made possible by new media.

So, here's the key question. Would Don Draper embrace new media?

I think he would. He'd take a drag on a Marlboro and embrace technology and social media for what it is. It's a tool (an extremely powerful one) to connect. Draper would throw back his head, drawing down a shot of Scotch whisky, and offer the opinion that "you need to get connected and stay connected."

I think Don Draper would use this wonderful resource sampler as the authors suggest it be used—to jumpstart his journey into the exciting world of new and social media.

I think you should too.

Sincerely,

Michal Lorenc
Google, Inc.

INTRODUCTION

How to Use This Book

Whatever your job title, the skills you can develop with assistance from the resources in this book can help you go far in this new world of digital media. This book will help you use social media to:

- *Build your personal brand*
- *Sell products or find new volunteers*
- *Start a new blog or develop content for blogs that already exist*
- *Write and place digital news releases*
- *Master social media sites like Facebook, LinkedIn, Twitter YouTube, Pinterest, Instagram, and others*
- *Build communities of interest with customers or other audiences*
- *Practice search engine optimization and search engine marketing*

This book won't make you an expert in social media just by reading it. You need to practice social media day-in and day-out.

Our goal is to get you ready to venture into the world of social media on your own, visit some new territory and explore the best of the thousands of resources we've reviewed for this second edition of our *New Media Driver's License® Resource Guide.*

You won't be alone on this journey. You will have the advice and commentary of great bloggers, professors, journalists, and social media practitioners who have freely shared their experiences on the Web, and which we have highlighted.

During the past five years we have helped more than 1,500 students obtain a New Media Driver's License® certificate—certifying them as a successful operator in social media and new media marketing. In our hybrid class, our students work online, start blogs, practice SEO, and develop online marketing plans. They have also been of great help in identifying myriad wonderful resources on the variety of subjects we explore through this guide.

This isn't a book for the unmotivated, and it's not a "book for dummies" either. This book is an outline for ongoing exploration and self-instruction. To get the most out of it, the book requires your active participation.

We said this before, and it bears repeating: If you take this challenge seriously, you'll begin a lifetime process of learning and teaching and developing new uses for social media as a business tool that so many of us already take for granted as part of our *social life.*

PART 1

SOCIAL MEDIA

To get more detail on the resources in this book, follow our advice and Google the phrase followed by (G).

CHAPTER 1

What Makes Social Media Social?

There are about as many definitions for social media as there are definitions for public relations, and that's a lot. About.com says the best way to define the phrase social media is to break it down:

> Think of regular media as a one-way street where you can read a newspaper or listen to a report on television, but you have very limited ability to give your thoughts on the matter. Social media, on the other hand, is a two-way street that gives you the ability to communicate too.

Social media are part of the fabric of our everyday lives. They have been able to accomplish, almost overnight, what other media have struggled with for centuries as they've tried to be increasingly social. After all, newspapers created "Letters to the Editor" pages to hear from their readers and therefore to become more social themselves.

In order for true communication to occur, newspapers knew they needed to introduce *listening and responding* to their audience, as well as just reporting the news and offering their opinions. Radio stations also have long understood the importance of giving voice to their audiences by incorporating another media into their programming—the telephone. The call-in talk show and all-talk radio station is a concession to the importance of the give and take that creates customer engagement, an attempt to become more social.

But it wasn't until the Internet that media could become truly "social," and our world has changed. The "socializing" of all media is expanding daily and as dramatically as are the new uses for these media.

Consider what we learn from the *"The Social Habit 2012" (G)*, the study conducted by Edison Research and Arbitron.

> Social Media reaches the majority of Americans. This figure is driven by Facebook, which is now used by more than half of Americans 12 and older. The use of Twitter is also expanding rapidly. Roughly 50 million Americans 12 and older check their social media sites and services several times every day.

In what is described as the most-viewed Social Media video series, *"Social Media Revolution" (G)*, author Erik Qualman provides clear evidence of the significance and size of the social media revolution. Google it, and take a look.

To find out what's driving this unprecedented adoption of social media, we turn to social media maven Brian Solis who says we need to understand what he calls "*behaviorgraphics*" *(G)* in order to understand that the many reasons we "share and interact online, and the motivation for doing so, changes with circumstances, intentions, and experiences."

> The social landscape is populated by individual presences, but charted by its connections and how in turn they move information between them. These conduits represent the opportunities for brands and media to participate in and steer the sharing of usefully and mutually beneficial content.

Solis credits Forrester Research's introduction of *Social Technographics (G)*, detailed by Charlene Li and Josh Bernoff in their best-selling book *Groundswell (G)*, with providing a template for better understanding different use patterns among social media consumers.

Reminiscent of Everett Rogers's *Diffusion of Innovations (G)* scale, Forrester characterizes social media consumers as moving up a "Social Technographics® Ladder from Inactives through Spectators, Joiners, Collectors, Critics, Conversationalists, and, ultimately, to Creators."

Brian Solis believes that good content creation is an essential component of a brand's or individual's likeability in social media. He worked with *Vocus (G)*, another significant force in American research, to test his theory that it is the discovery and consumption of compelling content that helps a consumer move into the role of curator. Becoming a curator creates consumer engagement by balancing content creation with conversation.

"There's a reason why people 'like' you. The networks realize that as our networks both grow and contextualize, your presence increases exponentially in value and they can sell against it," Solis says.

Stephanie Schwab told SocialMediaExplorer.com that the first question any brand manager should be asking is: "Are we in the stream?"

"People are going to be much more diligent about curating their own content into a more manageable form. Consumers are realizing that following 'eleventy-hundred' brands on Twitter and Facebook is getting them some good coupons and deals, but it's also turning their walls into malls, which is getting overwhelming."

Figuring out solutions to being overwhelmed by content is one of the new trends in social media, Schwab says: "For brands, this means it's not going to be enough to create content. You have to create content that gets curated into people's streams. If your content is truly compelling and share-worthy, it'll get noticed and 'liked,' it will generate 'comments' and 're-tweets,' and you'll be okay. . . ."

Kip Bodnar, writing for Hubspot, posted *11 killer social media presentations (G)* that are freely and conveniently available to view on *Slideshare (G)*. First on his list is a great presentation from Rohit Bhargava on the 25 basic styles of blogging, and when to use each one. This is followed by a presentation of Olivier Blanchard in which he outlines the basics of social media return on investment. Do you need to answer a skeptical boss who wonders why you are spending so much time and company energy on Facebook? This might help.

Social Media: The Phenomena Revisited

Did You Know 4.0 (G) is one of many videos available in cyberspace that attempts to put numbers on the immensity of the impact of new. By the time you read this, we expect to see a version 5.0, but this immensely popular video remains a reminder of the speed of change in the world of social and new media.

While there's no shortage of conversation about the speed with which social media are changing, there doesn't seem to be much reflection about *the top three ways social media has changed our lives (G)*. Brett Greene's recent post on SocialMediaToday.com ponders this issue. Facebook, for example, has rapidly emerged as a *force majeure*, a great force with world-changing implications. But has Facebook and other social media summoned the grim reaper to the villages of all traditional media, killing off newspapers, radio, and TV? And are social media causing us to do our daily jobs at such a rapid pace that they are killing off the thinking that yields innovation and creativity? And, oh yes, is privacy a thing of the past?

Like us, Greene puts a lot of stake in the wisdom of Brian Solis, and he leans upon this social media maven to remind us that the question may not be so much as to whether or not privacy is dead, as to whether social media have created conditions in which privacy, and many other things with which we are comfortable, will never quite be the same.

You can believe that what goes on in Vegas stays in Vegas—or not—but BlackEnterprise.com writer Janel Martinez warns us that what goes on in Facebook may be a whole lot less private than our "settings" might cause the uninitiated to believe. She details information rolling out in FB's Data Use Policy and in its statement of Rights and Responsibilities to give us her take on why *new Facebook privacy policy ruffles feathers (G)*. "The more you 'like,' the more you will be tracked," she says.

Social media are changing and evolving so rapidly that for many—even experts in the field—coming up with a single simple definition is a difficult and complex task. "If you ask a heap of different people, 'What is Social Media?,' they will all give you a different answer," according to Matthew Tommasi. He compiled a list of *50 social media definitions (G)* from different industry websites to help.

If nothing else, Tommasi's list helps you frame your own definition of social media. It might also cause you to consider purchasing a copy of Tomassi's *The Social Media Guide (G)*, within which you'll find his preferred definition: "Social media is user generated content that is shared over the Internet via technologies that promote engagement, sharing and collaboration."

So, now we have that definition for social media we've been looking for, right? Well, not so fast. As Patrick Keane points out, as the Web becomes more social, the meaning of different social terms, including the term social media itself, becomes blurred. "Today, there is a lot of *confusion about terms such as social media and social networking (G)* buzzing through the Twitterverse."

Keane, CEO of Associated Content, uses an Adage.com post to explain the differences between the two phrases. And he stresses that these are not distinctions without differences. In fact, Keane says, how you understand the terms will, to a large degree, govern your behavior. How you behave in the commercial Internet will govern your success. "Until brands understand how to authentically join, rather than crash, the conversation, they will continue to throw their money away."

Once we decide on the social media terminology that best suits us, it's time to start winnowing down the list of the most effective and *essential social media resources (G)*. There's no more agreement on this subject than there seems to be on finding a single definition of what social media are. Google away and you'll find a range from nine to 90, literally—from SocialMediaToday.com's top *nine essential social media resources (G)* to the *90+ essential social media resources (G)* of Mashable.com.

Sarah Perez begins her ReadWrite.com column entitled *Social Media U: Take a Class in Social Media (G)* with the observation that many of the folks who are required to incorporate Facebook or Twitter or other new media into their business procedures could benefit from her free web class.

"Of course," Perez says, "the entirety of social media can't be summed up in any one blog post . . ." (nor can it be summed up in any resource guide or class, for that matter). But she does provide a handful of subjects ranging from using social media for personal branding to learning to podcast—many with embedded videos that help make her point.

Do you understand the concept of "six popped-collar cool"? Neither did we until a June issue of Ragan's PR Daily hit our screen with a photo we thought was of the author of the 2012 edition of *52 Cool Facts and Stats about Social Media (G)*, Danny Brown. (We checked out his Facebook page to see the real picture of this award-winning marketer and blogger. He's better looking, or at least, better shaved.)

Brown's column is a compilation of often hard-to-substantiate stats from sources as far ranging as The Economist and CNN to Google Investor Reports.

They cover five fun "facts" in 10 categories (there are two bonus facts at the end of the article) and ironically the subject areas track pretty closely to the chapters in this book.

We get into the details of weblogs, now called blogs, a bit later in the book, but if you want to be inspired on everything social and viral, you can join in the conversation on Viralblog.com. The blog is ranked 41 (up from 53 last year) in Ad Age's Power 150 as a top media and marketing blog and is a very interesting and credible spot to check out fresh, hot, and up-and-coming social media topics.

The goal of Viral Blog is to bring interested businesspeople the newest and best social media marketing ideas and strategies, and to examine viral campaigns. It's a great resource for social media entrepreneurs and experts to share their wisdom, predictions, and suggestions.

There's little doubt of the power of this new and social media, but a huge number of questions remain as to when it works, and how it works best. This is a question several of our academic and business colleagues are committing a large number of their working hours to trying to figure out.

In a comprehensive *"Case Study—Social Media's Effects on Marketing"(G)*, USA Today writer Jon Swartz uses the example of how Ford Motor Company went social to launch a new subcompact model, the Fiesta.

We can't help but think about how much the "social work" of Ford social media gurus reminds us of how a young *Lee Iacocca launched the original Ford Mustang in 1964 (G)* by filling an entire Midwestern town with loaner Mustangs in the hands of volunteer test drivers. This time, however, to prepare for the American re-introduction, *Ford gave 100 of the most influential bloggers a new Fiesta (G)* to try out. Ford's social media analysts had identified a variety of social media niches from which to draw their volunteer test drivers.

We remember a day when the Republicans seemed to be dominating the close political contests by using market segmentation and targeting tactics to use direct marketing to mop up the political street with their Democratic rivals. Well, the modern political landscape sure has changed. Now businesspeople who want to use the most modern social networking technology to gain a political advantage seem to looking to the Democrats for guidance.

Google this phrase: *What President Obama can teach you about social media (G)*. Brett Relander didn't wait long after the 2012 returns were in to deliver a clear assessment of how Barack Obama and his team used social media techniques to keep the moving vans away from the White House. This widely circulated article shares some of the key political techniques that should easily transfer to many a business that wants to deliver more to its bottom lines.

Old McDonald may have had a farm, but social media is the tune marketers are singing today. Nonetheless, Bill Seaver went to great lengths to tell the readers of SocialMediaExaminer.com *what Old McDonald can teach you about social media (G).*

Evolution, some say revolution, has taken a toll on advertising as consumers are developing the ability to block and ignore promotions they are confronted with every day. They are shunning persuasion in favor of conversation and fluff in favor of facts. "Consumers have developed extremely sophisticated filters. As a marketer, you're fighting that filter every day," says Seaver.

Founder of *Micro Explosion Media, (G),* a social media marketing consulting firm, Seaver provides the benefit of his experience in getting the attention of an increasingly reluctant and discerning audience of media consumers.

To break this barrier, he uses the pre-school song *Old McDonald Had a Farm* and "E-I-E-I-O" to remind us that we must Entertain, Inspire, Educate, Inform and (even occasionally) Outrage if we want to create valuable and memorable content.

Differentiate or die. That's been said in a lot of different ways, but we can't imagine it ever having been more important than today. One key to the social media success drill involves finding more ways to target audiences. Targeting, of course, allows us to build more direct communication channels with the people we need to reach while we avoid bothering those who don't want to talk.

Ad Age gave us access to tremendous advice on segmentation, telling us *which boomers are using social media the most (G).* More importantly, it showed us how social media consultant Laurel Kennedy zeroed in the most likely boomers to buy her book, *The Daughter Trap. (G)*

The book discusses the plight of the baby-boomer, generally people aged 50 to 65, often referred to as members of the sandwich generation. They feel like meat being squeezed between their children on one side and their aged and ill parents on the other. Kennedy worked with market research firm comScore to study a group of "Boomer" caregivers. She found "a great niche for marketers."

Roughly 20 percent of the country's boomers fall into the category of caregivers, and they are increasingly turning to social media, viewing 70 percent more pages per month than the average Internet user. It turns out that the number one reason caregivers are turning to social media is, well, the social aspect of it.

Says Matt Carmichael, "Being a caregiver, especially for the parents that always cared for you, causes all kinds of relationship stresses."

It's pretty easy to see how finding the sandwich segment within the social media boomer group was a powerful and direct way to sell books.

Strategies and Campaigns in Social Media

A lot of people are wary of social media's usefulness for business and marketing. Developing a campaign will alleviate some of this fear and start a social media campaign in the right direction.

SamHowat.com is among a rather strong list of experts available to show you *how to start a social media campaign (G)*.

> Though establishing a social media presence for your business can be a daunting task, there are several proven strategies for both establishing your campaign and tracking its results that you can use to get started on the right path.

For the kind of basic training a business manager might find useful as an *overall guide to social media (G)*, we're partial to the SocialMediaExaminer.com. Google that phrase and you'll find a starter kit that includes videos and articles that begin with the *2012 Social Media Marketing Industry Report (G)* by Michael Stelzner. This free report is full of "valuable information and includes answers to important questions such as 'How much time does social media marketing take?'"

Forget about the four or five P's of marketing. Paul Chaney, writing in PracticalECommerce.com, says as far as social media are concerned the four P's don't count, but these *four steps to an effective marketing strategy (G)*—his four C's—do: content, communication, conversation, and conversion.

A good deal of professional advice in this space gets down to understanding the shift that is occurring in buyer-seller relationships from a persuasion-based model to one in which conversation is infinitely more interesting, and profitable.

Gregg Crawford is a world-renowned strategy execution specialist, a keynote speaker, and founder of the successful BayGroup International, a consulting and performance improvement firm. His best-selling book, *The Last Link*, has helped thousands of entrepreneurs close the gap "that is sabotaging your business." Crawford says, "Every day, all over the world, businesspeople struggle to transform top-line strategy into bottom-line results." That's what Crawford's book is about, and that's largely what this book is about also.

The key to the drill, whether you're a devotee of Gregg Crawford, or *Sun Tzu's Art of War (G)* for that matter, is good strategy. Take it from the experts at Forbes.com who love to give us capitalist tools like *A Strategic Guide for Social Business (G)*. "Nothing in business today is more beneficial than developing a social business strategy. When we think of today's highest growth companies . . . there's one common denominator that permeates most of them, and that's the ability to quickly adapt to new market opportunities." They want the ability to "wow" people.

Forbes suggests going to Jacob Morgan's book, *The Collaborative Organization (G)*, for a detailed process for transforming a traditional business into a social one.

Founder of Converse Digital, Tom Martin works with companies and ad agencies, helping them monitor, create, and engage in digital conversations to grow market share or increase customer loyalty. Martin believes that "knowing how to use social media isn't enough." Effective companies understand *how to integrate social media with traditional media (G)*.

> So instead of asking how to integrate all of it, maybe a better question would be to ask 'how to think' about integrating social media, digital media, old media and the blending of all of it. We need to be asking for a framework, not a solution.

The post on SocialMediaExaminer.com provides tips to integrate social media marketing with traditional marketing in the right way.

Learning a strategic planning approach and identifying the goals of a social media marketing campaign is something marketers and advertisers should think about when meshing together social media and traditional media.

If you want to examine the issue from a slightly higher altitude, but with significant attention to detail, Debbie Hemley offers *26 Tips for Integrating Social Media (G)*. Her A-Z guide begins with Apps that are designed to build brand awareness and moves through the alphabet to Pam Moore's linked description of a Zoom agent—someone who takes responsibility for transforming a traditional business into a social one.

Remember, however beneficial you see the social transformation of your enterprise, money matters, and according to Ray Spellerberg, *Social media budgeting is one of the hardest tasks facing the marketing world at this moment (G)*.

Creating a budget for a social media campaign is often difficult because it is hard to determine how much money actually is required to do the job. Remember this, however. Spending only half enough of what your organization needs is worse than not doing anything at all. Think of this like taking only half the dose of medicine your physician prescribed to cure your illness. Half a pill won't be enough to cure you, and by shorting the dose in this way you may end up believing that the medicine was useless. You'd be wrong.

Mark Schafer, writing in BusinessesGrow.com, describes a long discussion he had with an analyst as he tried to answer the question: *How do you budget for social media marketing? (G)* He contrasts the cost curves for traditional media spends with a very different shaped curve for social media. The gist of his thinking seems to be that with traditional media, once your spending stops your awareness numbers begin to drop off. Contrast that to social media where the objective is to develop and sustain relationships with constant small engagements, rather than flamboyant, interrupting advertising. It's a great point.

Contrasting traditional advertising and its value to that of social media marketing is not easy and not entirely fair. Nonetheless, a variety of social media outlets are being used to pull customers in for a sale—and the targeting of these customers can be quite precise. The bottom line, however, is always the bottom line, in business circles called the return on investment (ROI.) *Enhancing social media ROI (G)* is the objective of a great deal of the resources available through EzineMark.com. Talk about resources! This free article directory is a large library of hundreds of bright and brief videos, and many more interesting articles, on virtually every aspect of social marketing.

Library of Congress look out. The world is changing so rapidly that it doesn't seem possible that even our greatest institutions could possibly keep up with the information freely available online. Come to think of it, many of these great institutions (read: dead newspapers) haven't.

One of our favorite "library" resources is CommPro.Biz. In fact, not a day goes by that they won't send you any number of great articles targeted to your needs and interests and delivered via good old-fashioned email.

Suppose you've made a Twitter account, Facebook, LinkedIn, and created some Search Engine optimized content. Now what?

Using these platforms is only a small piece of the social media marketing pie. A larger piece involves understanding how these tools can be incorporated into your overall marketing strategy.

Marc Meyer, a digital and social media strategist, writing in his personal blog, said his clients were requesting "that I should supply a document that mapped out the ways that you can blend social media into your marketing mix." So Meyer provided a list of *ten blended social media marketing campaigns (G)* a company might want to consider. As you can see from his graphic, Meyer uses the logos of a wide variety of networks to highlight the types of conversation being facilitated on the Web.

We know it's starting to sound repetitive, but we simply have to push you to another great resource from Altimeter's Brian Solis. His *Mashable.com (G)* posts are the cream of the crop, and he did it again with this *ten stages of social media business integration (G)*—a model patterned after Elisabeth Kübler-Ross's stages of death and dying sequencing the phases of grief a business should go through to fully integrate its social strategy.

Solis never really defines what he means by integration, but he obviously knows what it is when he sees it. It will become clear to you as you walk through the steps he feels are necessary for a business to be on the leading new media edge of its business segment. One point is most clear. Solis believes, as does KD Paine (who you will read more about later) and others, that true business inte-

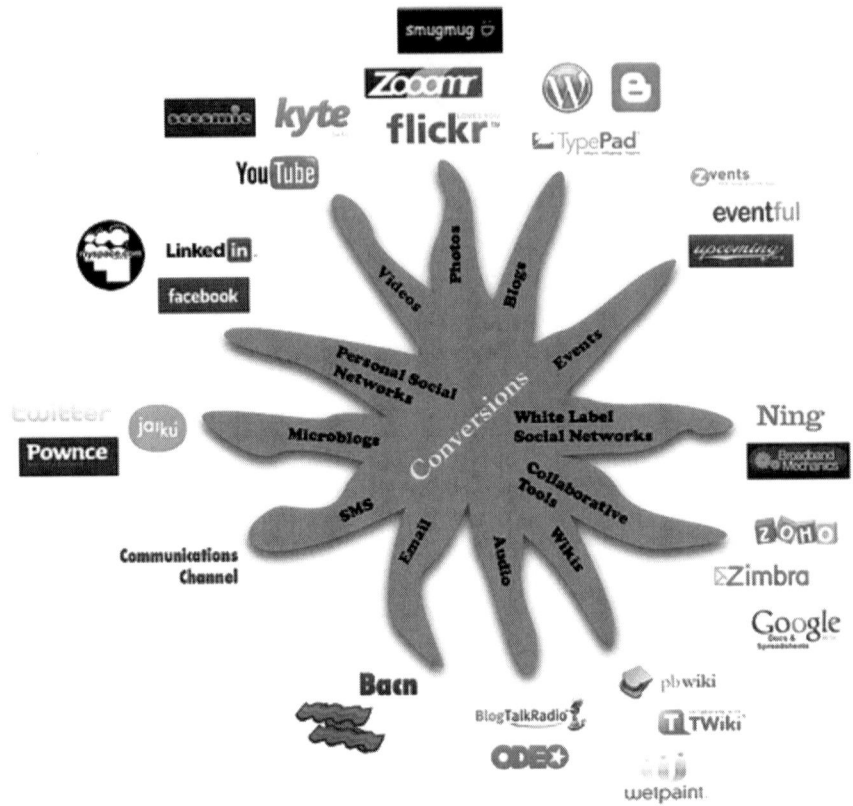

Source: Marc Meyer (Direct Marketing Observations blog)

gration of social media cannot occur until you have a full understanding of the "volume, locations, and nature of online interaction, the true impact of our digital footprint, and its relationship to the bottom line. . . ."

"Business Performance Metrics" is the tenth stage in the Solis model. Getting from steps one to nine may involve lots of grieving. It is never, ever, as easy to do this stuff as it seems on paper, but Solis makes a very credible case that there's something very important to experiencing all the stages along the way to full acceptance.

Adrants.com "provides marketing and advertising news . . . with insightful, informed, experiential, no-holds-barred commentary on the state of advertising. . . ." Its publisher, Steve Hall, has "done time" (in his words) in a variety of advertising agency-related jobs.

His list of *seven traits of successful social media campaigns (G)* is a common sense way to approach this issue because almost every trait focuses on the concept of authenticity. This post was repurposed by Chris Martin and appears on

BmPR.com. From "platitudes don't work" to the importance of avoiding "blatant self promotion," Hall's no-B.S. approach to campaigns should be required reading.

Jared from Subway, the Snapple lady, and the mothers of Walmart are benefitting from effective social media campaigns that follow a few basic principles.

Stephanie Marcus, posting in yet another Mashable.com site, describes how and *why social media is perfect for brand ambassador campaigns (G)* by amplifying "real people" advertising:

> The public, having grown wary of traditional advertising, has become more difficult to convince. That's where the brand ambassador—the person who creates a sense of credibility, likeability, or interest—comes in.
>
> Brands have realized that people like real people, and social media have the ability to take that one step further.

We suspect that it's the "dialogic-ability" of social media—when I get a tweet from a celebrity it feels like it's from her to me—that is the driving force behind this phenomena.

Marcus praises successful ad campaigns that mix social and traditional media. Her Mashable.com post describes how to create a lasting image, generate positive feedback and share content with others to promote your brand using ordinary people as the face of a social media campaign.

Well begun is half done, right? The international team at Virtual Social Media sure thinks so. Here's what they say:

> The social media marketing campaigning may get you noticed with prospective customers more quickly, leading your business to grow and build meaningful lasting relationships with people. But successful media campaigning requires sound knowledge about social media and other networking technologies.

If you want to know *how to start a social media campaign, Virtual Social Media (G)* outlines five basic principles that will get you on track to developing the kind of campaign that can make any business or nonprofit infinitely more effective.

As if you need a demonstration of how much free advice you can get on the subject, start with this phrase: *five ways businesses can use social media (G)*. You'll find approaches businesses can use to leverage social media productivity, to provide tools for progress, to build traffic at trade shows, to generate sales leads, and (an issue that seems to be of great interest to our students) to get jobs. There's more, and we recommend you start with a Forbes.com guest post written by Ryan Homes who spells out the *five ways social media will change the way you work in 2013 (G)*. Did you know that by the end of 2012, 73 percent of Fortune 500 companies were using Twitter, or that more than eight in ten executives believe that engaging in social media has led to increased sales for their businesses?

Not all social media campaigns work—or at least work the way you hope they would. And with social media marketing as with other things in life, finding the right answer might involve correcting a couple of wrong ones first. But when it comes to brand image, one thing worse than having no social media campaign might be having a weak one. The truth is that a weak social media campaign may be capable of dealing a setback to your organization's brand.

"Instead of watching a train wreck hurt your brand, there are *five warning signs of a weak social media strategy (G)* that you need to be aware of before things really get bad," says social media and marketing enthusiast Nehal Kazim. You may be able to fix a failing social media campaign if you know the warning signs.

Kazim's list of warning signs contains a bit of a tautology—using a bunch of different words to say the same thing—but we can handle that. His warning signs bear repeating. For example, sign number five of a weak social media strategy is "There is No Social Media Strategy in the First Place!!" And that's a point worth emphasizing.

"Ask yourself or your team, 'do we really have a social media strategy?' If you're not honest about this, all of your hard work will mean nothing. If you don't have a social media strategy, stop putting it off and get started," Kazim says.

What are the key components to consider?

- "Why are you participating in social media? Exposure? Sales? Creating bonds with your clients?
- "What's the expected ROI (Return on Investment)? Are you expecting too much too soon?
- "What's the content strategy? What will you post? Why are you posting that content? How is the content aligned with the reason why you're on social media?"

In Top Rank, the online marketing blog, Lee Odden reinforces Kazim's main point in laying out *the best and worst practices (in) social media marketing (G)*, saying, "Social media is hot . . . Along with that hotness, there's good and bad when it comes to the way companies are beginning to engage social media channels."

What's the worst of the worst according to Odden? "Being fake in any way isn't good for anyone on the social web."

Social Media: The Emerging Tool for Business

One of our favorite resources is *Business Wire (G)*, a Berkshire Hathaway Company. We don't see everything that they put out—they are a news release distribution enterprise, of course. But what we do see from BW is normally in plain English, capable of being understood by a man who would say, as would Berkshire's Warren Buffet, "never invest in something you don't understand." Business Wire seems to feel that if done right, *social media profiles increase consumer trust in e-commerce sites (G)*.

"With three million fraudulent or fake websites entering the World Wide Web every year, consumers are understandably wary about buying from sites that are away from the mainstream," PR social and search agency Punch Communications said in a presser released through Business Wire.

Source: Geico.

So what's the answer for companies in a category that may be a bit suspect, if you will, or at least seen as being too large to fail, like Buffet's GEICO, for example? Social media, that's what. And, now that you know this little GEICO gecko has a Facebook page, doesn't that make you "like" the company just a bit more?

Turns out it might. Social networking blogger and creator of Kikolani.com, Kristi Hines, lists *eight ways business should use social media (G)*. This resource can help you identify different ways your business should be using social media, for sure, but you have to put her ideas into practice. Hope is not a strategy.

Hines offers ways businesses can go social to learn more about themselves and their industry. It's also a key to better engagement and involvement with clients and communities that might be interested in the business's products or services. Start out, Hines implores, by monitoring conversations about your business through *Google Alerts (G)* and *Social Mention (G)*. A new service, *Talk-Walker.com (G)* has been getting good buzz as an alternative alert service.

"Many businesses hear about the advantages of social media in terms of marketing their products or services, but some forget to look at other major benefits of social media beyond finding leads or making a sale," says Hines.

Her Kikolani.com post gives you customer-service tips and ideas for monitoring industry trends through social media to help your business thrive.

Sometimes the only thing keeping you from controlling content and driving traffic to your website is just doing it. You might say: "Well, there's not much new here." We think that's right because this article applies traditional business principles with traditional social media models to help you create a marketing plan that will work for your business.

And like we said earlier, hoping won't make it happen.

Every organism has a life cycle and matures through different stages. Social media aren't any different.

Bill Ives, consultant and writer on SocialMediaToday.com and elsewhere, examined the natural cycle social media goes through as they adopt new technologies.

His article, which outlines *five stages of social media maturity (G)*, is based on the Forrester research that was the basis for the strong-selling book, *Groundswell (G)*. It would be very easy to misinterpret both the Forrester research and Ives article to suggest that there is a single logical sequence of development that companies go through in adopting social media, but that's neither true, nor is it Ives's point.

Ives sees companies moving from the Laggard stage, through testing to coordinating "where management recognizes the risks and rewards of social media." From there, he says companies move to "scaling and optimizing . . . when firms 'have already coordinated their social organization and are now focusing on optimizing their social media activities.'"

"Finally," Ives says, "the Innovators are truly empowering their employees. This final stage is where an easy to use social media awareness tool . . . can have a real impact."

Communications scholar Everett Rogers spent three or four decades of his academic career expounding upon and elaborating the *Diffusion of Innovations theory (G)* for which he became internationally known. A very similar concept to the one described above by Ives, Rogers looked at the adoption of processes, consumer products, ideas, even the Internet of which he wrote in 2003, as moving through stages, for sure, with increasing percentages of a population acquiescing to the innovation over time.

Innovators, those who are inclined to embrace change first, may constitute as low a percentage as 2.5 percent of a normal population while Rogers's laggards—the last to move—may be more than six times that many (16 percent). In between are early adopters, early majority, and late adopters.

As you are examining the resources presented, it might be wise for you to ask yourself where you fit on Ives's adaptation of Rogers's scale. Are you willing to make the changes necessary to get on the cutting edge of the curve? You might also correctly observe, the cutting edge is not always the best place to be. Just ask Julius Caesar.

Social media marketing and its role in the business mix are often misunderstood. In fact, that's a bit of an understatement. Given the embryonic stage of social media compared to other forms of media, for example, most effective social media applications for business have not yet been discovered.

Most good campaign answers spring from a good question. In this case, *10 common social media marketing questions (G)* are answered. Magdalena Georgieva posted on Hubspot.com to help us clear up some of the obvious misconceptions about social media and business.

In her post, she gives some strong hints as to how she goes about judging the effectiveness of a social media campaign; how to create and maintain a blog; and even details like how to incorporate social media buttons into web content. Georgieva's blog post also discusses how to evaluate the best channels to use for reaching your target audience.

That people are using social media for business may be old news. But exactly how are the *top five enterprises using social media (G)* is a different issue entirely.

Zachary Sniderman, an editor at Mashable.com, provides examples from The National Wildlife Federation to Ann Taylor and Whole Foods to show how these for-profit and not-for-profit organizations create a sense of community using individualized forms of social media.

"There are countless enterprises—from mega brands promoting campaigns, to small business owners growing their presences—maximizing social media in their day-to-day," says Sniderman. His insightful post will help you generate your own ideas to take control of your brand's online image through social media marketing. And his article also reminds us of the great flexibility of elegant social media strategy as it's used in social marketing and commercial marketing alike.

Elegance is often best defined in strategy, as it is in writing, by its simplicity. In an elegant post on *three steps to improving client retention with social media (G)*, Chrometa co-founder Brett Owens makes a point we should never forget.

Probably nothing will create a stronger bond with a client than accurate and timely activity reports—or that will lose a client's trust faster than late or insufficient ones. We got that, but we're partial to Owens's second point in this post: "Set up a Blog and Write Informative Articles on a Weekly Basis":

> You have a lot of expertise floating around in your head, so much that you might not realize it. Your clients tap this vast pool of knowledge when they meet with you and engage your services—it's the value they receive from doing business with you.

Remember it takes a good deal more money, generally, to get a new customer than it does to keep an existing one. So, on our list of ways that companies can use social media, lowering company costs by retaining existing relationships scores number one.

Inc. magazine reporter April Joyner describes her best *30 tips for using social media (G)* in business as a "social media cheat sheet for the time-strapped entrepreneur."

Here's tip #8.

> Don't try to create a stand-in for yourself.
>
> With all the other tasks required within your company, it's tempting to outsource managing your social media or even to try automating the process. That can easily backfire, as Joe Pulizzi, founder of Cleveland marketing firm Junta42, learned when he tried sending automated welcome messages to new followers on Twitter. His online contacts quickly called him out for sending out what they perceived to be spam.

Here's another of Joyner's tips—this one that may help resolve a persistent business question. Should we, or should we not, allow people to post comments on the Internet that haven't been pre-screened by management?

Joyner answers the question rhetorically this way:

> Interact with visitors—really?
>
> Just putting up a blog or a Facebook fan page won't do much good if visitors sense the flow of conversation only goes one way. In fact, Matt Mullenweg, founder of blogging platform WordPress, lists not participating in comments as a surefire way to kill an online community. Mullenweg and his team field the many suggestions users have for WordPress through his blog.

Joyner's issue may, at first, seem to be all about policy, but if you are beginning to believe that social media can be an effective tool in supporting and expanding your business, then it should be obvious how much difference policy, when well conceived, can make.

Ask Susan M. Heathfield who advises on *how to develop a social media policy for human resources (G)*: Our employees are participating in social media. What are we going to do about it? Her answer; "Use social media to your company's advantage."

Shama (Hyder) Kabani, author of what we understand from colleague Allie Siarto is a great book, *Zen of Social Media Marketing (G),* asks a company's customers, clients, employees, and other key constituencies:

> What are they saying about you, your company, and your practices? Better yet—how are you responding? Having a social media policy in place does not mean that you get to dictate your image. But, you do get to interact responsibly in the conversation that forms your image. And, you get to help your employees do the same.

Beyond this, Kabani says there are benefits to blogs and Twitter and other social media, but there are risks. Without a clear policy, you and your company can get into trouble with other government agencies, customers, or the general public. In other words, without a policy, you can allow your company's brand name to be diminished, or worse. Heathfield, again drawing heavily on the work of Kabani, lays out a step-by- step process for analyzing what your policy should be and how you should convey it. But don't expect the post to ruminate on whether or not such a policy should be put in place. It absolutely should.

New Tools, Tips, Tactics, and Tricks of the Trade

You simply have to love Matt Silverman for putting together a list that links you to *90+ essential social media resources (G)*, most of which you will use:

- To turn a profit. The design community is always hungry for content, inspiration, and tutorials. These nine networks are a great place to discover and share creative resources.
- Boost nonprofits. The National Wildlife Federation has been getting creative with their social media awareness campaigns, particularly when it comes to location-based technologies. This post discusses some of their innovations.
- Curate content. At times, content creators and content curators have been at odds, but the sheer volume of "stuff" and noise on the Web has made curating essential. This post discusses the status of the curator on today's social web.

Accidental status updates, tweets, and photos on a social network can be deadly, in part, simply because they are permanent. Twitter saves every tweet even after it's deleted, and, anyhow, instant dissemination to followers and friends means your message—with special emphasis on the "mess" part —has already been broadcast. Corporations using social media need to be aware of what messages are posted and who is posting them.

Tanzina Vega, media reporter and multimedia journalist for *The New York Times*, describes important *tools to help companies manage their social media (G)*.

In the rush for businesses "to leverage the keyboard," many companies are finding an unwanted side effect—an inability to keep track of all the ephemeral thoughts and ideas they are sending into cyberspace.

"But," says Vega, "a small suite of emerging technologies [are] offering solutions to help companies manage their social media presence by archiving business communications or managing individual employees posts on sites like Twitter and Facebook."

Besides every other reason for keeping track of every social media message released from a corporate account, one major argument is that it provides a way to avoid legal issues. Here's the basic message. Archive, archive, archive! Understand how to use important new tools to keep track of everything on social networks and to prevent harming the company brand, and your job security.

New social media websites seem to be popping up everywhere. And there is a social media site for just about everything. The SEOmoz.org social media marketing guide to find the *101 social media websites to help market your business or yourself (G)* is a great resource to steer your marketing efforts for a brand in the right direction.

The list ranks the popularity of various social networking, social bookmarking, social news, social directory, and education websites.

"Using this list, you can determine which sites to target and how to engage with them to earn mindshare, branding, customers, and links," SEOmoz tells us, encouraging readers to copy and paste the snippet (above) and others to your website or blog.

Each social site in the SEOmoz ranking is categorized by website primary value and size, and a link to more information about the website is provided. The top 25 social media sites are accompanied with marketing tips to help you create a social media marketing campaign.

New tools are coming to social media much, much faster than we are able to keep track of them. That's why we put together this book. We, and our students, have found most of these resources, and we are reporting on them, among the many possibilities, to help you get started. This CommsCorner.com post showed us a couple of tools of which we'd never heard in listing the *11 Twitter and social media tools to try (G)*.

Here's an example about MentionMap, a "conversation-visualization tool." Post author Adam Vincenzini, PR Daily Europe contributing editor, puts it this way: "I think PR people will really like this one."

"MentionMap provides a 'live' analysis of what a particular person is talking about on Twitter and who they are talking to. When you take a look at a blogger's or journalist's MentionMap, you can get a really clear idea of what they have been Tweeting about lately."

Vincenzini shows you how another clever new tool, Twylah.com, can "turn your tweets into a fan page" and how Likester.com can help you "see what the world 'likes.'"

This social media maven leads you to five incredibly useful social media tools making a splash that you might want to use to get your feet wet.

Here's another valuable trick-of-the-trade list that we believe is well worth the read. Is there one thing we can show you to help you *improve your chances of going viral? (G)*

"Going viral refers to the fact that your content resonates so enormously that it catches on fire," according to wikiHow. And it all begins from a clear appreciation of the varying degrees of going viral, and understanding the limitations of virality.

> You can hope for it, you can position your content to be at its best and most interesting with the underlying wish that it will catch on, but you cannot make it go viral.

Going viral is actually all about *tactics for building an audience via social media (G)*. Mike Brown posted a great resource in SocialMediaToday.com on this very subject.

Direct and to the point, Brown, the founder of BrainZooming Group, is described as a strategic brand builder, and we can see why after reading this piece. Here are just three of his key points:

1. **Regularly share strong, intriguing content, especially news & interesting links**—It's easy to say, "Don't be boring." Work hard to make sure it's also easy for your audience to see you really follow the advice. And don't think you can share content once and then stop! Be consistent in your presence and sharing.

2. **Share content from intriguing people**—If you struggle generating enough rich content on your own, at least share and link to rich content others are creating.

3. **Don't overpromote yourself**—Nobody likes an aggressive salesperson in real life or online. Cool the sales pitch.

"Infographics help communicate information in a digestible manner as they creatively present data in an understandable and engaging format," says experience web designer Grace Smith. You might ask: "What do you expect a graphics designer to say? Did you ever ask a barber if you need a haircut?"

But, seriously folks, Smith's article on Mashable.com is much deeper than you might expect. She compiles a list of *10 beautiful social media infographics (G)* that are actually designed and, she says, tested, to help you learn and make sense of social media.

The list of infographics engages your inner creativity by organizing data into a colorful and playful format. Social media are represented on infographics like the Conversation Prism, which categorizes and organizes how people use social media according to how they are used for finance and human resources. This list can make social media even more fun and interesting then you already think it is.

Creating a blog, a Twitter account, and Facebook account is hardly the start of a social media marketing campaign.

"Sure, you can start publishing updates and sending friend requests, but those communications are just the preliminary steps to social media marketing success," Susan Gunelius pointed out in a recent BusinessInsider.com article.

Terri Seymour identifies her *top ten social media marketing tips for 2013 (G)* in a post appearing in SeymourProducts.com. At the top of her list is an item that we think of as a universal: If it's not important to say, then don't say it. People look at businesspeople who insist on telling them where they are planning to vacation or about the cat they almost hit when picking up their kids from school as . . . well, frivolous, at best.

> Social media marketing is expected to reach new and unequaled heights in 2013. Don't let your business be left behind. Become active with social media. Really get involved. Make new connections and post relevant visual items. Make it about your followers and clients, not about what cereal you had for breakfast!

This is a great online business resource for learning how to mold information about your company brand, or your personal brand, to the customer and how to keep them wanting more.

We often joke that this book is not social media for dummies, although who can argue that the dummies franchise hasn't been a huge success. And there is, in fact, a social media glossary for dummies available on the Web, but we found that, as with nearly all resources, you don't need to open your wallet to get the information you need.

So we recommend you start with the *Social Media A-Z Glossary (G)* put out by BlurGroup.com. As they say, with social media "it's always going to be a challenge to produce a glossary as fast moving as social media . . . "

But, if you're challenged, for example, to get a basic understanding of cloud computing or a tag cloud, you need go no further than this handy and very accessible guide. It's a good one.

In our first edition, we led you to Pete Blackshaw's 2010 jargon refresher. We're hoping he's refreshing his refresher, because we love the humor he put forward in his 2010 entry. For example:

A hash bragger is "a person who consistently (and annoyingly) uses hashtags to brag about exploits, exclusive conferences, or envious travel—often uses multiple hashtags."

Then there's the App rat: "A relentless app collector who is known to download apps and then leave them to gather cobwebs. Related to Appotato, a compulsive app addict."

Add to that the trail marker. Picture the central character in Disney's version of the great Farley Mowat book *Never Cry Wolf.* You know, it features the guy who drank excessive amounts of tea so he'd have enough ammunition to mark off his territory from the wolf pack—the way the wolves do.

And after all is said and done, and you get supercharged on the idea of exploiting every possible social media tool that is at your disposal, you come to a point where you ask yourself the question: "How can I possibly manage all of my real-live networks?"

Well, again we turn to Mashable. This time it's Rich Aberman making the contribution with his list of *11 essential apps for managing your real-life social network.*

His "essential apps" include the likes of TeamSnap for iPhone, and Facebook Groups, and for formal groups, GroupSpaces. There is GroupMe, Facebook Events (which, according to Aberman, is not the greatest RSVP-management tool, but like many things in life, is defined by its "redeeming qualities.")

Link to this Mashable.com site, and while you're at it you might consider signing up with Mashable.

Event planners spend countless hours organizing and planning events, picking the invitations, selecting a caterer, picking a venue, addressing budget issues, and picking the décor.

You'll see that we have selected Mashable.com editor Ben Parr's writings as among many of the best resources for social media and marketing we've found.

One of Parr's examples provides a step-by-step guide for *how to plan and promote events with social media (G).* It's his attempt to teach you everything from choosing the right social media tools for an event to tips for e-invitations: "Whether you need to work with organizers, generate buzz, or share post-party photos, social media should be a primary weapon in your arsenal."

He describes how using social media for an event is a great way to create conversation and keep people updated before, during, and even after the event is over. The Children's Trust Fund of Michigan has used some of these techniques in generating buzz for its annual *Pam Posthumus Signature Auction (G)* Event. Google it and you'll see how the CTF team is making this a "must attend" event in the state of Michigan's capital city.

Social Media for Personal Brand Building

You know the expression that the cobbler's kid goes without shoes? Well, you do now, and you really ought to think about this within the context of social media.

Here's a thought: "If you can't find yourself on Google, maybe you don't exist." That may be a bit of an overstatement, but think about it in this way: You have to understand the positive power social media has for building your personal brand, and your personal brand is undeniably connected to your professional success. And parents and grandparents shouldn't forget what Business Wire and other online sources have pointed out in reporting the findings of international security company AVG—that *92 percent of U.S. children have an online record (G)*. So, we've included just a couple of good resources to keep you and your family from going shoeless, in the Internet sense.

What could be more important, after all, than learning *how to use social media to improve your career? (G)*

In a guest post in Money.USNews.com, author Sharon Reed Abboud tells a variety of real-world stories about how people all over the country have landed jobs using social media.

By the way, we have several similar success stories from young people, and not-so-young people, who have taken our New Media Driver's License® course at Michigan State University, so nothing in this article surprised us.

Abboud's post connects to articles in several digital venues. It's a great read if you are interested in making sure that the career crystal ball you're juggling doesn't hit the floor, or if it already did, how you might get a second chance to juggle it again, this time more successfully because of your new social media skills.

Denying that your online presence builds your personal brand won't make that reality go away. "Most people online are building 'a brand,'" says Dan Schwabel in a Technipedia.com post in which he discusses *how to use social media for personal branding, (G)* "but sometimes people forget whose brand they are building. . . .

"For instance," Schwabel says, "if your Twitter handle reads @fastcar, then you aren't building your own personal brand. When people retweet you, they are viewing @fastcar, and not your full name.

"And please don't think the Twitter handle @needajob will land you your dream career."

Marketing expert Heidi Cohen provides *seven tips to give your social media career a facelift (G)* in a post on b2cmarketinginsider.com:

> To develop an effective social media marketing presence requires accepting that social media has become an integral part of how we communicate and share information. Not participating means that you're missing a large part of the conversation.

So, begin with yourself: "You must take control of own social media footprint."

Cohen's second point includes a link to an inventory of her favorite available social media marketing resources (newsletters, books, handbooks and posts, and special sections on Facebook, Twitter, LinkedIn, blogging sources, and more).

Her list of newsletters begins with Mashable.com and moves to a great daily newsletter round up of the top social media stories of the day: *"Smart Brief on*

Social Media."(G) Just going through Heidi's resource list is a great education and is bound to make you a better social mediator.

Geeksugar.com's compilation of *what your social network says about you (G)* is one of the rare posts that runs through a summary of academic research in social media. In fact, it is the only example we found of academic research that built a best resources list published in mainstream social media.

Here's a highlight of their list of 10 studies:

- A group of researchers in Germany found that Facebook status messages "make us feel more connected with each other."
- Another study, this one from Hewlett-Packard Laboratories, demonstrates that most of us are relatively passive consumers of information on the Web, and it discusses the marketing implications of this information.
- A Malaysian business school study demonstrated that peer or "friend" movie recommendations seem to matter more than critics' reviews.
- A study from the Psychology Department of Tufts University is both encouraging and, also, somewhat common sense: "We like people more if they are expressive" in both real-life situations as well as online.

You know right now if you don't need to know *what companies want in a social media intern (G)*. But, if you are a student (or a young worker in an unsatisfying job) and you think that you may want to consider a job in the rapidly expanding world of social media, this Mashable.com post is for you. Or if you are in a business or a nonprofit organization and you're considering bringing in an intern to help you get up to speed of social media, this post might be for you also.

Thank you, Amy-Mae Elliott, for what is bound to be a career-expanding piece of work for a number of our readers.

First, we love how Elliott organized this piece. The first graphic—the one with the young lady holding up a cardboard handwritten sign that says "I heart to work!"—is precious, and it also emphasizes the first thing we tell our students. You simply have to learn how to show that you love to work, you love social media, and you are enthusiastic. The picture is worth one thousand words.

Elliott's first point about good communication skills is followed by the warning that you better become a good writer if you're not one already. That statement is supported by our experience and some research we did in the *national assessment of the perceived writing skills of entry-level PR practitioners (G)* in 2009. Here's what we found:

PR supervisors are often shocked and largely put off by the poor quality of writing they are seeing among entry-level practitioners in several different categories of writing, including on blogs and other online vehicles.

Our advice: You simply have to make yourself a better writer than you are today. Danny DeVito's character asked Billy Crystal's in the movie *Throw Mama from the Train* what it takes to be a good writer.

Simple enough, Billy Crystal replied: "Writers write."

Writers write. That's it. That's all. And there has never been a greater time than now or an easier way to practice your writing skills than in this age of social media. So write away. While you do, avoid developing bad habits. Learn to be accurate, grammatically correct, and always brief and to the point.

Write, for sure, but make sure that you remember that once words and pictures get into cyberspace, as far as we know, they'll be there forever. And now is as good a time as any to ask this question:

Could you pass a Facebook test with a prospective new employer? It's been said that one test every employer should give a prospective new hire is to stop by her or his apartment and pay a surprise visit. Would the employer, or recruiter, see anything that might cause her to not want to go through with the hiring?

A surprise visit to a prospective employee's home might sound like a great idea, but it might also open up some legal challenges. Homes are private, after all.

But Facebook isn't home. And Facebook isn't Las Vegas either because what goes on in Facebook doesn't stay there. It might be a lot of fun for you to post photos of your weekend parties, all right, but *Facebook is fun for recruiters too (G)*.

Jennifer Waters opens her *Wall Street Journal* online entry with this question: Could you pass a Facebook background search?

> The next time you apply for a job, don't be surprised if you have to agree to a social-media background check. Many U.S. companies and recruiters are now looking at your Facebook, Twitter, Flickr, and other accounts and blogs—even YouTube—to paint a clearer picture of who you are.

One employer told Waters he's not terribly concerned about party shots—as long as they are not outrageous.

> I look at their Facebook and see how they approach what they put on it. Is it immature? Is it appropriate or inappropriate? I'm not judging their activity but looking at how they communicate what they do and their thoughts and their judgments to the public as a reflection of what they will do with their clients and team members.

Monitoring, Evaluation, and Security in Social Media

If you really want to become an expert in social media (and/or public relations) modern measurement techniques and applications, you simply have to meet KD Paine. She's a firebrand on the subject of measurement, and you should consider her to be your first and, maybe, your last source, but certainly you should consider her one of your best sources.

"If you've ever wondered how to measure social media, public relations, public affairs, media relations, internal communications, or blogs," her KD Paine's Measurement Blog announces, "you are in the right spot."

As we write this, Paine's blog post from the Lisbon Amec European Summit on Measurement (July 2011), in which she gives a complete rundown on the conference, provides a great list of the five measurement books you could take to the beach. (See list below.)

As you might expect, Paine, who is a shameless promoter of measurement, listed her own book. But if we were coming up with our own list, we'd have listed Paine's book first. (We'd also list a sixth book that's being published as we write under the working title of *The Social Current—Monitoring and Analyzing Conversations in Social Media*, by Allie Osmar Siarto and this book's first author, Richard Cole.)

By the way, Paine says: "O.K., I don't really expect you to take these measurement books along the next time you go to the beach."

But any serious student of measurement should consider this a must do reading list.

If you want to find *20 free tools to evaluate social media (G)*, check out Dirk Singer's post on his site "devoted to social media, stats, data, and research"— LiesDamnedLiesStatistics.com. In this post, Singer says the first thing we have to understand is that there is a big difference between measurement and evaluation. He's interested in evaluation tools "that will give you some form of meaningful data that you can use in reports."

We won't tell you what free tool is first on Singer's song sheet, his list is alphabetical after all, but you'll be amazed at the great tools that have popped up over the past couple of years—many of which are accompanied by the ability to create infographics guaranteed to dazzle your co-workers and boss.

If you haven't yet figured out *why you need to monitor and measure your brand on social media (G)*, Maria Ogneva, Director of Social Media at Attensity, answers that question and shows how she does it in this Mashable.com post.

KD Paine's 5 Measurement Books You Could Sure Take to the Beach

1. A great place to start your social media strategy is Stephen D. Rappaport's, *Listen First!: Turning Social Media Conversations into Business Advantage*. It's a detailed workbook of how to begin listening to your customers, how to manage a social media listening program, and how to use the research correctly.

2. Your next step up the measurement ladder is Katie Delahaye Paine's *Measure What Matters: Online Tools For Understanding Customers, Social Media, Engagement, and Key Relationships*. It takes you from first steps all the way through how-to-measure procedures for each of your audiences and projects. If you're a seasoned pro, it's your all-purpose reference: As Lee Odden says, "This is a measurement bible for the social media and public relations savvy professionals of the world."

3. Philip Sheldrake's *The Business of Influence: Reframing Marketing and PR for the Digital Age* is definitely not for the newcomer to social media. It does start with a great overview of where we are, but then quickly gets into the nitty-gritty of defining and mapping the influencers that are important to your strategy. Says Katie Delahaye Paine: "The Business of Influence *should be found, dog-eared and jam-packed with marks in the margins, on every successful CMO's desk.*"

4. If you're in the B2B space, *Social Marketing to the Business Customer: Listen to Your B2B Market, Generate Major Account Leads, and Build Client Relationships* by Paul Gillin and Eric Schwartzman is an great read. It removes the "This doesn't apply to me excuse" beautifully. Chris Brogan says, "Finally, the book I was too lazy to write. Gillin and Schwartzman have broken open the code to how to approach B2B marketing with social media."

5. Finally, for anyone in marketing or media—practitioner or teacher—you must read Timothy Wu's *The Master Switch: The Rise and Fall of Information Empires*. Every new communications medium or technology begins with an idea, an entrepreneur, and an explosion of free exchange of this technology. But, sooner or later, it is taken over and monopolized by a single person or company—too frequently with the collusion of the U.S. government.

(Reprinted with permission: KD Paine & Partners)

> Although there is no shortage of social media monitoring tools, each one is a bit different in its approach, methodology, metrics, depth of analysis, channels measured, reports, and UI. The existence of this many tools and the fragmentation of the tools market is evidence of the fact that the space is not quite mature, and doesn't yet have a set of agreed-upon metrics and best practices.

To prove her point on the wonderful world of social media monitoring, Ogneva links to Ken Burbary's *Wiki of Social Media Monitoring Solutions (G)*. The current, but building, count of resources on this list alone is 229 items.

Priit Kallas provides a thinned-down version of a list of what, in his opinion, are the best *54 free social media monitoring tools (G)*. He breaks the tools into two groups: the group of business tools he uses most regularly and the group of tools he loves to play with.

And as "Kelly" points out in a piece for ProCommunicator.com: "There are lots of places you can go to find social media monitoring tools. A lot of them cost bucks $$$. Here's a list of *10 free social media marketing tools (G)*. Try them out and see what works for you."

Unfortunately, traditional web analytics don't reveal anything about user social media habits. Tracking the page views and bounce are not particularly valuable.

Tim Trefren, founder of real-time analytics service Mixpanel, helps companies understand how users behave with web applications. He posted his article to help you find *three new ways to measure the social web (G)* and understand how and why social web companies are developing their own data collecting systems:

> There's a reason for this: Social media are highly competitive, and the biggest advantage you can have is data. To improve and grow, these companies need to gather as much information as they can, and they need more than simple page view tracking.

If you're interested in learning about new social web measurements, this resource will help you understand what these new systems are, why they are useful, and how you can use this for your social media marketing campaign.

Trefren says, "There's a lot to learn about analytics from the frontrunners in social media. The intense competition has resulted in many new and innovative ways to track and analyze visitor data."

Nick Lucido, one of our stellar graduates, who became president of the national Public Relations Student Society of America (PRSSA) while he was at MSU, is now in Edelman PR's office in Chicago.

One of Lucido's specialties, when he was still at MSU, was setting up what he called social media listening posts for Edelman clients.

Alina Halloran, writing in the OpSecSecurity.com blog, opens her commentary on *how to catch the social media buzz by monitoring your brand online (G)* with these questions:

> What are you doing? What's the latest trend? And what are you buying? These are just some of the questions being asked and answered through online platforms.
>
> As brand owners monitor their online presence, it is an opportune time to mine intelligence . . . weeding through vast amounts of information on social networking platforms can be cumbersome, but there are guidelines to help make your search a bit more manageable.

Halloran shows us what we should be monitoring for and renders her expert opinion on what we can learn from the conversations that are occurring about our brand online.

Metrics can provide valuable information. Metrics can tell you what's working, what isn't, and what needs to change. There are many different kinds of metrics besides return of investment that are important for any social media marketer, and it will be helpful to look at this list of *eight social media metrics you should be measuring (G)* before you start.

Nichole Kelly is a social media measurement speaker, consultant, and coach. Her SocialMediaExaminer.com post asks this: "Are you struggling to find measurements that are meaningful to your organization? Do you feel like you're searching for a needle in a haystack of metrics?"

If you've answered yes to either question, Kelly's post can help. There are many tools used for measuring data and the article describes what resources are used for different measurements.

Learn the importance of conversion rates and how these calculations are made, the importance of a control group, and how to measure social media growth against what's happening in the control group. You can use your conversion rate to measure customer acquisition costs and retention rates once you understand how to calculate it. And this information may help boost the rate the success of your marketing campaign.

All the information in the world won't help you much if you can't find it. That's why Cody Barbierri's post on *four must-have social media dashboards for your business (G)* is such a valuable post.

> While big brands and agencies have the luxury of resources and money, local businesses don't. What they need is a social-media dashboard—an all-in-one, Web-based monitoring tool for Facebook, Twitter, and other social sites where customers hang out. . . .

Barbierri identifies three dashboard criteria: cheap, easy to use, and automated. HootSuite is one of the original players in the dashboard market—allowing users to monitor all of their social profiles like Facebook, Twitter, and LinkedIn.

Social Media: Some of Edelman PR's Nick Lucido's Favorite Social Media Resources

Nick Lucido joined Edelman Digital in May 2009 after receiving the Daniel J. Edelman/PRSSA Outstanding PR Student Award while in Michigan State University's Department of Advertising and Public Relations—home of the New Media Driver's License® social media sequence. He is a member of Edelman's digital strategy team, providing strategic counsel for clients in the technology, pharmaceutical, consumer packaged goods, and restaurant industries. Prior to working for Edelman, he also completed internships in mid-sized and boutique agencies.

Lucido completed his undergraduate degree from MSU in December 2010. At MSU, he assisted co-author (Professor) Cole in redesigning a graduate course in media relations to include a new media component, which he then co-instructed. He served as national president of PRSSA in 2011–12.

ComScore.com Insights Blog (G)

"One emerging trend has been how an organization can leverage social media to improve SEO—or search engine optimization—rankings. This post lays the foundation on how an organization can use Facebook and Twitter to not only improve its social page ranking, but also to help your main website rank higher."

Darmano.Typepad.com The Six Pillars of Influence (G)

Nick likes this resource because his colleague, David Armano, points out the six key sources of influence. "This is particularly important to remember in order to identify influencers within your community, as one pillar has no more weight than others," Nick says.

The Digital Influence Mapping Project (G)—Evaluating Markets for Social Media Readiness

"One of the most daunting aspects of social media is how people use different online networks in different countries. It makes executing a global social media strategy seem very challenging, so I often reference this post from John Bell that encourages you to evaluate your program through a critical eye."

Techipedia—17 Digital Marketing Experts Share Their Top Tips, Tricks, and Tools (G)

"While it's important for companies and brands to find their own way in social media, looking up to see what the experts are doing and using in digital marketing is helpful." This post, written by Blue Cross Blue Shield of Michigan social media manager, Shannon Paul, lists what Nick believes to be some relevant tools and tricks to help any new PR or digital professional navigate the space a little easier.

Jeff Esposito—23 Social Media Facts to Share with Executives (G)

Although stats are constantly changing, Nick feels it's important to know what kind of stats to share with someone you're trying to sell social media to. This is a solid guide on what stats executives care about and can guide you in the right direction if you're trying to sell in an online program.

Avoiding Mistakes in Social Media

Orlando Business Journal columnist Michael Coudriet outlined *six social media mistakes to avoid while job seeking (G).* Since this book focuses upon social media for business, we think help getting a job might be a good subject to cover.

> [Avoid] mixing personal with business. Unless you are the brand, separate your personal social media accounts from your business accounts. From a business perspective, most people don't want the details of your personal life. They are more interested in your products and services rather than pictures of your family vacation.

Controlling the conversation between consumers on social media websites is hard enough without generating complaints because you can't keep the main thing—business—the main thing. But some complaints are inevitable in any business.

Read *BlineMarketing.com's five great tips for dealing with complaints on social media (G):*

> Social media can be a tricky endeavor and maintaining your accounts is the most important aspect.
> What do you do when someone leaves a negative comment?

The manner in which you deal with these complaints, if done correctly, can be beneficial to your brand. If complaints are handled incorrectly or not taken seriously, they can really hurt your image.

It's been well over a decade since Karl Albrecht, in his classic book *Service America, Doing Business in the New Economy (G),* observed that it's not only when things are going well that relationships with clients are strengthened. In fact, it's at that "moment of truth" when something has gone wrong that the customer relationship is both in greatest jeopardy and is also given the opportunity for lifetime loyalty. It's then, when something goes wrong, that the retailer or service provider has the opportunity to demonstrate just how important the customer relationship really is.

"Just how important is my business to you?" That's what the customer is thinking, and that's the time the supplier can show him—or not.

Negative comments online are often harsher than face-to-face because cyber-distance seems to provide a safe, and quite spontaneous, way to emote. The first thing any business needs to remember is not to take the complaints personally. And it's equally important to not be impersonal when responding to customer complaints.

Donald M.D. Thurber, a former board chair at Blue Cross and Blue Shield of Michigan, would tell company executives: "Every knock is a boost." Complaints give you a chance for redemption. It's when the customer doesn't feel like it's worth his or her time to complain that the business is in trouble.

Social media give any retailer or service provider a wonderful opportunity to hear the customer talking and to join in the conversation with real results. But just like anything in life that's worthwhile, becoming socially skillful in cyberspace isn't easy.

There is this crazy idea that social media is easy and that it will work just because everyone is doing it. Wrong!

Listen to Anna Mack and let her help you clear up these kinds of misconceptions as she points out *seven reasons why your social media marketing efforts are not working (G).* Her advice might prevent you from wasting a good deal of time and money in a half-hearted pursuit of new business in social media.

Mack's post on McKremie.com/blog may just help your online social media succeed. For example, she identifies a major reason for a social media failure lacking clear goals for your campaign.

> If you are someone who is just sharing content with no goal in mind, this is the reason as to why your marketing efforts are not paying off. Social media marketing is just like any other type of marketing—you must have an outcome that you are working towards. For example, are you trying to get more subscribers to your website or do you want more traffic to your website? Once you have a goal in place you then know what you are working towards. Without one, it is obviously going to seem as though your marketing efforts are going to waste.

In any event, once you choose to go into social media, you have to recognize this. Operating successfully in social media isn't as simple and clear cut as many try to make it out to be. It's hard work, and after all: If it were all fun, they wouldn't call it work.

Bianca Male wrote BusinessInsider.com's *eleven social media mistakes your company must avoid (G):*

> In reality, there are common mistakes that business leaders unfamiliar with social media marketing seem to stumble into. These errors reveal a lack of social media savvy and often negate the effectiveness of those marketing efforts.

You might think the examples she cites are pretty much common sense, and they are. But then, how often have you felt that common sense isn't always all that common, like when you bump into sites that don't have "enough fresh content"? Do you return to those sites? We don't—common sense.

Or what about spamming? To some degree spam is in the eye of the beholder. But you shouldn't take chances.

Male advises:

> Tools like Twitterfeed allow you to automatically send certain updates to your account. Convenient, yes, but beware: If those are the only posts you have, your account is going to feel impersonal, and it will completely negate the interactive element of social media marketing. Think rescue marketing.

To some people social media have become such a religion that screwing up can be sinful. Unfortunately, fixing a social media screw-up is not as simple as showing up once a month to confess your social sins and being absolved of responsibility for them.

Social media experts Eric Boggs and D. J. Waldow posted a slide share that is so clear and concise Lucifer himself could have written it. They call their presentation *the seven deadly social marketing sins (G)*.

They aren't the first ones to translate biblical references into a modern context. Much of their advice is common sense, and some of it is absolutely no different than that which you would give a mentee who was looking to avoid a trip to the woodshed.

The only thing worse than making a mistake is making a mistake and not knowing enough to go back to apologize and try to fix it. Heather Dugan hit a very large national audience with a HuffingtonPost.com article in which she details *eleven social media mistakes you don't even know you're making (G)*.

> Spotting the mistakes of others is easy: The cringe-inducing Facebook status message. The ill-advised "after hours" tweet. Using Foursquare to check in at an establishment of questionable repute. While social media provides a multitude of opportunities, the flip side is indelicate revelations are always just a click away.
>
> We know, we know . . . YOU would never do that. But there are other social media blunders that are far less egregious you might be committing. And those mistakes could be holding back your job search or attempts at advancement.

What's the biggest mistake you can make? "Never engaging in real life," according to Dugan. "We're not saying you need to set up face-to-face appointments with the hundreds (and possibly thousands) of people who follow you. But it's never a bad idea to hand-pick a few people you want to impress and set yourself apart by creating mutually beneficial relationships that go offline from time to time."

Why is it that tragedy is often the underlying basis of stuff we think is funny? We don't know the answer to that and Sam Laird didn't address it directly his Mashable.com brief history of *social media screw-ups (G)*. But that doesn't make the article less funny, or the screw-ups less humorous.

Who could forget former U.S. Representative Anthony Weiner whose tweeted crotch-shot set a new standard for political pratfalls in the social media age? Among brands, there's the Red Cross employee who accidentally tweeted about "#gettingslizzerd" from the charity's official account rather than her personal one. Ragu, Nestle and Kenneth Cole have all showed some Twitter or Facebook ineptitude of their own as well.

Use protection and be safe.

No, this isn't advice from Planned Parenthood or the National Rifle Association. It's social media advice on *how to stay safe in a social media world (G)*.

Learn how to protect yourself against the dangers in social media. Child predators and identity thieves thrive on social media websites, where the age of users gets younger and younger, and the amount of personal information posted online gets larger and larger.

Steve Olenski, Creative Director of Digital Services for The Star Group, a marketing communications agency, says: "In today's social media gone amok world, everyone thinks they need to be and should be social and sociable with everyone.

"For some reason many of us think of the Internet as somehow being different than the real world."

This Olenski post will explain some of the dangers of social networking and when and where we need safeguards to protect our families, our children, and ourselves. The post describes how to make a strong password, status updates you should never post, and how to use privacy controls.

Extra Point—Tracking the Trends

As if we need more evidence of the important role social media is playing in worldwide business, international PR firm Burson-Marsteller reports that the 100 largest international firms were mentioned more than ten million times during a one month period alone in 2012.

The firm's *global social media check-up 2012 (G)* took a snapshot of social media activity—Facebook, Twitter, YouTube, Google Plus, and Pinterest—of the Fortune 100 during February 2012. Commercial social business among the world's most powerful corporations has expanded since the data began being collected in early 2010.

This year, researchers at Burson-Marsteller found 87 of the 100 companies on the Fortune list using at least one platform to communicate online with various stakeholders. One interesting trend—39 of the Fortune 100 had developed branded YouTube channels during the past year alone.

Speaking of trends, in our first edition we went to a Brad Howarth Indesign

Media post to help us project into the future of social media. Howarth can't possibly know everything there is to know about social media. No one could. But his projections in 2010 showed that he knows his stuff.

This year, we're turning to Patricia Redsicker who used *Nielsen's Social Media Report 2012 (G)* to post *seven social media trends for consumers (G)* in SocialMediaExaminer.com.

How could anyone be surprised that Nielsen researchers would identify an increasing tendency of consumers to go mobile? "The survey found that consumers are increasingly looking to their smartphones and tablets to access social media."

And unless you just rode into town on a load of pumpkins, you probably won't be surprised to see that Pinterest usage is on the rise also.

"One of the interesting findings in this survey," from Redsicker's standpoint, "was that 76% of the participants said they experienced positive feelings after engaging in social networking," while 21% reported negative sentiments after social networking, describing the experience as time wasted.

Another of the Nielsen questions found mixed results on the acceptability of ads in social media.

Social Media Resource: Top Five "Picks" of Social Media Expert and Author Greg Verdino

Greg Verdino is the author of *microMARKETING: Get Big Results by Thinking and Acting Small* (McGraw-Hill, 2010), a recognized marketing thought leader, and a popular conference speaker. His company, Verdino LLC, provides clients with strategic consulting and business innovation advisory services. His "top picks" reflect his interest and his reputation as a top advertising, direct marketing, digital, and social media marketing consultant. Greg blogs at www.gregverdino and tweets as @gregverdino.

Six Pixels of Separation

http://www.twistimage.com/blog/
"Written (and recorded—Six Pixels is a blog *and* a long-running podcast) by Twist Image president Mitch Joel, Six Pixels casts a realist's eye on the latest in social media, mobile and more, all from the perspective of a seasoned digital marketer and recognized marketing thought leader. Mitch's book—also called *Six Pixels of Separation*—is a smart, easy-to-digest introduction to social media marketing, and he can always be counted on to look at new technologies and approaches within the context of digital marketing strategies that stand the test of time."

PR-Squared

http://www.pr-squared.com/

"Todd Defren is a principal at *SHIFT Communications* and the man who conceived the original social media press release. After more than seven years blogging about social media from the PR practitioner's perspective, Todd still consistently delivers smart, no-nonsense thinking on the current and future state of public relations."

PSFK

http://www.psfk.com

"PSFK isn't a marketing or PR blog per se, but it is my go-to source for a wide-ranging look at trends, ideas, and cool new stuff in general. Piers Fawkes and his team assembled dozens of short, inspiring posts each day — covering everything from branding and business to culture and design. If you're looking for a spark for your next innovative idea or simply want to keep your finger on the pulse of what's new and what's next, PSFK is a fertile field to sow."

Darren Herman

http://www.darrenherman.com

"I first met Darren when he was running his in-game advertising startup, *IGA Worldwide*, and I was running the emerging channels group at Digitas. He has since gone on to become chief digital media officer at New York ad agency *kirschenbaum bond senecal + partners*, and looks at the media, marketing, and advertising scene with a compelling blend of big budget ad guy plus entrepreneurial spirit. His blog is a great source for marketers looking to understand the tools and technologies shaping the future of the ad business, and for sell-side startups interested in getting inside the head of one of the most innovative digital media buyers in the industry."

We Are Social

http://www.wearesocial.net

"This one is worth reading for two main reasons. First, *We Are Social* is among the top social agencies in Europe and Australia, so their team (led by managing director Robin Grant) brings a uniquely international perspective to their posts about the latest social media marketing campaigns, news, and trends. Second, their Monday Mashup posts provide fantastic one-stop-shop reviews of each week's interesting global stories, technology developments, platform plays, marketer moves, and new social initiatives. While there's plenty of U.S.-oriented content, this blog provides American marketers with a nice little reminder that there is plenty of interesting, innovative (and sometimes surprising) activity happening beyond the States."

MAKING YOUR PRACTICE PERFECT

Some tasks that will help you understand the ideas and concepts talked about in Part I.

Exercise 1: Join LinkedIn and build your profile to 100 percent (or close to it). Every step of the way, LinkedIn tells you how to do it. Building a credible profile, loaded with keywords, may help propel your business career. Invite your friends. Request recommendations. Upload a photo. Your LinkedIn profile is your connection to the business social media world—and you need to be there. We'll show you more about LinkedIn in that section of the book later.

Exercise 2: Start a Twitter page. Choose your handle (username) and launch your Twitter presence. Then you can tell your friends about your Twitter. Log in to your Yahoo or Google mail and see how many of your friends are on Twitter. Make your first tweet. Follow some people. Join in the conversation. More is coming on Twitter later too.

Exercise 3: Create your Facebook profile. You need to have a presence there to understand this social media giant. Your Facebook profile can lead to hours of entertainment as you surf and connect with past people you thought you would never see again. You can also create a Business Page or a Professional Page instead of a profile if you wish to use Facebook strictly for business. Read more in our upcoming Facebook section.

Exercise 4: Join Google+ and see what it's all about. This new entry into the social media space gives you a nice alternative to Facebook. Invite your friends. See who is already on there. Group your friends into circles and play along. You may just like it.

Exercise 5: Now that you have built all these profiles, commit to using them once a day for the next 90 days. If you really want to immerse yourself in social media, you need to do it. And a 90–day regimen will be a good start in joining the conversation, and building your social media brand.

PART II

SOCIAL NETWORKING

CHAPTER 2

The Ins and Outs and Ups and Downs of Blogging

As you must know by now, blogs were described as web logs when they first hit the Internet scene in the late nineties.

Some people think about blogs as websites—simple websites perhaps, but websites nonetheless. But for those of you too young to remember, trust us when we tell you that much of what can be done on a free blog service today would have required hundreds, perhaps thousands, of programming hours to have been able to do on a website only a few years ago. In fact, a good deal of what goes on blogs—even the free services—simply could not have been done at all.

Why would someone want to set up a blog?

The basic motivation for setting up a blog is because the blogger wants to conduct a public conversation on a subject that is important to her and she wants to have that conversation in real time. The blog also will provide a running record of the contributions of other experts.

Bloggers may have a variety of different motivations. Some want to be recognized by their peers as experts. Others want to collect information that will be useful to them as they pursue their hobby, their job, or their politics. Some will use a blog to help them sell books they have written. Some bloggers have a long-term goal of generating enough traffic on their site so that they can eventually sell advertising or build up enough traffic to sell it off to an entity that wants it in order to expand their subscription or advertising base.

Arianna Huffington started her blog—Huffington Post—in 2005 to provide a liberal-leaning alternative to the right-leaning Drudge Report. Within just a few short years, The Huffington Post was ranked at the top of the most popular political websites. Along came AOL with a strong need to reestablish its relevance—and a check for $300 million—and Arianna Huffington had a big payday and a new boss.

Normally, entries in blogs go in what is called reverse chronological order. In other words, the most recent comment is at the top of a string of comments related to the particular subject of interest. There is much more about blogs available to you through a variety of online sources. Here's a useful Wikipedia entry on blogs:

> Most blogs are interactive, allowing visitors to leave comments and even messages to each other via widgets on the blogs and it is this interactivity that distinguishes them from other static websites.
>
> Many blogs provide commentary or news on a particular subject; others function as more personal online diaries. A typical blog combines text, images, and links to other blogs, web pages, and other media related to its topic. The ability of readers to leave comments in an interactive format is an important part of many blogs. Most blogs are primarily textual, although some focus on visual or commercial art, photographs, videos, music, and audio. Microblogging is another type of blogging, featuring very short posts.

One thing we recommend is that you can broaden your perspective on blogging by going to the *Technorati (G)* home page and clicking on the "blogging" button. Here you'll find a steady stream of conversation and posts on a wide variety of issues you might want to consider—from why people are blogging to the benefits of a company blog, and well beyond.

One reason for the proliferation of blogs is the ease with which they can be set up and operating in less than an hour's time. WordPress has been a leader in providing a free and open access blogging platform and content management system providing the vehicle for nearly one quarter of all blogs.

Especially if you are "visual learner," there's a great way to get an overall feel for just how easy it is to go about setting up to *launch a self-hosted WordPress blog (G)*. A free tutorial by Michael Hyatt is very much biased toward WordPress, but so are we, and this is a wonderful self-help resource.

Hyatt assures you that he can get you going on WordPress in 20 minutes or less. Even though we share Hyatt's bias toward WordPress, there are a growing number of alternative powerful blogging platforms. In fact, Adam Cornell has developed a list, with some of the pros and cons, of *33 powerful free blogging platforms (G),* and Nadine Myrick offers her list of the *12 best free blogging platforms of 2012* (G).

But before you spend even 20 minutes setting up your blog, you really should focus on just how likely it will be that you'll be blogging in the future. Mathew Ingram, writing in Gigaom.com, commented on a February 22, 2011 *New York Times* article that cited research from the Pew Center's project "Internet and American Life" to conclude that *blogging is dead just like the web is dead (G).* At least, the headline in the original article seemed to imply the demise of the blog.

Except Ingram believes the actual *Times* story said something quite different: "Even according to the figures used by the *New York Times* itself, blogging activity is actually increasing, not decreasing. What blogging is really doing is evolving."

Not so fast, says Francine Hardaway, writing about why, in fact, *blogging is dead—and what's next? (G)* in *Fast Company* magazine's online daily newsletter, which we contend is, itself, a blog.

"The blog is dead," Hardaway says, and as proof she points to the fact that she finds herself originating many of her posts in Google+ and Facebook, and she says, "I can't really blog on my phone; so when I am at an event, I'm more likely to live tweet, and then convert those tweets later into a Storify."

"News is a river," she says, "that happens all day and night, all over the world, which is why Twitter is so compelling." And although Hardaway says blogging is dead, she goes on to say: "It won't die all at once, but just you wait."

One of the reasons that it's a bit complicated to predict exactly what the future of blogging is relates to the fact that it's not all that easy to say what is, and what is not exactly, a blog.

Twist Image President Mitch Joel says *the future of blogging might surprise you (G)*, and put it this way in his Six Pixels of Separation blog:

> It's interesting to note that the true growth of blogging is not coming from individuals using this empowered publishing platform to share their insights with the world. The credibility and growth from blogs moving forward seems to be coming from the mainstream media's desire to have a cheaper, faster, and near-real-time platform to distribute their content.

As it turns out, the leading lights in the online world don't seem to agree on the future of blogging. So we turn to Technorati.com's *State of the Blogosphere Report 2012 (G)*, which provides a mixed view into the future of blogs.

On the one hand, more than 30 million Americans fit Technorati's defintion of a blogger and 43 percent of them now use WordPress as their blogging platform, and other 35 percent use Blogger. One of the reasons for the popularity of these free platforms, however, may be the fact that only 8 percent of bloggers are able to earn enough money to be able to support a family and more than 80 percent have never made $100 from blogging.

According to the Technorati survey, 60 percent of U.S. businesses have a company blog of some sort, yet 65 percent of these businesses have not updated their blog during the past year.

So when it gets to the future of blogs, it appears that the only thing we know for sure is that no one appears to be able to predict it.

Well, there is one more thing we know for sure: If blogs are like almost anything else related to the Internet, what they are today is not much like they are going to be five years from now. And if this is true, then being able to take advantage of whatever that next thing is that is going to evolve from blogs requires knowing as much as possible about this current thing we call blogs. The best way, maybe the only real way, to do this is to start participating in blogs that interest you. And at the very least, this will make you a better writer.

Becoming a Better Blogger

Anyone can be a blogger, but not everyone can blog well. Bloggingbasics101.com is Melanie Nelson's attempt, and a good one at that, at showing us everything we need to know to get started blogging. Her orientation page answers this question: *How do I start a blog?—Blogging Basics 101 (G).* Nelson takes you to a series of articles covering everything from helping you choose the blogging platform for you to the extremely big decision you must make as to what you want to name your blog.

You can click through to her five-point checklist for beginning bloggers.

Once you make the decision to try your hand at blogging, you need to decide that you are going to learn to both write well (or better if you're already a five-handicap writer) and to provide valuable content to get your blog and blog posts noticed. In short, focus on content first.

A guest blog on mastermindblogger.com lays out a list of 10 *quick blogging tips for enhancing readership and success* (G).

> While there's nothing wrong with sharing interesting, informative content that your readers will find valuable, there is something wrong with just regurgitating the posts of others. Don't do it. Be unique, original and creative.

That's point one. Another of the 10 quick tips we like advises the blogger to write like you talk.

> You have one important asset in communicating with your audience via your blog—and that is YOU. Make sure you use your voice. Don't be afraid to post in a personable way. Your audience expects you to be down to earth, approachable and personable. Don't put on airs and don't write in corporate speak. Blogging is not about that. Blogging is about connecting with your audience on a personal level. Once your readers start seeing you as an authority, you will strike gold.

Let's be clear and concise, which is Copyblogger's tip number one in a post entitled *seven ways to improve your writing (G)* . . . right now. Copyblogger is a cool service that you should check out for many reasons. This recommended writing resource gives you a few easy tips for making your blog a better read. Check this post out for yourself and let us know what you think, and then take a look at what Chris Lake has to say—in a bit more detail. Chris Lake's post begins by suggesting that he lucked into a job as a technology journalist.

Reading his column on *how to write for the web—23 useful rules (G)*, it occurs to us that rather than dumb luck, Chris is a good example of what happens when preparation and opportunity collide. The advice he offers is spot on. We don't want to give too much away because we want you to Google his post, but we will share Chris's first rule. It should give you a little insight as to why we think his column on Ecoconsultancy.com is valuable enough for you to drop everything and check out.

Chris says that one of the "best ways of writing an article is to quickly pour out your thoughts, and then to finesse the finer points once you have a structure for your post. That's how I'm writing this one: I've written out the rules and am now filling in the detail."

Well, Chris, that's exactly the strategy we are using to write this book, and we thank you for the advice.

By the way, we feel pretty lucky too, and what we've found out is how true the statement is that the harder we work, the luckier we get.

Not to be outdone, copywriter and technologist George Passwater says: "Well, if you are like me, then you probably don't remember everything, all the time. This is why I have a checklist I use when I write my blog posts. It's just a simple reminder of the points I need to check off before I hit that publish button."

SocialMediaToday.com is another one of those cool companies that provide a wealth of free information like Passwater's *10 key points to remember in an effective blog writing checklist (G)*. It's absolutely free to anyone trying to get better at what he or she does on a blog. It even offers a free newsletter to keep you up to speed on the latest and greatest in social media.

So, you may want to start with the Passwater checklist and move from there to becoming a SocialMediaToday.com regular.

Paul Chaney and PracticalCommerce.com give you eight clear and precise suggestions for *writing SEO-friendly blog posts: eight suggestions (G)* that meet Google's "Farmer" algorithm, thereby resulting in more favorable search results.

Google's so-called farmer algorithm update emphasizes original, unique content for favorable organic search results. Frequently updated, keyword optimized, topically relevant blog posts can provide your ecommerce site with original content, and improve its search engine rankings.

Rule number one is to frequently update your content.
Here's what Paul says about this:

A question I am routinely asked about blogging is, 'How often should I post?' The answer is, 'As often as you can.' If you are planning to use a blog for marketing and search engine optimization purposes, the more frequently you can update content, the better. Google thrives on fresh content. I recommend a minimum of three to five times per week. And blog posts don't have to be long—350 words is a good average length.

Other recommendations include how to "think keywords," including eight very specific recommendations for how to select and use keywords for maximum impact. And if being good is not enough, and you want to be great, check out the post (below).

If you don't have any idea what you should be blogging about, consider the possibility that you should not be blogging at all. And, as Tracy Gold told us in a marketingtrenches.com post we used in the first edition, if you are a "horrible writer, or even worse, you hate writing, you probably shouldn't blog either."

But if you are simply struggling with keeping a consistent blog on a great topic going, and being good is not good enough, ScoutBlogging.com offers *10 tips for becoming a great corporate blogger (G)* that are just as relevant for mommy blogging, daddy blogging, or any other kind of blogging.

Begin with understanding the fundamentals of blogger relations.

> While anyone can set up a blog in a day and start publishing articles, it takes far more work to be a great blogger and see the real benefits of blogging. First, you need to have a blogging strategy that is in line with your PR strategy and business goals. Next, you have to provide relevant content. Most importantly, you must conduct what is called Blogger Relations.
>
> Blogger Relations is what blogging is all about—starting and maintaining a conversation. As the conversation progresses, you get to know the other players in your industry; you gain credibility by listening as well as commenting; and you gain new readers as other bloggers provide links back to your blog to give you credit for your ideas.

OK. So you simply cannot be deterred. You are going to become a blogger come hell or high water. But you need to get started, and you are looking for a little help.

Librarian Lisa posted a very important set of ideas on her blog designed around the premise that well begun is, well, half done, and we don't think she was fooling around. She answers the question in her post title, *What to blog about? It's all about confidence (G)*. Start out with a theme. Write four to six simple blog posts that fall under that theme and make sure you include a bit of helpful information in each post—useful tips and tricks that people can follow.

But what if you can't seem to come up with even four to six blog posts off the theme you've selected. Well, every once in a while, we come across a resource on the Web that has a value that exceeds even their promise.

Here's an article by Carol Tice writing for Copyblogger.com that promises *50 can't fail techniques for finding great blog topics (G)*. One quick read of this post and we think you'll agree that this would be just as valuable for Stephen King's plot ideas or Leonard Cohen's poetry as it for people who are trying to become successful bloggers.

That's right. Whether you are a great novelist, poet-songwriter, or blogger, you need ideas that capture the attention and the imagination of your audience.

You need ideas that resonate with your fan base, ideas that have the ability to attract new readers or listeners.

By the way, Copyblogger.com is a service that is all about getting traffic and gaining readers and, as they say, helping their clients "sell stuff."

> People want valuable online content, so compelling content becomes your advertising. And using the right words in an engaging, persuasive way (that's copywriting) determines not only how well your site converts visitors into sales, but also how much traffic you get and how well you rank in search engines.
>
> Delivering quality online content is the smartest strategy for growing an authoritative website and your business, so it's your copywriting and content marketing skills that will set you apart for success.

Making Your Blog Hum

Here's another post from a familiar name, one of our favorites, Darren Rowse, founder and editor of ProBlogger.net. He identifies five strategies that he says if pursued together would give you a long leg up in becoming a viable blogger. It begins with the question: *If you were starting out in blogging from scratch, how would you promote your blog (G)?*

Again, our book is more of a sampler platter than a main course, so we don't want to do anything that might distract you from going to Darren's site and getting the full scoop, but here's what Rowse chose to make first on his list.

> Perhaps one of the most powerful ways of exposing your writing to a new group of people is to put some of your best content on other peoples' blogs—and not your own.
>
> Guest posts have long been a feature of blogging, but it has been in the last year or two that I've really seen some wonderful examples of bloggers launching their own blogs and raising their own profiles through focusing their attention on writing guest posts on other blogs.

Good point. And this might imply that if you don't have anything valuable enough to put on other blogs, why would you even consider starting your own?

Once you start your own blog, you'll want to know *how to grow a blog community with social media? (G)* Again, we turn to Darren Rowse, one of the world's blogging experts. His best-selling book, *ProBlogger*, is a must read for anyone who wants to be a competitive blogger. And after all, we're all competing for the attention of limited audiences. The Rowse video, introduced by social media guru Michael Stelzner through his SocialMediaExaminer.com, is a great way to get started moving to the next level.

You'll get some great tips from Rowse on the video for sure, and you might even decide to enroll in his latest project, the ProBlogger Academy, a platform that takes bloggers through the various aspects of blogging.

It's an old saying in business (especially heard in sales departments): Nothing happens until somebody sells something. That's what generating visits to most websites is all about. At some level, it's about selling something to somebody.

In this neat list of *eight ways to drive more traffic to your blog (G)*, Rich Brooks, president of Flyte.biz, a new media company, gives a world of useful information in just a few hundred words. And if you want more detail, he provides links to many others in his column inventory, all of which are designed to make you a better blogger.

We particularly liked his recommendation that bloggers need to make sure that you write blog posts that "don't suck." While defining "not sucking" posts may be a little tricky, Brooks emphasizes that people who write vanity posts— posts that brag about their achievements or talents or posts that rave about the products they make and sell—that kind of thing—will end up writing for just one reader, themselves.

Susan Young's Ragan PR Daily post in which she describes *12 things every business blogger should know (G)* is both useful and entertaining. She lays out everything from why you should make up your own rules to how to identify your key audiences.

Rule seven encourages potential business bloggers to use more video. "Video continues to be a hot trend in social media. Not everyone is a writer, and not everyone is a reader," Young says.

"We all learn through different communication modalities. Some of us are more visual; others are more auditory." Enter video blogs (vlogs). Young describes one business blogging bonus as recording your own video and later transcribing it to repurpose it for your blog.

In the blogosphere, being findable is "where it's at." We talk more about search engine optimization later in the book. But, since we're talking blogs now, author Jim Ludico begins this important article with this question: "Are you looking to get your blog highly ranked on Google?"

His answer is in the form of *six ways to optimize your blog for search engines (G)*. It begins with making sure you are starting with high-quality content. We think he's right.

The selection and use of keywords is also a big part of the drill, and you'll benefit by looking at all six tips and trying to figure out imaginative ways to get them incorporated into your blog.

Ludico's tip #3 is to "Write Strong Meta Titles and Descriptions." So, we ask, just exactly what does that mean?

> Meta titles and descriptions tell both the search engines and the reader what's on the page. The Meta title and description also show in the search engine results, so they need to convince readers to click through to the website. Good content management systems and blogging programs include a place for meta information.

That's the kind of crisp, clear response that caused us (and our students) to list this SocialMediaExaminer.com post as among our favorites.

We'll give a number of kudos to Copyblogger.com during our presentation of key resources. We hope they appreciate the plug. Brian Clark got more than 500 reactions to his post asking the question: *Is commenting on blogs a smart traffic strategy? (G)* His answer went beyond a simple yes or no. And he did emphasize that in any event you need to be careful on this issue.

> If one of your primary traffic strategies is to leave fast comments on the posts of larger blogs in your niche just to get a few clicks from the passing traffic, stop. You could get more traffic from one piece of stellar content than months of that type of comment strategy. And without good content, there's no reason to attract a few 'curiosity clicks' under any circumstance. What's going to make them stick around after the click if your content sucks?

"Nothing," Clark says, and we think he's right.

"Plus, the root motivation for those curiosity clicks is often bad to begin with. The nature of the game makes it that way."

This is just the kind of advice we wrote this book to provide. But don't stop here. Go to Brian Clark's post, and then check out some of the comments that it has generated so far.

Don't be bashful in letting Clark know you appreciate his advice, but don't you dare use this as a way of trying to crap-trap big-shot bloggers back to your site.

We have found a great many wonderful resources on the subject of *blogger outreach best practices (G)*. Simply stated, blogger outreach is to social media what good media relations are to organizational-public relationships. Reaching out to the leading bloggers in your product niche can be a cost-effective vehicle for elevating your brand presence and clarifying its identity.

One of the tools that is getting some play in blogger outreach ironically was initially developed as a vehicle to match up PR practitioners and their clients with traditional news reporters who are looking for sources for a story that they have in process. Called *HARO (G)*—as in help-a-reporter-out—this service puts together lists of requests from reporters and bloggers who are looking for experts to fill out their stories. It's free and according to Stacey Politi who posted on Mashable.com, was pushing toward one million story topic listings by the beginning of 2012.

Mallory Woodrow from NetvantageMarketing.com epitomizes a phenomenon in public relations that has yet to be documented, much less written about in any detail.

Not too many years ago, journalists were a dominant force in public relations. Drawn to big dollar jobs, ex-journalists saw their role as schmoozing editors—convincing them to write about their client's business in the daily papers. Somewhat ironically, today it's the PR practitioners who are becoming the journalists, writing client-oriented stories for niche blogs.

Clients seem to be catching on to the notion that the "R" in PR is relationships and that relationships are built through the kind of authentic dialogue facilitated by social media—especially through blogs. But finding the right blogs remains a challenge. That's Woodrow's take on blogger outreach—how to get links, build relationships, and not get murdered.

> We use tools in the office to locate guest blog opportunities and places to review products, but sometimes I use other methods. Obviously, you can take a look at your competition and see where they are getting links and blog reviews or you can just go in blind. I like Google Blogs for this particular task.

Here's more advice from Jeff Korhan who appears to be deeply interested in providing useful and important ideas about blogging with anyone who shares his interest. He shares advice for *Getting your blog read: five tips from 150 posts (G)*.

Korhan's first principle is hardly novel, but that doesn't make it any less important to be said:

> Frequency sets expectations. I put this one at the top for a reason. Very few bloggers are consistent. Therefore, frequency is an approach that creates new expectations that are—well—unexpected. This keeps your blog fresh and your readers engaged.

That's a great point, simply stated: To stay relevant, you have to be sure your blog stays fresh. Everything important flows from that.

Make sure the stories you share on your blog are original, or at least uniquely told, and, by all means, avoid ranting.

"There is nothing fresh about a rant," Korhan says. He's right.

One of our students discovered a resource that reminded us to emphasize that writing your blog post and putting it out there is just the beginning of a process of helping it find readers who will appreciate that you took the time to write it in the first place.

"Randy" put *12 things to do after you've written a new blog post (G)* on the

Cool Infographics site, and cool infographics they are. And just like any infographics, the graphics are never any cooler than the info. Here's point #5:

> Most social networking sites and online forums let you promote content as long as it is relevant. A great strategy is to write a compelling headline or question as your forum title, then include some thoughtful commentary followed by your URL. Lastly, ask readers to provide feedback on the forum to continue discussion.

Blogs are media and dealing with bloggers requires the same attention to media relations as public relations has paid, and still pay, to traditional reporters, editors, and publishers.

Blogging for Business

Like so many of the other "dress for success" articles about blogging, the major focus seems to be that a successful blog is deeper than appearance alone—although appearance matters. But there's much more to it than that.

Michael Reynolds, posting on the globalstudio.com blog begins his discussion of *blog strategies: blogging for business success (G)* this way:

> The introduction of the Gutenberg press in the 15th century changed the world by making the printed word available to the common man. But perhaps an even greater revolution is underway today as the proliferation of the Blog gives every common man his own printing press.

OK. So we'll accept a bit of hyperbole here, but why would the average business care about getting engaged in blogging? Well to begin with, Reynolds feels that there's a big difference between telling clients and prospects that you are an expert and showing them that you are by publishing expert testimony on the blog.

Beyond your expertise, a well-constructed blog will also display your personality and the interaction that occurs will create the "relational glue" that can develop a community of customers.

No doubt, several bloggers have interesting ideas about what it takes to create and run a great blog, and almost all of them agree that there's no substitute for the power of a great name.

Chris Garrett, a blogging and Internet marketing consultant, tells readers and fellow bloggers *how to create a catchy blog name (G)*:

> Naming your blog is an important aspect of blog branding, or blog success for that matter. It seems very important to my visitors too. Ever since my original 'What's In a Name?' post, people have been asking for advice on how to select the best name for their blog.

So here are a couple of his tips. And like most of the websites we reference, you're smart to check Garrett's blog out for yourselves:

When choosing a domain name there are some factors to consider:
- How original and unique is it?
- How descriptive is it?
- What image does it convey?
- Would you remember it after seeing it once?
- Could you spell it after hearing it once?

We've already mentioned that there seems to be a developing sentiment in the new media world that Facebook and Twitter—the microblogs as they are sometimes called—will eventually make traditional blogging a thing of the past. We're not convinced.

Neither is Michelle Salater, author of an article on obtaining *business blogging success through Facebook (G)*. Salater is an award-winning writer and president of Sumèr, LLC, a company that specializes in web copywriting, SEO copywriting, and the promotion and marketing of websites after they launch.

According to Salater:

Expanding the reach of a blog has become increasingly easy thanks to growing social media platforms. Not only do social media sites allow you to share content that isn't necessarily appropriate for a blog, but they also enable you to reach various markets that your blog might not reach.

So rather than seeing Facebook as a competitor to blogs, Michelle sees an evolution occurring that is a harbinger of good things to come for all of social media. "In particular, Facebook is one of the most powerful ways to extend the reach of your blog."

Time will tell.

We've already given you some indication that a variety of free blogging platforms are available to you, and that you can get a blog started on one of these free sites in as few as 20 minutes. But if you still are wondering *how to choose a blogging platform (G)*, check out the SocialMediaExplorer.com white paper that reviews the most popular blogging tools across the most important criteria for success.

Thanks to Kat French who reminds us: "Even those who have been blogging for a while need to periodically review their tools to make sure they still make sense."

SocialMediaExplorer.com has also published a white paper that you can get to via a link in this resource. The paper reviews eight of the most popular blogging platform judged against "nine important criteria for blogging success."

BlogTrafficExchange.com features a post arguing that in order to get a competitive edge in the competition for bloggers, you should consider *ten benefits of hosting your own blog (G)*. With arguments ranging from "professional appearance" to "recall ability" to increasing your ability to generate revenue, this subscription service provides a seemingly endless string of tips for successful blogging.

We think there may be a point for some folks to set up their own blog rather than using one of the great free or low-cost services available to you. But you probably ought to make sure you have the expertise and the time to support your own set up before you venture off into this space.

Here's one example of why setting up your own blog, rather than relying on a free supplier, may make some sense to you.

We have some former students from Michigan State who started an amazing web business a few years ago. The business, called *Texts From Last Night (G),* is as close to an "overnight sensation" as any business we've ever seen.

If you're not afraid to read some stuff you'd not want your mother to see, have at it. Our point in mentioning TFLN is because it began as a simple blog that Ben and Lauren started on one of the free blog hosting sites. As they tell it, their little experiment got so big so fast that one Friday afternoon they got an urgent message from the free-blog host. They were going to be shut down within a couple of days because their volume was crashing the blog's servers.

So literally overnight, they had to build their own TFLN website.

Fortunately, the TFLN team had the funds and friends to pull this off over a weekend. But the record will show that they were quite vulnerable, finding themselves at the mercy of a free service that proved incapable of keeping up with their growth.

A significant advance in the world of blogs arrived in 2007 with the invention of Tumblr. Tumblr is a social media site that lets users post a variety of content to what is called a short-form blog, which allows users to follow other users' blogs.

In a Mashable.com account, writer Lauren Indvik described *why fashion's top brands are flocking to Tumblr (G):*

> Fashion brands are creating increasing amounts of visually rich, branded content to share via their websites, blogs and social networks like Facebook, Twitter, YouTube and Flickr. Tumblr provides, among other things, another outlet for distributing that material. And, best of all, the native fashion community on Tumblr is highly receptive to it.

According to Jolie O'Dell, the "subject matter is a perfect fit for the arts- and community-focused mini-blogging platform." Tumblr sources say nearly 200 of the top 1000 Tumblr blogs are fashion-related.

We remind you that only a very small percentage of bloggers, fewer than 10 percent, report that they are making enough money blogging to support a family. Arianna Huffington, of course, is a notable exception to this rule. So, what's the answer to the question of *how to blog for a living (G)*?

We think the Squidoo.com sums it up pretty well in two words—ads or products. You'll either be placing ads for others or selling products if you want to make your blog financially viable.

Tenacity: That's what we think is the first requirement for working your blog into a place where it can make some real money. If you're not willing to be tenacious, don't quit your day job. In fact, don't quit your day job until your well down the road to having a financially viable blog.

But be careful. We once heard that there's a sure-fire way to make a small fortune blogging for a living: Start out with a large fortune.

Here's some good advice from one of the Internet's true wizards, Seth Godin, about the five things you need to include in your blog bio. You can find it by checking out his *five rules for your about page* (G).

By the way, if you wanted to learn as much as there is to know about social media and could only go to one source, Godin would be a pretty good choice.

Godin says to avoid jargon and stock photos. Humanize your bio and use lots of third-party testimonials to establish your credibility. And don't forget to make it easy for someone who finds you to get in touch.

Remember, the trick to success on the Internet may be as simple as making yourself the most findable source within your niche.

Study guys like Seth Godin, David Meerman Scott, and Eric Swartzman if you really want to know how that's done.

We touched on this earlier in the book, but we think it bears repeating. One common list of the *seven deadly sins of blogging (G)* is anger, greed, sloth, pride, lust, envy, and gluttony. If somebody just took this list and translated it into stupid things people do on blogs, you'd come up with a pretty useful list of things you could do if you wanted to see your blog fail.

Our friends at Copyblogger.com came up with a great list. It's another one of our students' favorites.

Here is the kind of useful information you'll get from checking out this post:

> It's lovely to put your heart into your content, to infuse it with your personality, to come across as a real and likable human being, but . . .
> The game still ain't about you, baby.
> Some people are naturally attracted to topics that other people care about. Others aren't. Don't try to sell broccoli ice cream, even if that's your favorite.

More on search engine optimization later, but here's a *concise list of must have SEO plug-ins for WordPress (G)*.

The article is a collaboration of material from SEO specialists Lorna Li and Joost DeValk. Use the article to help you boost search rankings and utilize the many SEO tools on the Web.

"I can help you with buzz marketing and online reputation management. And I know a great deal about blogging," Li says as she tells a story about how she figured out how to identify and install the best plug-ins as a result of some fortuitous tweeting.

In the true spirit of social media, the aforementioned Joost DeValk volunteered to thin down her original list of 30 recommended plug-ins.

You can see his picks by linking in to Lorna Li then jumping over to Joost's site to read his WordPress SEO bible.

The most anthropomorphic resource we came upon asks this question: *Is your blog the unpopular kid (G)?* It's also one of the most useful resources we've found—falling under the category of "how to make sure your blog doesn't suck."

This post got big-time play with CNN as high-flying news editors Andrea Bartz of *Psychology Today (G)* and Brenna Erlich of Mashable.com team up to show you how to make sure your blog doesn't end up being taken to the prom by her stepbrother.

"Why?" they ask.

"Last year the total tally of blogs hit 126 million, according to BlogPulse. That's a big class to climb to the top of. We're not saying you have to be head cheerleader, but it would be nice to be noticed among the digital masses."

Among their best advice—and there's lots of it in this column—is to pick a narrow niche—one you can own—and own it:

"You're a jock? Write all things jock-related. You dig D&D? There are scads of kids out there just waiting at their computers to read your stuff.

"A narrow subject is best. If your theme is, say, 'mental health,' you're competing with gazillions of more-established blogs. But 'bizarre psychological conditions,' you can totally own."

The Best of the Best Blogs

One of the amazing things about the world of social media is that great people are freely sharing great information—caring and sharing and showing us all what it means to "pay it forward," as Jeremy Porter says in one of his notes about the best PR blogs out there.

In this section, we provide a few examples of the "best of the best blogs" lists in categories ranging from the biggest and best in business to lists specifically targeted at public relations or social media marketing.

Look these lists over, and take some time to explore some of the picks. This is a great way to get a sense of what's going right and, maybe, what's going wrong in the world of blogs.

One thing that is going right is that the public relations community is demonstrating how blogs are helping build better relationships between organizations (or in this case, a discipline—PR) and audiences of practitioners, students, and researchers. This is happening because the basic nature of blogs is to build dialogue, and dialogue is what it's all about in organizational-public relationships.

So, if you believe in the importance of picking good examples to live by, check out the lists that are available—all of which contain links to the blogs they are reviewing.

And don't forget that imitation is the best first step in innovation. Most competitive people recognize that imitation is a high form of flattery, and they are more than willing to help a future competitor get started on the right foot.

In the first edition of our book, we asked you to take a look at the Kissmetrics *list of seven awesome corporate blogs (G)*. We couldn't resist starting off this section by suggesting that you google your way back there and check out the reference to *Zappos.com's CEO and COO blog (G)*.

What sets this blog apart is the transparency it offers to Zappos.com customers. Internal emails, memos, and other corporate news—everything Zappos is shared.

The fact that internal emails are copied in their entirety is something a lot of corporations would scoff at—in fact, they'd be downright frightened by such exposure.

Zappos gives you the impression that both the blog and the company are dedicated to building trust. For instance, in 2010 they shared an internal email in honor of the first anniversary of their deal with Amazon.

Zappos's CEO and COO blog is just one of the blogs that you can check out to get a sense of what Kissmetrics.com says is corporate state of the art.

You can start with Kissmetrics.com, but don't wait too long before you check out *Technorati's top 100 blog list (G)*. It's probably the best way to see what the big guns are doing.

As of the day of this writing, Huffington Post rules, as it has for several years now, as number one. Second on the Technorati list is a blog we cite several times in this book, Mashable, the " leading tech blog focused on Web 2.0 and social networking news with more than five million monthly page views."

The first thing to do to find some good blogs to investigate and, maybe, imitate is to go to the *blog-a-logs (G)*—the blog catalogs.

Alltop.com (G)—the granddaddy of all blog discovery tools according to Mashable. Alltop allows you to customize the service by creating your own blog dashboard. *Technorati.com (G)* also allows you to "search by keyword for specific posts on a topic or by entire blogs devoted to that topic. . . ."

If you are interested in connecting with one or more good PR blogs, it's not hard to find the *best PR blogs (G)*. *Blogrank (G)* is a good place to start. They use more than 20 different factors to rank blogs in any category they list. Their methodology includes assessments of RSS membership, incoming and indexed links and pages from Yahoo and Google, monthly visitors and pages per visit, and Alexa and Technorati rankings, to name a few.

First place on the Blogrank list goes to *The Future Buzz (G)*, "a blog about web marketing and PR strategies that spreads buzz in the social web and builds long-term visibility for your brand, business and art in a fragmented media society." The Buzz's Adam Singer writes much of the content daily, as he's done for more than a decade.

Jeremy Porter put out a great list of his favorite PR blogs in 2010, and if he's done a revised list recently, we haven't found it yet. But his list is still current and the blogs he covers appear to be more a matter of his personal taste than any Blogrank type volume and quantity measures.

One of the things we like most about his listing is Porter is a PR guy who covers PR blogs like a good journalist would. His reporting has an objective ring to it, and he covers everything from blogs operated by major public relations firms to PR blogs operated by individual authors like one of our favorites, Deirdre Breakenridge.

Of Breakenridge, Porter says she exhibits "great insight on PR 2.0 strategies" (personally, we think her stuff is more like PR 3.1).

Also on Porter's list is Brian Solis.

Brian offers so much more than PR knowledge these days, it's almost unfair to put him on this list. That said, he's one of the leading innovators in our industry and is somebody you should pay attention to when he posts (he's also a pretty nice guy). If you want to know what people will be talking about next year, just read Brian's blog today.

As far as general social media blogs are concerned, we like SocialMediaExaminer.com's *top 10 social media blogs (G)* listing. Social Media Examiner describes itself as your guide to the social media jungle, and their annual social media contest may not be the biggest or the most objective in town, but they did get more than 600 nominations for the best social media blogs.

What we like about this list is the subjectivity—the color and detail that they provide in their write-ups.

Their current #1 is SocialMouths.com, which offers "kick-ass social media advice for the real entrepreneur." Didn't we say this list offers color?

Go through the list and you'll see what we mean.

Here's an important posting from Mendel Chuang, product marketing manager at Google Blogspot:

> At Blogger we're passionate about helping communities form around blogs. To further that goal, we've introduced a new feature that lets you easily follow your favorite blogs and tell the world that you're a fan.

Extra Point—Blogging in 2020

Stop the presses—this just in. You think it is strange that Ronald Reagan is said to have had an astrologer assisting him in White House decision-making during his eight year, two-term presidency?

Well, how about this—fortunetelling in social media? And what better name for a fortuneteller than Mars, that's right, Mars Dorian. Dorian describes himself as a "creative marketeer with a moon-melting passion for human potential and technology" who blogs at www.marsdorian.com on subjects like *what blogging will be in 2020 (G)*.

"If you want success in the present, you must anticipate the future. No crystal ball is required," Dorian says in opening up his April 2013 post in Ragan's PRDaily.com.

He opens the outline of six possible futures for blogging with this appeal:

> If there's a time traveler from the future in the audience, don't eliminate me with your ray gun because my predictions didn't all come true in 2020. Cool?

Here's one of Dorian's blogging predictions we think is a good way to end this section of our book:

> Mobile optimized content psychology—
> I'm not talking responsive design and bigger fonts. I mean writing specifically with the mobile person in mind.
> In Japan, for example, cellphone novels are popular. They are romance and paranormal-based short stories in messaging style, created in a way that makes them readable on the go. Smirk if you want, but these sell up to 400,000 units per digital novel. Even if you don't plan on writing e-novels, this comes with mass inspiration for possible blogging ideas . . .

Dorian provides a couple of quick tips, including one thought per paragraph and simple structure and bite-sized chapters.

Makes sense to us.

CHAPTER 3

Everyone's Friend—Facebook

If you are not a current Facebook user, all we can say is, "What are you waiting for?" Everyone is on Facebook. Well, not exactly everyone, but almost.

Let's start out with just a little history. Less than twenty years ago, in 1995, the Center for the People and the Press issued a statement regarding a study it had conducted. Their conclusion may provide an insight into why the U.S. newspaper industry seemed to sleepwalk into an era of tremendous disruption:

> Few see online activities as essential to them, and no single online fea-ture, with the exception of E-Mail, is used with any regularity. . . . Among those who currently use their modems, the study detected a decided soft-ness in attitudes toward online activities and a fragile pattern of use. Only 32% of those who go online say they would miss it 'a lot' if it were no longer available.

Five years later, in 2000, the Pew Research Center published the results of its first Internet & American Life Project. Then, email was clearly the dominant force in the Internet.

The *Pew Internet & American Life Project (G)* recently reported that two-thirds of online American adults (67 percent) are Facebook users. This makes Facebook the dominant social networking site in this country. They also found that on a typical day 59 percent of American adults use a search engine to find information, 59 percent send or receive email and nearly as many (48 percent) use a social network site like Facebook, LinkedIn, or Google+.

One of the more interesting statistics about Facebook is that more than half of the world's Internet users (outside of Asia) use Facebook today.

A fun project in a college dorm room has become a global, publicly traded, Internet juggernaut. And perhaps no networking site demonstrates the degree to which business has climbed on board better than Facebook. Intuit.com's report on *how small businesses are using social media (G)* stresses that more small businesses than ever are "turning to social media to generate new business and connect with customers. With over 9 million small businesses on its platform, the most popular social network for building brand awareness is Facebook, which just unveiled its new Timeline format for businesses." And why would this not be the case?

Social media are "inexpensive, easy to use, their customers use it and it doesn't take a lot of time."

A recent Zoomerang.com survey says: *small businesses use more social media (G)* every day. Zoomerang polled small and midsize business owners about their biggest challenges for 2011 and their plans for 2012:

> Not so coincidentally, the challenges they overwhelmingly say they faced this year—attracting new customers and clients (cited by 44 percent) and retaining existing ones (cited by 32 percent)—are the same ones they plan to work on in 2012. Sixty percent say attracting more customers will be their primary focus, and 38 percent plan to focus on customer retention. So far, only 33 percent of those small businesses surveyed are using social media, but 40 percent say they intend to use it next year. Surprisingly perhaps, a sizable percentage of entrepreneurs (25 percent) don't feel comfortable yet with social media.

Intuit.com provides a wonderful infographic demonstrating *how small businesses use social media (G)*, and why they might be getting it wrong.

The great majority of small businesses who use social media invest less than $100 a year in it, and only 10 percent have a full-time employee assigned to social media marketing

If you want to go to the source for *how to use Facebook for business (G)*, here's what the company has to say about itself:

> Over one billion people like and comment an average of 3.2 billion times every day. When you have a strong presence on Facebook, your business is part of these conversations and has access to the most powerful kind of word-of-mouth marketing—recommendations between friends.

Here's an example of Facebook.com's *Four Steps to Business Success on Facebook (G)*:

> Step 3—Engage Your Audience
> When you post content and have conversations on your Page, you're building loyalty and creating opportunities to generate sales. Learn how to create content that will keep your audience interested.

If you want a slightly more objective analysis of the data, we return to a most trusted source for social network demographics: *Pew Study shows who uses Facebook, Twitter, Pinterest and others (G)*.

As a MarketingLand.com customer newsletter pointed out in September 2012:

"There are stereotypes attached to certain social networks about the makeup of their user base. LinkedIn is for business people. Facebook has a lot of older Americans. Pinterest is for girls. That's the conventional wisdom."

But how true are the stereotypes? According to the Pew Study:

- 58 percent of U.S. Internet users that earn at least $50,000 per year are on LinkedIn, while only seven percent of those that earn less than $30,000 annually are.

- 56 percent of Internet users 50 years old or older are using Facebook.

- 19 percent of female Internet users are on Pinterest, compared to only five percent of male web users.

About Facebook—The Big Kid on the Block

With more than a billion users worldwide, if Facebook were a country it would be third on the population list—close to catching up with China and India, and three times larger than the U.S. Trying to identify individual resources to get you up to speed on what's going on with the worldwide, publicly-traded social network is not possible so we won't try, especially when there are so many other great sources to satisfy your curiosity.

First, we're recommending that you take a cyber trip over to *Allfacebook.com (G)*, the unofficial Facebook blog:

"AllFacebook.com is the online guide for everything related to Facebook. We provide everything from tips to how-tos, and the latest news for Facebook users as well as brands, marketers, and anybody else looking to take advantage of Facebook."

Describing itself as an "insightful blog to learn more about Facebook," All-Facebook.com is owned by Web Media Brands, a conglomerate that also holds the trademarks to such well-known cyber brands as AppData, Inside Network, Social Times, and Stock Logos. They also own and operate the powerful Facebook Marketing Bible we'll fill you in on later in this chapter. AllFacebook.com is a powerhouse loaded with useful information.

Just picking one day at random, here's a taste of what you'll find as the top stories in the blog.

The Pros and Cons of Facebook's Domain-Sponsored Stories (G):

More companies are catching on to a Facebook ad product that used to be mainly used by Amazon: domain sponsored stories . . .

Register Early for Inside Social Apps and Save (G):

Explore the hottest topics affecting social and mobile platforms at Inside Social Apps, June 6–7 in San Francisco. Network with industry-leading developers, marketers, investors, and analysts for two days of in-depth discussions, while learning monetization strategies from the most forward-thinking minds in the field.

Mark Zuckerberg and Priscilla Chan Among Biggest American Philanthropists in 2012 (G):

We all know that Facebook Co-Founder and CEO Mark Zuckerberg is one of the richest people in America, but he's also one of the most generous. The Chronicle of Philanthropy announced Monday that Zuckerberg along with is wife, Priscilla Chan, the second-biggest American philanthropist in 2012, behind Warren Buffett.

There's more—about how *Facebook users buzzed about Rihanna and Justin during the 2013 Grammys (G)*.

A second source for the inside scoop on Facebook is *Inside Facebook (G)*, which bills itself as "the leading source of news and analysis on Facebook's global growth, corporate developments and product innovations," providing "dialing news and analysis for developers, marketers, and investors."

Today we learned about *Facebook testing new 'buy tickets' buttons (G)* on events, but these buttons send users to other sites around the Web and do not allow users to conduct transactions directly from an event page. That has to make *Ticketmaster (G)* a bit nervous. Other stories include one revealing that *Facebook News Feed ads aren't always clear who's paying for them (G)*, and extensive news on what's going on "Inside Mobile Apps."

How Business Exploits Facebook's Potential

Maybe it's time for you to get religion, or at least to pick up a bible.

The Facebook Marketing Bible is by no means a free service, and it's not even inexpensive as Internet services go. But if you are serious about the salvation that may be linked to getting the most out of Facebook's potential, you need to know about this resource.

Put together by the publishers of Inside Facebook, this Bible is a most direct way to get the complete rundown on Facebook marketing. They offer strategic marketing advice and detail on four different levels from beginner to expert.

"*The Facebook Marketing Bible (G)* is a comprehensive guidebook of marketing and advertising on Facebook. Each month, the Bible is updated with new content so that you stay current with the ever-changing Facebook ecosystem." That's how Web Media Brands describes their service. Here's how they describe the benefits of using it.

The Facebook Marketing Bible provides a wealth of high-value information, including:

- strategies for maximizing impressions, social reach, and conversions
- expert insights unique to the product

- case studies of successful and unsuccessful Facebook campaigns
- technical how-tos on installing plugins, building OpenGraph apps, and more
- how to conduct small-scale experiments to refine your audience and marketing strategy
- an in-depth survey and comparison of ad-op services, social media services, SaaS solutions, and other providers
- It also teaches you key marketing skills such as how to:
- demonstrate ROI for Facebook marketing
- generate successful calls to action and increase conversions
- maximize ad spending through targeted ads and optimization
- build websites with meaningful Facebook integration
- grow a loyal fanbase on your Page and maximize the reach of your content
- make the most of new and upcoming Facebook marketing and ad features.

Katie Adams, head of interactive marketing at 1–800–Flowers, isn't bashful in her endorsement: "The Facebook Marketing Bible and Inside Facebook are my lifelines! As the head of social media for my company, I rely on it to keep me up to date on what's going on with Facebook. Complete dependency!"

Meryl K. Evans brings us *32 ways to use Facebook for business (G.)* This has withstood the test of time. The tips are fairly basic and they cover essential categories of activities with links—most of which take you to official Facebook applications and resources, making it extremely easy to work through the list, line by line.

Read the rules first, Evans says, so you can "stay out of trouble."

Demonstrating the beauty of a blog post, you can see how others—everyone from students to professional marketers—reacted to Evans's advice.

If you want to go a little deeper, check out Justin Stravarius's *25 tips for killer Facebook marketing (G).* He does a masterful job of doing exactly what the title of his post suggests. Not only are the tips well thought out, they are beautifully presented. This is a "how-to" mini-manual for anyone with a product or service to sell.

His "Design a Custom Facebook Page" tip, for example, shows the Dunkin' Donuts page that includes free offers, a fan of the week feature showing a couple of over-caffeinated fans jumping for joy, and compelling photos of lattes.

We also liked his "Keep the Conversation Going" tip: "Conversations help foster the sense of being a community and that will do wonders for your brand."

There's no shortage of cyber advice available regarding Facebook advertising. And as is often the case, there are two sides to the story about the effectiveness of

Facebook advertising (G). So before you embark on a major Facebook ad campaign, you'd better do more than just read a few of the many tip columns out there. And make sure that you go beyond Facebook developed and sponsored articles.

You'll have to decide for yourself if Facebook advertising fits the marketing model that will work for your business. But be sure to google the phrase *how effective is Facebook advertising (G)* if you want to get a full picture of the various viewpoints on the subject.

Time.com writer Sam Gustin reached out to Andrew Lipsman, VP of industry analysis at comScore.com and co-author of the recent study and whitepaper, *The Power of Like (2): How Social Marketing Works (G).* ComScore.com and Facebook collaborated on the study.

"Yes, Facebook's ads can work. But there are different types of ads, and certain types work better for some marketers than others do," according to Lipsman. "Facebook ads can absolutely drive advertising effectiveness," he says, "but there aren't enough data points to generalize yet with a broad brush statement like 'Facebook ads work,' or 'Facebook ads do not work.'"

According to Gustin and Lipsman, there just isn't enough information in yet to be able to compare the effectiveness of Facebook ads to established online publishers like Yahoo and AOL.

But there's more to the story as Gustin emphasizes:

> The study looked at online and offline purchase behavior of fans and friends of fans for Amazon, Best Buy, Target and Walmart during the 2011 holiday shopping season. The researchers measured that purchase behavior against spending by the general population. Not surprisingly, the study found that 'fans' of retailers, on average, spent significantly more at those stores than did the general population—more than twice as much at Amazon, Best Buy and Target, and almost that much more at Walmart. Much more impressive and to the point, however, is that 'Friends of Fans' also typically spent more—only 8% more at Amazon, but a striking 51% more at Target and 104% more at Best Buy. That would seem to be a clear-cut, if modest, early validation of the social advertising thesis.

As Gustin emphasizes, there's just not a lot of data in regarding Facebook advertising effectiveness, but his examples of successful Facebook ads are not the only ones that exist. In fact, Dan Slagen provides *10 examples of Facebook ads that actually work (G)* in a HubSpot.com article:

> While there has been quite a bit of controversy surrounding the effectiveness of Facebook ads lately Ford and Coke recently gave their seal of approval in a Wall Street Journal article about Facebook ads, with both saying they were finding value in Facebook ads, and with Ford planning to expand its use of Facebook's advertising platform.

Slagen highlights four factors that he uses to assess an ad's Facebook effectiveness and then evaluates each example ad against these factors: relevance, value proposition, call-to-action, and disruption factor.

His article ends with a link to a free E-book, *How to Create Epic Ads (G)*, and another link that subscribes you to *HubSpot's Inbound Marketing Blog (G)*.

If Slagen's evaluation factors seem vaguely familiar to something you may have heard decades ago in an undergrad advertising class, you're probably not far off. In fact, in a *Fast Company* magazine article from June 10, 2102, E. B. Boyd answers the question: What is *the secret to marketing success on Facebook? Advertise like your grandfather (G)*:

> A new study by Facebook brings some big news that, curiously, at first blush might not seem like much news at all. It's this: If you want to create successful ads for the social network, just do the same thing you would do if you were advertising on TV, or in magazines, or on the radio.

The Facebook study upon which Boyd's article is based—*What Traditional Principles Matter When Designing Social (G)*—was presented at the prestigious Advertising Research Foundation's (ARF) Audience Measurement Conference in June 2012. "The study found that the ads that performed best were the ones that also did the best job of hewing to advertising fundamentals, especially focal point, brand link, and tone. The most important criteria," says Sean Bruich, "was that the ad needed to have some kind of reward."

We love the phrase "ad ownage" even if our spellchecker doesn't. Nickycakes lights a fire on his blog, and he's no less reserved in his article on *five killer tips for Facebook ad ownage (G)*. He's a shameless promoter, and we'd be a bit careful taking absolutely everything he says as gospel. But isn't that true about everything you read?

The Nickycakes theory is that the advertising is the thing. Rather than worrying about how to use Facebook advertising to get your company running at a better level, he says just go find a product, any product, and sell it on Facebook.

We've heard that imitation is the highest form of flattery, even that innovation always starts with imitation. Nickycakes comes right out and says it. Want to find a product to sell, he says, "Spy on other people's ads."

Some of his tips make us a bit squeamish; we're not certain we'd advocate selling everything that he would, but much of his advice seems very solid.

Business reporter Candace Beeke provides a business take on Facebook in an MLive.com post on *five rules of Facebook that companies should be thinking about (G)*. This is a little more elementary than some of our previous recommendations—it is, after all, written for a newspaper audience.

Here's what Beeke calls her first rule:

> Thou shalt focus on Facebook. Otherwise, you'll find yourself writing on someone else's wall things you meant to write on your own, posting information publicly that you meant to keep between certain friends, and other social media faux pas.

In other words, you really need to understand this new media, including the consequences of acting without thinking, before you venture into Facebook as a business tool.

Using Facebook as a business tool suggests that it has the capacity to help you sell a product or a service. Now that you are becoming familiar with Facebook as something other than a way to communicate with family and "friends," you might be asking yourself, just *what are Facebook ads (G)* anyway? You've also noticed the strips that appear down the right sidebar of your homepage, and the thought may have occurred to you that the ads seem to somehow correspond with your interests, or the interests that someone in your demographic—gender, age group, income level or location, that kind of thing—might be reasonably expected to have. SocialAdStool.com provides a great tutorial that answers basic questions about the ads and gives you three fundamental issues you have to resolve in getting an understanding *what are Facebook Ads? Social Media Tools (G)*

Here's more from SocialAdStool.com on *how Facebook ads work (G):*

> Facebook ads are targeted according to your Facebook profile information. Depending on their goals and the product that they are advertising, advertisers can set a targeting filter to select which group of people will see their ad.

Rob Fore blogs about a variety of social media issues and provides a concise explanation of what *Facebook Ads Cost (G)*.

His column begins with this statement: "Done correctly, Facebook PPC advertising should not cost you a dime."

Before you run off and start placing Facebook ads, you have to understand that Fore is talking about net costs—costs of the ad after the sale of the product or service:

> First thing you'll want to understand is that advertising on Facebook is not free. There is a 'Facebook ads cost per click' upfront, but the goal is to turn those clicks into likes, leads, sales and profits.
>
> You can estimate the Facebook ads cost per click (CPC) during the set up process of creating your ads. You can simply enter various targeting criteria and continue through the process until your reach the last step—which deals with pricing. It's at this stage the system will present you with a suggested bid price of other ads competing in your same niche.
>
> When your ads actually run on their network the only Facebook ads cost you incur is when a prospect actually clicks on your advertisement to

get more information. So these can be highly targeted prospects if you do it right.

Fore goes on to provide a good example of how to calculate Facebook ad costs, and how you can come to the conclusion he suggests in the beginning of the post. If you are able to convert the clicks into sales, the net costs of the ads should be zero.

Bloomberg.com's news service writer Brian Womack breaks down how in one quarter in 2011, *Facebook increased ad prices 40% on rising popularity (G)*. "The increase was on Facebook's self-service ads, not the higher priced premium ads that run on user home pages," according to the post.

To get a clear understanding of the differences between various ad forms, we turned to Merry Morud's SearcheEngineWatch.com article on *advertising on Facebook: Self-serve ad units explained and examined (G)*.

We need to be very clear on this point. A simple search of the question why some *Facebook advertising doesn't work (G)* will surface articles from a variety of skeptics that make it clear that if your business is searching for a silver bullet, you probably won't find it on Facebook.

For example, BehindCompanies.com says *Facebook advertising is fool's gold (G):* "People don't buy because of who they are, they buy because of circumstances in their lives, jobs that need to be done. The concept of *jobs to be done theory (G)* answers the question of 'what are the circumstances where a customer is most likely to buy my product."

That having been said, however, even the most skeptical people will admit that by engaging in Facebook advertising in an energetic and effective manner, you are increasing the chances that the better mousetrap you built will find its market.

Brian Carter lists what he says are *five proven ways to generate revenue from Facebook (G)* in a more recent, and perhaps more modest, Mashable post.

Here's the big picture. Start with advertising-based Ecommerce.

Marketers can leverage the massive reach and highly customizable targeting of Facebook's ad platform. They can create ads that take clickers straight to an ecommerce site, bypassing fan marketing entirely. The ads-direct-to-websites option is often overlooked, but can be immediately profitable. If you're not 100% sure about committing to the time and creativity required for fan marketing, then test direct-to-site ad traffic first.

Carter's great resource provides four additional potential income generators, and all of them have clear infographics like the one on the following page.

"Which revenue model should you choose?" Carter asks.

Think it over carefully, he advises. Remember, "companies that jump into

Source: Brian Carter (Mashable.com)

fan marketing without that understanding and a good plan usually post in a way that doesn't lead to much interaction."

Our lawyers would remind us from time to time to point out that we are not endorsing any specific advice that you may get from any of the wonderful, or even not-so-wonderful, resources we are urging you to visit. And this makes especially good sense when we're talking about ways to make money on Facebook. But it is happening—some people are making money through Facebook (other than Mark Zuckerberg, that is).

One popular article that is easy to google is called *12 ways to make money on Facebook (G.)* We first came across it in the very money-oriented blog BlogStash.com, and assumed that this was the original source for the article. It's been reissued on a number of blogs, and frankly, it's not all that easy to be sure who published the article first. You'll have to do some of your own independent research to determine if any of the chosen methods make sense for you. But be careful. Some of the information in this resource is (how you say?) dated.

For example, take a look at method #1—Radical Buy, which contains this cryptic note: "RadicalBuy.com has discontinued its widgets and apps and doesn't work any more. I will try to find another good app that can help you make money with your Facebook account, as soon as I can."

But hey—this is only one of twelve tips. You can spend hours just cross tracking through this post alone and who knows, by the end of your trip here you may have figured out a way to use Facebook to get you that Ferrari.

The main point in this post—wherever it originated—is the case that if you are a regular Facebook user, and have developed some of the basic Facebook skills, you may be passing up a chance to become the business of YOU.

Some Important Information about Facebook Users

Engagement has been a pretty big concept in public relations during the past decade in no small part because of the influence of the Internet. Generally, we think of someone being engaged if they are interacting with us, and if they increasingly show signs of being dependent on us to fulfill some aspect, however small it might seem, of their professional or personal lives.

Andrea Vahl recently summarized *nine Facebook marketing tips to improve engagement (G)* for SocialMediaExaminer.com. It all begins, she says, with getting personal.

> *Smart Passive Income (G)* with Pat Flynn does a great job with a variety of posts but also adds some of his personal life. You can throw the old 'don't tell them what you had for lunch' advice right out the window with this tip. Your community wants to get to know you and wants to be able to relate to you and your company.

Now we go back to one of our favorite sources, Mashable.com, for this simple but profound reminder that there are some basic things we need to do to maximize engagement by using these *three tips for maximizing engagement with Facebook likes and shares (G)* (you can find it by googling *Social Media Informer (G)* and entering David A. Yovanno under search):

> When it comes to Facebook, if you're uncertain where and when to place a 'Like' button on your site and when to use 'Share,' you're not alone. Social sharing technologies have evolved significantly in the past several months, but it's not as complicated as it may seem.

Facebook.com places a *value of a liker (G)* by making the case that "the average liker has 2.4 times the amount of friends than that of a typical Facebook user. They are also more interested in exploring content they discover on Facebook—they click on 5.3 times more links to external sites than the typical Facebook user."

And if you are aiming your product or service at a younger group, Facebook finds that the average liker on a new site is 34, compared to the median age of a newspaper subscriber, which is approximately 54 years old.

More than just citing the stats, Facebook identifies the best ways to reach likers. Here's a couple of their top tactics:

> Implement social plugins, beginning with the Like button. When a person clicks Like, it (1) publishes a story to their friends with a link back to your site, (2) adds the article to the reader's profile, and (3) makes the article discoverable through search on Facebook.

Optimize your Like button. By showing friends' faces and placing the button near engaging content (but avoiding visual clutter with plenty of white space), click-through rates improve by 3–5x.

It's pretty difficult to overstate the value of Mari Smith's *21 creative ways to increase your Facebook fan base (G)*. And if you look at the comments from others—there should be more than 400 by now—you'll see that we are not the only ones who appreciate these suggestions.

Again, some of the material is not new—it would be crazy to think that it could be—and almost all of it is useful.

Her tip #17 reminds us to use the share button:

The share button is all over Facebook and is a very handy feature. It only works for sharing on your personal profile. So periodically go to your fan page, scroll toward the bottom left column and click the "share+" button. Add a compelling comment along the lines of exciting news, recent changes, special incentives, etc., happening on your fan page and invite your friends to join if they haven't already. I find the Share button far more effective than the Suggest to Friends approach. And, if you'd like to Share content from the Web on to your *fan page* vs. profile, I highly recommend using the Hootlet bookmarklet tool at *HootSuite.com (G)*.

Smith also gives a great tutorial on *how to add a custom landing tab to your Facebook fan page (G)*—"a video that explains exactly (a) what your fan page is about, (b) who it's for and (c) why they should become members. The result: you'll increase your conversion rate from visitors to fans."

When are Facebook users most active? That seems like an important question for a variety of reasons. Christina Warren gives an excellent overview of a three-year study by the social media company Vitrue that answers the question.

Here are some of the big takeaways:

- The three biggest usage spikes tend to occur on weekdays at 11:00 A.M., 3:00 P.M. and 8:00 P.M. ET.
- The biggest spike occurs at 3:00 P.M. ET on weekdays.
- Weekday usage is pretty steady, however Wednesday at 3:00 P.M. ET is consistently the busiest period.
- Fans are less active on Sunday compared to all other days of the week.

So we know when Facebook users seem to be most (and least) active, but what if we want to know *what's a Facebook follower worth (G)* in dollars and cents terms?

Sarah Needleman and Evelyn Rusli took a look at this question for the *Wall Street Journal online (G)*:

> Under a program rolled out in May (2012), businesses pay Facebook Inc. anywhere from $5 to hundreds of dollars to promote a post to the news feeds of users who have 'liked' their page, plus Facebook friends of those users. The price depends on how many users a business wants to reach.
>
> A July survey of 400 U.S. businesses with between $5 million and $50 million in annual revenue found that 77% spend a quarter or more of their marketing efforts on social media. Slightly fewer, 73%, said they have added social-media management to the duties of at least one employee in recent years. The survey was conducted by Edge Research and commissioned by the software company Vocus Inc.

Facebook says the new promoted posts are beginning to be accepted by the small business community, which had previously seen these fan contacts as free. But some small businesses are complaining that having to pay for social media puts them at a competitive disadvantage over their larger rivals.

Jeff Bullas, writing in his blog, has a more optimistic take on the question of *how much is one Facebook fan worth? (G)*. He believes that the equation for online stores is "quite simple?more traffic equals more sales!"

The challenge for all business, large and small, is to drive traffic to your website.

A recent study by *HitWise.com (G)* in the UK has revealed that a Facebook fan is worth 20 additional visits per year to an on-line store. From there it is easy to calculate the direct benefit in cold hard sales.

Time, as they say, will tell.

New Facebook Tools

If you want to get a good look at the top new Facebook tools, you should begin by tuning in to Mari Smith. We've referred to her earlier in this chapter. She's a recognized speaker and co-author of *Facebook Marketing: An Hour a Day (G)*. She's also a major contributor to *SocialMediaExaminer.com (G)*.

In her December 2010 post on the *top 75 apps for enhancing your Facebook page (G)*, she sets up a great index that will give you a head start on knowing where to look for what's new. The categories she has set up include:

- Apps for adding custom content/branded landing tab
- Full hands-on customization service for designers/developers
- Enterprise-level customization tools and apps
- Your blog, which includes her favorite app for important blog feeds
- RSS Feed and Content Publishers
- Video—YouTube and Viddler

- Twitter, which includes her favorite app to publish select tweets (only) to your Fan page
- Photo Apps including Flickr and SlideShare
- A Reviews app that you can add to your Fan page
- Live Video, which includes her favorite Vpype and four alternatives
- Live Chat to offer live chat sessions with your fans
- FAQs, the FAQ Page app that allows you to have a FAQ tab on your fan page to which you can direct fans
- Polls and Quizzes, which include some free and some priced apps
- Contests and Promotions, including a dozen third-party apps from which you can choose
- Local business apps, appointment scheduling apps, contact forms, email marketing apps and her five favorite Ecommerce apps to help "sell products on your page."

Lisa Mason wrote about the *ten best Facebook page apps for Timeline (G)* in a recent posting for SocialMediaSun.com, an impressive blog of Adam Justice.

"The landing pages that were once a favorite of small business will be replaced with the cover page." Lisa suggests that you google *Facebook Page Timeline Tutorial (G)* to get more information on how businesses are "resorting to Facebook page apps to engage customers on their own terms."

In his January 2013 Mashable.com post *Facebook Timeline Change: It's Starting (G)*, Chris Taylor takes you directly from a New Zealand beta test to a description of the Pinterest-like *new Facebook collections manager (G)* feature "that let's you customize all that content at the top of your Timeline, as well as (giving) you the ability to rearrange the right-hand column."

You might also be interested in the new suite of Facebook safety tools—not quite so new at this writing—but described in April 2011 on the Facebook blog by Arturo Bejar. In that post, Bejar described *Facebook two-factor authentication (G)*, a then-new feature to prevent unauthorized access to your account—a particularly sensitive issue to Facebook business users.

Lifehacker.com's post by Whitson Gordon describes *everywhere you should enable two-factor authentication right now (G)*.

He quotes Google's "spam guru," Matt Cutts:

Two-factor authentication is a simple feature that asks for more than just your password. It requires both 'something you know' (like a password) and 'something you have' (like your phone). After you enter your password, you'll get a second code sent to your phone, and only after you enter it will you get into your account. Think of it as entering a PIN number, then getting a retina scan, like you see in every spy movie ever made. It's a lot more secure than a password that anyone can hack, and keeps unwanted snoopers out of your online accounts.

Facebook describes its mission as making the world more open and connected. In early 2013, Facebook wiz Lars Eilstrup Rasmusson announced that the company founder and CEO had given him a challenge. The result was Graph Search. He talked about it in an article posted on Facebook.com, in which he took us *under the hood: building graph search beta (G)*.

> In 2011, Zuck asked the search team to design and build a new system that would recreate the ability to search the entire social graph. This was an interesting challenge because—compared to large document collections like the Web—the data in our databases have significantly more explicit structure than free-flowing text. Therefore, a traditional keyword-based search product might not be the answer.
>
> This project presented two parallel challenges: what would such a product look like, and what infrastructure would we need to build to support it?
>
> For the product part, we discussed and debated, and built several simple prototypes of graphical UIs that allowed users—click-by-click—to build up structured, database-like queries. But they all seemed too complex and not quite up for the full scope of Zuck's challenge to us.
>
> Then an idea emerged around the title of each page on Facebook. We wanted people to be able to construct their own views of the particular Facebook content they were interested in. If a person simply entered the title of the content they were looking for, could we then build a system that would understand the searcher's input and find the content for them?

The rest, as they say (whoever "they" are) is history.

Graph Search will appear as a bigger search bar at the top of each page. When you search for something, that search not only determines the set of results you get, but also serves as a title for the page. You can edit the title—and in doing so create your own custom view of the content you and your friends have shared on Facebook. And by the time you read this, both Timeline and Graph Search should have most of the bugs worked out.

Enhancing Your Facebook Page

Thank you SocialMediaToday.com for sharing *eleven quick tips for enhancing our Facebook page (G)*.

We are big boosters of a number of nonprofit organizations in the mid-Michigan area. And when we found Frank Barry and Jeff Patrick's post in the fall of 2011, we just couldn't wait to send it off to the Children's Trust Fund. We think they put it to good use.

Because of Facebook's large user base and incredible popularity, businesses and nonprofits are using the services in increasingly effective ways. Nonprofits specifically are figuring out how to connect with their supporters, donors, volunteers and advocates in new and interesting ways. Some are even using Facebook to successfully raise money.

Jeff Patrick and I had a chance to speak to over 350 nonprofits a while back. We shared a Facebook 101 for Nonprofits type of presentation that was focused on highlighting what a few nonprofits are doing well in hopes that others would see the possibilities and be inspired to take action. Here's the presentation followed by 11 useful tips to get you moving in the right direction with your Facebook presence.

Speaking of nonprofits, John Haydon provides a wonderful PDF version of his book—*The Complete Facebook Guide for Small Non-profits (G)*—as a service to that sector of the economy least equipped to hire consultants, and most in need to new ways to build their Facebook fan base.

The Haydon book covers the waterfront from a solid introduction to a step-by-step approach to creating a Facebook page, customizing it in a way that embeds a volunteer or fundraising widget, and making your Facebook page "do tricks" like linking it to your Twitter account.

Not everyone cares how many followers they have on their Facebook page. If that's you, skip on past Ching Ya's *ten ways to grow your Facebook page following (G)* and on to the next section. But we love Ching's post because it answers, for us, a question that he gets from his clients on a regular basis.

From the day you set up a Facebook page, it does require an ongoing commitment to brand, monitor, and network with people who find interest in your product. Besides quality service, it's important to build close-knit relationships with visitors.

Like he said and we have said elsewhere, this stuff takes work, and it is certainly not something you should do unless you intend to do it well.

But if you're looking for some great tips on how to get people to like your Facebook page, take Ching Ya's advice. The common theme throughout his tips is fan engagement.

Putting your face on milk cartons is no longer the premier way of being found in America. How about the possibility that making yourself findable to the search engines might be a better way to get your brand out there?

This post is more than a couple of years old now, but it's still among the most useful we've found. Marty Weintraub, writing in SearchEngineLand.com, admonishes readers to think about *ten SEO tips for maximizing Facebook visibility (G)* to take you and your organization beyond basic Google and other mainstream engines, and to start thinking about Facebook:

> Little-to-none of Facebook's activity is indexed by Google and other mainstream engines. It's easy to see why Facebook's members-only organic search results deserve attention!
>
> At the root of this new consideration is the reality that Facebook is now allowing users to search the last 30 days of their news feed for status updates, photos, links, videos and notes being shared by friends and the Facebook pages of which they're fans.

Some of the specific data may have changed since Marty's 2009 post, but the principle remains the same. "Facebook is quickly becoming a massive walled-garden parallel organic Internet."

Matt Sullivan, client services manager at MoonToast, used his post in Social-MediaToday.com on the *anatomy of a shared link on Facebook (G)* to show us how he nearly doubled click-throughs to his clients' stores by properly promoting sharing to a Facebook Fan Page. His advice is thorough: "Needless to say, giving our clients the ability to customize the title, message, and image specifically for sharing to their Facebook Fan Pages made a huge impact, and drove even more qualified leads to their stores."

You need to understand that we're not shilling for Mashable.com, but we have to admit we love it. And since it's an advertising-based service, we have to assume they don't mind us referring to them as often as we do.

If you go to the "About" page at Mashable.com you'll find out they have been around since way back in 2005. Here's how they describe themselves:

> Mashable is the top source for news in social and digital media, technology and web culture. With more than 40 million monthly page views, Mashable is the most prolific news site reporting breaking web news, providing analysis of trends, reviewing new websites and services, and offering social media resources and guides.

Here's one reason we're "Mashablephiles." Stephanie Marcus provides some wonderful advice we're sharing with our students (and our children, by the way) in her post on *how to score a job through Facebook. (G):*

> While Facebook is better known for helping people lose their jobs, it's largely an untapped resource when it comes to job hunting. With 500 million users, it has the potential to be one of the largest. But finding a job through Facebook isn't about pestering your friends and junking up their news feeds with status updates like 'Unemployed and Looking For Work—Help A Dude Out.' It's about making the most of your network in a positive way, not by being a nuisance.

Stephanie lays out six major steps that you can take to use Facebook to help you get that job of your dreams. Each step provides wonderful advice and practical examples that just might do the trick for you. And as soon as we complete our Facebook section, we'll take you on a guided trip through a social network—LinkedIn—that's increasingly known for finding jobs.

Here is what we call a throwaway resource. If you don't care about whether you ever get a decent job or whether you'll be promoted in the job you have, throw this resource away. If, on the other hand, you don't want to be in that category of almost hired or almost promoted (but for the fact that the employer used social networks to screen candidates and employees), you might consider getting into *SocioClean.com (G)*.

This is also not a free service, but it may be more than worth your while to figure out just how offensive is your Facebook profile: "Socioclean.com crawls through your Facebook profile photos, groups and wall posts, and alerts you to anything inappropriate."

But before you get carried way scraping your Facebook page, you might want to read the Forbes.com post by Meghan Casserly who warns about *social media and the job hunt: squeaky-clean profiles need not apply (G)*.

She describes a young friend of hers who got a job as an intern at a New York City job-recruiting firm. Her job: to review the Facebook accounts of applicants.

> She's become the gatekeeper to employment for thousands of New Yorkers, and I was surprised to hear about the barriers to entry. Wedding pictures? Great. Baby photos? Even better. Photos with friends at parties, beaches and concerts? An absolute must.
>
> There's a sense that a profile with no character has probably been scraped of some racy stuff or else the person has no social skills and won't fit in. Either way, she says, that candidate has been moved to the bottom of the pile.

Let's wrap up the Facebook love fest with an alternate point of view. Dan Yoder, writing in BusinessInsider.com, is mad as hell, and he just isn't going to take it anymore.

Yoder ticks through a list *ten reasons to delete your Facebook account (G)*— objections ending with #10, which is, according to him, Facebook's "completely one-sided" terms of service, which leads back to his objection #1—"The Facebook application itself sucks." He leaves no stone unturned or should we say "un-thrown"?

But all is not lost. As he is signing off this column advocating deleting your Facebook account, he sends us to a second column sharing *10 Reasons You Will Never Quit Facebook (Even If You Think You Want To) (G)*.

"You may feel a slight twinge of anxiety," Yoder says. "But you'll stay on Facebook forever."

Extra Point—Facebook in the Future

Sporting an image of a blue Pac man with a Facebook "f" gobbling Google, Pay-Pal, Skype, and Groupon, Adam Rifkin's TechCrunch.com post a few years back made a bold prediction in making the case for *how Facebook can become bigger in five years than Google is today (G):*

> I have been mulling over data from both companies, and I'm ready to declare in public my belief that Facebook will be bigger in five years than Google is right now, barring some drastic action or accident.

Perhaps that reveals why Google at the time we wrote this seems to be putting all their vast resources behind their new social media platform called Google+. Google may see the writing on the wall and realize that they need social media if they want to truly become too big to fail.

Rifkin continues:

> Facebook will inexorably grow as big as Google is today and maybe bigger, because Madison Avenue's brands are less interested in targeting than they are in broadcasting to vast mother-loving buckets of demographically correct eyeballs, and Facebook has become the perfect platform for that.

Not so fast, says Peter Da Vanzo in a post in SeoBook.com, *Facebook Vs. Google: No Contest. (G)*

> Google wins because Google's advertising is closely aligned with the users' primary activity, which is to seek topics and click links. The primary activity of a user on Facebook is to socialize. Translating this activity to a commercial imperative in a way advertisers find profitable is the challenge Facebook faces.

We're not sure who's right here, or how important the debate really is. Time, the most correct prognosticator ever invented, will (eventually) tell. And the way we see it, the cyber world seems, at this moment anyway, to be big enough for both of them.

CHAPTER 4

LinkedIn—"The New Resume"

First, we have to credit John Hill, the LinkedIn Higher Education evangelist (and former Michigan State colleague), with turning us on to describing LinkedIn as "the new resume." We hadn't thought of it exactly that way before we saw Hill's reference, but that is, in fact, what LinkedIn has become—the new resume. It's that, for sure, and it's become so much more than that.

We find one of the first uses of the phrase *LinkedIn—The New Resume (G)* in a column by Mike McCready from his social media marketing blog in October 2011. His advice for getting started is exactly the same thing Derek and our other instructors, Graham Davis and Ross Johnson, tell the students in our opening New Media Driver's License® class at MSU:

> Fully complete your profile. Make sure you've added your education, experience and skills. Also include a professional photo and links to your social network and websites.

McCready goes on to identify four or five other important considerations as you get started, or rejuvenate your interest, in LinkedIn.

The ultimate business social networking tool, LinkedIn is a 200 million member website, said to be active in 200 countries, and it's all about making business connections. Put your resume online, and you are on your way to connecting on LinkedIn. But *optimizing your social media/LinkedIn profile (G)* is key to you managing your social brand.

Another key is recognizing that LinkedIn is a "button-down networking site," as Cindy Krischer Goodman called it in a column that first ran in *The Miami Herald*. Her main point, and the title of her piece, was that LinkedIn is all business so treat it professionally. Don't make the mistake of treating it like Facebook:

> If you had a hard day at the office or your child just won an award, you may want to share it with your personal network elsewhere, but not on LinkedIn. Experts advise only sharing what you would share at a professional networking event. Another etiquette pitfall on LinkedIn is the hit and run—making a connection and not following up.

By the way, if it weren't for LinkedIn, this book would not exist. Neither would MSU's New Media Driver's License® class, at least in the form it is in today, which to date has taken more than 1,500 students through a pretty thorough introduction to every subject we touch upon in this book.

Early in author Richard Cole's five-year term as chairperson of MSU's Department of Advertising, Public Relations and Retailing, he got a call from Internet guru Toby Trevarthen. Here's Rick's version:

> Toby is both an MSU alum and an Internet-business pioneer. He called to offer to help me set up a department LinkedIn site. In fact, he volunteered to do most of the work to get the site off the ground. Not long after, he messaged me through LinkedIn that there was a young entrepreneur in Ann Arbor who was doing interesting things in social media, and he thought our students might like to meet him. Using our LinkedIn connection, I asked (now co-author of this book) Derek Mehraban to come to East Lansing to speak about how businesses are using social media at our "Promotions Commons" speaker's series, and the rest, as they say, is history.

Mehraban is a stickler for getting your LinkedIn profile right. He's not alone in this thinking.

Gerry Moran has posted some great advice on the subject in Business2Community.com on *social branding: how to create the perfect LinkedIn profile blueprint (G)*. And it all begins with understanding what the current (2013) LinkedIn profile character limits are. Moran walks you through the limits, category by category, and includes some brief hints.

Here's one example: "Honors and Awards—1,000 characters to shine the spotlight on YOU. Even if you won a sales award, it's a great accomplishment to list!"

Building your LinkedIn profile is your first step. Be sure to follow the guide and build it to completion. Here are a few other things to consider when building your LinkedIn profile:

1. *Create a custom LinkedIn URL—Shelly Roth (G)*—an important marketing tool for you. The best way to get this done is to go to Roth's wonderful YouTube tutorial. Having your name as part of your LinkedIn URL will make it easier to find you.

2. Write a keyword-rich description of yourself in your professional headline at the top of your profile. Be clear and impactful. Avoid the simple and short description like "accountant." Check out this advice on *how to optimize your linked in profile professional headline—Des Welsh (G)*, and you can find other advice by Googling that phrase.

3. *Importing your email connections to LinkedIn (G)*. This is easy with Gmail or Yahoo mail to upload all your contacts and see who is on LinkedIn. Then if they are there, you can select them and invite them

to connect with you. Invite all business connections, and even friends who you could do business with.

4. Ask for recommendations. One of the best things you can do is to get recommendations from your peers. Laura Rubenstein will tell you all you need to know about *how ask for a killer recommendation on LinkedIn (G)*. Past bosses, colleagues, clients . . . Remember, the best way to get a recommendation is to give a recommendation first.

5. Build links to your profile. Use your profile URL in your email signatures. Link to it from your website . . . Take a look at Pamela Vaughan's *ultimate cheat sheet for mastering LinkedIn (G)* to get a head start on expert link building.

Since you are taking this journey with our book, building and maintaining a strong LinkedIn presence is a good first step and a great way to build your personal and company brand.

Turns out that the line between business and personal gets very thin on LinkedIn. And that fact becomes quite clear as you examine the comprehensive resource list LinkedIntelligence.com provides in their post about *100+ ways to use LinkedIn (G)*.

This site covers a smorgasbord of individual articles that makes us somewhat envious. Not all the resources listed are top-of-the-line, but this crowdsourced "Encyclopedia LinkedIn" covers everything from business development and marketing to using LinkedIn in for job search and recruiting.

Using LinkedIn for Business

Way back in 2007, in an article on *How to change the world: ten ways to use LinkedIn (G)*, Guy Kawasaki told us: "Most people use LinkedIn to 'get to someone' in order to make a sale, form a partnership, or get a job."

Kawasaki is a founding partner and entrepreneur-in-residence at Garage Technology Ventures. He is also the co-founder of Alltop.com and was an Apple Fellow at Apple Computer, Inc. His blog *"How to Change the World (G)"* is, in his words, "a practical blog for impractical people."

Kawasaki's post provides tips stemming from years of experience in the business and technology industry, and despite its advanced years, remains a great resource to on ways to differentiate yourself from the millions of other LinkedIn users.

Want a quick resource guide to help you understand and capitalize on the power of LinkedIn in your professional life? Then google the phrase *ways to use LinkedIn for business (G)* and you'll find a variety of great resources dating back to Gigaom.com's blogger Meryl K Evans 2009 post: "You can do so much more with it than simply look up contacts: find gigs, sell products, expand your networks, grow your business and gain free publicity."

If you like the idea of reading a brief and well-written PDF on the subject, HubSpot.com makes its book on the subject available with the click of a mouse.

We like to use real-world examples to get a point across, and so does FoxBusiness.com as evidenced by their post showing how *three small business owners use LinkedIn effectively (G)*.

> When 39–year-old Ralph Carlone wanted to start his own management consulting company, he turned to LinkedIn to create a group for those who shared his business interests. He started the 'Small Business and Independent Consultant Network' in 2009, which today has grown to more than 5,000 members.

If you get a chance, you might want to sign on to one of the sponsored LinkedIn seminars on how to use LinkedIn for Business. A recent seminar conducted by SocialMediaDirectors.co.uk focused on UK business and covered the following subjects:

- Why LinkedIn is an increasingly key business tool
- How to get the most out of LinkedIn
- Key considerations when creating a Profile which really works for you
- Developing your network and integrating your current one
- How to best connect with people (and how not to)
- Tools on LinkedIn to push you and your business
- Targeting and approaching prospects using Advanced Search and other tools
- LinkedIn applications making your life easier
- A recommended weekly LinkedIn routine

Luke Knight, digital strategist for 4Ps Marketing, offered his advice and artwork in TheDrum.com on *how to use LinkedIn for brand authority and to generate leads (G)*.

> What many businesses miss out on is using LinkedIn to generate new business leads, and this should be an integral part of the sales and marketing process. LinkedIn has a number of original features that initially encourage professionals to sign up and these features are consistently developing, meaning that connections can be made with the right people, at the right time, for the right purpose.

Knight goes on to list six key elements of developing great LinkedIn content that begins with creating and implementing a company social media policy that

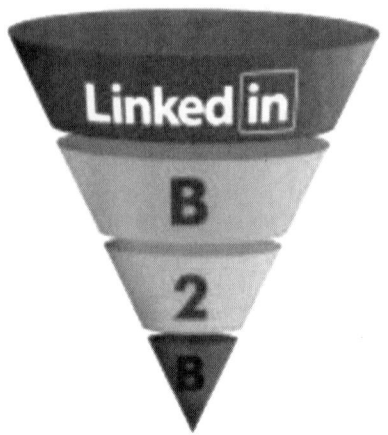

Source: Luke Knight (4Ps Marketing)

ties into the sales and marketing plan and ends with articulating a professional and timely content plan "so that every individual knows what content they need to be sharing with their contacts and when."

There's an old saying in advertising that's attributed to Philadelphia retailer John Wanamaker. "Half my advertising works," he said. "I just don't know which half."

According to a recent *Wall Street Journal* online article by Emily Maltby and Shira Ovide, a WSJ survey of 835 small business owners in January 2013 produced rather good news for LinkedIn. More than 40 percent of the participating *small firms say LinkedIn works (G)* as a valuable social media tool aiding their company's growth. This number is better than twice that of the other networks—16 percent for YouTube, 14 percent for Facebook, and a meager 3 percent for Twitter.

> Owners of small firms generally have limited money and time to figure out the most useful ways to tap into social media. In the survey, just four in 10 business owners said they have employees dedicated to social-media campaigns. Nearly half of them spend between one and five hours weekly on social media, and one-third spend no time at all.

HallamInternet.com provides a current and useful overview of *LinkedIn advertising: tips, costs, and how does it work (G)*.

> If you want to reach more business owners and decision makers, then LinkedIn Advertising may be a highly cost effective method for you to consider.
> How does LinkedIn advertising work?
> It is quite straightforward, really.

First you create your ad. Or better yet, you create three versions of your ads that LinkedIn will test, and you can learn which ads perform best.

Next, you identify the LindedIn users you want to target. Targeting options include industry sector, job function, company size, geography, gender and age.

And finally, you set your budgets.

If you are looking for a comparison between *Google ads vs. Facebook ads vs. LinkedIn Ads—a cost per click advertising comparison (G)*, check out the Business2Community.com column by Neil Sequeira. This post "could help you get a better idea of just how they stack up when it comes to running online advertising campaigns."

We agree.

So, if you're starting to be interested in using this social-networking juggernaut to zero in on tightly segmented business demographics, the company provides many tools to help you advertise on LinkedIn.

This resource will get you started, help you identify advertising goals, and teach you how to easily create an advertisement on LinkedIn.

Getting LinkedIn to Personal Growth

"Even after nine years [more than ten now] in the social media stratosphere, LinkedIn is still an elusive platform to master," Lauren Hockenson tells us in the introduction to her Mashable.com *LinkedIn boot camp infographic (G)*.

One graphic talks about the movers and shakers of LinkedIn. "When it comes to marketing yourself and your business, most people go straight to Facebook because of the sheer size if its user base. But demographically speaking, LinkedIn has a leg up."

Justin Levy worries aloud in a SocialMediaToday.com post that "It's very common to get sucked into social media networks other than LinkedIn." And he's concerned that with our fascination with YouTube, and Twitter, and Pinterest, and (of course) Facebook, we may be losing focus on the one network that is most closely linked to our professional futures.

One key about social media, especially LinkedIn, is how they allow us to connect with friends, family, and potential jobs. If you want to use social media to your advantage, then you'll want to pay attention to Dan Schawbel's ideas about *clever ways to get a job using social media (G)*. Schawbel is the founder of Millennial Branding, a full-service personal branding agency. His advice in this Mashable.com article could help you get the job you want.

Schwabel insists that "by understanding who you are, what differentiates you in the marketplace and establishing your personal branding online, you can compete . . ."

To the extent that we're looking at a network increasingly being billed as the new resume, we thought it wise to go to the job-hunt.org site to get their take on how to use *LinkedIn for executive job search (G)*. While the site doesn't look so great when you first go to it, remember you can't judge a book by its cover—or a website by its landing page, for that matter.

We didn't dig deep enough into this resource to be sure about its business model, but hidden within this landing page is good advice for execs seeking jobs on how to use LinkedIn to get them:

> If you're an executive, and you don't have a presence on Google, recruiters and employers are likely to dismiss you as a lightweight. Increasingly, if you're not on LinkedIn, the same thing happens.

There's a wonderful segment in this column about the importance of building a serious profile, starting to invite participation and getting endorsements, and using the variety of other available LinkedIn features.

Once you've made a potential job connection on LinkedIn what do you do? If you've answered this question with "Nothing," then you are going to want to read Linda Coles's ideas for *four LinkedIn tips to help you stand out (G)*.

Coles, of Blue Banana, is a sought-after speaker who also runs various workshops and seminars on how to use social media tools effectively and productively. In this SocialMediaExaminer.com post she asks:

> So how can you use social etiquette to really make your LinkedIn connections valuable and stand out from the crowd at the same time?
>   View LinkedIn as your own boardroom of connections versus your coffee shop connections on Twitter or Facebook. They tend to be managers, directors, business owners, CEOs and the like.

The key to LinkedIn's power may be this: Very important people are using LinkedIn daily. Many CEOs and business owners view it as a more valid form of connection than other social-networking sites. Learn how to make the most out of new and potential connections to build your network and stand out. As we've said before, and will again, differentiate or die.

We're pretty sure by now that you're getting sick and tired of hearing about how important LinkedIn is. So that's why were hoping you'll be interested in *building online credibility on LinkedIn (G)* for yourself. This resource will tell you why it's important and suggest the places where you should invest your time on LinkedIn, and will help save you time. Charlotte Britton used this column in SocialMediaToday.com to provide tips and to link you to a Slide Share presentation that expands on the article's key points.

Britton explains:

> Your online credibility is an increasingly important way of showcasing your specialized knowledge and expertise, which will build your online credibility. As more people engage with the social web, differentiating yourself becomes imperative.
>
> Most people understand the basics to setting up the profile, but beyond that they do not understand the potential of how they can use this online networking.

There is little, if any, room for error in your professional career. There are a lot of ways to make mistakes on various social networking websites, but, above all, LinkedIn is one where errors must be avoided.

Laura Smith-Proulx, a "resume expert" and former recruiter, asked a great question: *Are you making the top three LinkedIn profile errors? (G)* She posed her question as an article that answers it in Careerealism.com:

> . . . Using it [LinkedIn] incorrectly can actually reduce your chances of being hired. Here are three common pitfalls to avoid when setting up and using a LinkedIn profile for your job search.

Extra Point—Growing by Leaps and Bounds

"Like all the social networks, LinkedIn is growing by leaps and bounds," Stacey Acavero says in opening her February 2012 post in Vocul.com's blog. In it, she highlights *15 changes you might see in LinkedIn's future (G):*

> This year LinkedIn has undergone a few changes, including LinkedIn Today, an industry-specific news feed, a share function allowing users to send relevant information to members of their networks, and video functionality allowing professionals to incorporate video into their profiles. These new capabilities will be welcome additions for any professional looking to boost his or her social media strategy.

On the horizon:

- Content curating functions to help users create their own libraries of professional or industry-related information to augment their profile page
- Network connections to niche sites
- Geographic capabilities to help find new contacts based on your location, boosting your local reputation with nearby referrals and recommendations.

Becoming a Master of Your Twitter Universe

One of the things that made it difficult for some people to take Twitter seriously is the language—Twitter, Tweeting, and the latest, Tweeple, a word being used to characterize those people who are increasingly relying on Twitter and get messages out to increasingly large circles of Twends. Joe Markman, content manager @Factbrowser, acknowledges that he hasn't seen a percentage of the Twitter accounts that are businesses rather than personal accounts, and neither have we. *Joe Markman's answer to how many businesses are using Twitter (G)* ranges from 50 percent to 70 percent of U.S. business-to-business companies—a formidable number, for sure.

And regardless of what you may think of the wordplay (Twitter was named to mimic the sound birds use to communicate with one another), tweeting is having a huge impact in the world of social media. In fact more than that, Twitter is having a huge impact on the world! Now let's look at how it's being used as a new way to generate business.

If you're a high school kid, you can skip right over this next resource. But if you're in business, or going into business, or going into an occupation that may want to help businesses grow—even if you have an established Twitter program already underway—you probably want to review the basics.

PCMag.com's Jill Duffy does a good job of explaining *how to use Twitter for business (G)*.

Begin with this premise. You're most certainly not going to find that all of your customers or prospects are Twitter users. They are not. Not everyone uses Twitter, but those who do seem to have some things in common.

According to Duffy, "People go to Twitter to share what they know and learn in return. Twitter users are hungry for new ideas, opportunities, information, services, and products. If your business is not part of this exchange, you're leaving two huge opportunities untouched—growing your business and improving it."

Duffy recommends that you take these five issues into account if you want to "find your footing on the microblogging site":

- Define your purpose and goals
- Assign the right people in your firm to do the Tweeting
- Cultivate a voice for your company on Twitter by using real people with real names
- Follow the right people by keeping good lists and finding "connectors"
- Keep a sense of humor, and if you don't have one, find it before you start

Charlene Kingston provides a bit more detail by laying out *16 creative ways to use Twitter for business (G)* in her column in SocialMediaExaminer.com.

Her advice begins with the need to organize your lists and it ends with recognizing the need to expand the Twitter conversation to your blog:

"When you have a great conversation going on Twitter, or you find a topic that people respond to on Twitter, why not expand the conversation to the people who read your blog?"

If you are still unconvinced, ask Aaron Lee to share the *10 reasons why your business should use Twitter (G)*. By the way, Lee's blog is called AskAaronLee.com. The 10–part answer includes connecting with customers, building and advancing your brand, and generating customer feedback. The remaining reasons are just as basic and equally relevant.

Consumer Trends on Twitter

If you don't think the business world has caught on to the importance of Twitter, consider that the National Federation of Small Business, which bills itself as the voice of small business, has been teaching its members across the U.S. *how to use twitter to monitor consumer trends and tastes (G)*.

They begin their membership tutorial with advocating searching tweets by keywords:

Using Twitter's advanced search option gives you a great way to sample consumer sentiments. For example, let's say that partners in a sporting goods store in Cleveland want to get an idea of how many pairs of Kobe Bryant's new Nikes they will be able to sell in a city filled with LeBron James fans. (This post, obviously, was written before James said adios to MSU alum Dan Gilbert in Cleveland, and headed for Miami.)

First, the storeowners would want to go to search.twitter.com, and then click on the advanced option. They would type in the search phrase 'Kobe shoes' and select other useful options, such as 'place,' which allows users to read only the tweets originating from their chosen location.

It will become clear after reading the first few pages of Tweets that the

Source: Bird logo property of Twitter Inc.; adapted by Cara Pring (TheSocialSkinny.com)

majority of Twitter-using basketball fans in the Cleveland area will be sticking with the LeBron James Nikes. However, a few local users admire the looks of the Kobe model, which would be enough positive reaction for the storeowner to keep a few pairs in stock.

They also stress trend spotting through Twitter to follow industry tastemakers and popular topics, and show you some great shortcuts for doing this.

Twitter.com/search is the product's simple tool to see *what's happening on twitter right now (G)*. For example, we typed in LeBron James and got access to top videos and a variety of tweets relating to this basketball superstar. In fact, as we entered this paragraph, we saw a pair of cork LeBron Nikes showing up as a top photo. Fernando Ponce @FernandoPonce Jr., retweeted the photo that had been tweeted earlier in the day by Nike @KingJamesX.

The degree to which the Twitter business model has morphed from an easy way to keep in touch with people in your life to a serious quasi-news source was outlined on the official Twitter blog in November 2009:

The fundamentally open model of Twitter created a new kind of information network and it has long outgrown the concept of personal status updates. Twitter helps you share and discover what's happening now among all the things, people, and events you care about. 'What are you doing?' isn't the right question anymore—starting today, we've shortened it by two characters. Twitter now asks, 'What's happening?'

Here's what's happening with Twitter according to the most recent *100 more social media statistics for 2012 (G)* from Cara Pring. She runs a blogazine. (Is it a magazine or a blog?) We have happily joined the ranks of Pring's subscribers and have appropriated from her blog this lovely adaptation of the Twitter bird logo and the following fun facts:

- There are more than 465 million Twitter accounts
- Twitter is growing at a rate of 11 accounts per second
- On a busy day, Twitter sees about 175 million tweets
- The U.S. has 107.7 million Twitter accounts, Brazil has 33.3 million, and Japan has 29.9 million
- The U.S. represents 28.1 percent of all Twitter users
- The global average of accounts that are active (or those that have tweeted at least once in three months) is only 27 percent—which would indicate that less than one-third of Twitter's total accounts actually actively use the service
- Thirty percent of Twitter users have an income over $100,000

The *Pew Internet: Social Networking (G)* project's most recent usage study (February 2013) reports that two-thirds of American adults online now use social networking sites, with 16 percent saying they use Twitter. For a more detailed analysis, go to Pew Internet and American Life project's full report on the *demographics of social media users—2012 (G)*.

"The popularity of Twitter (and Instagram) among blacks in America is surging while white women under 50 continue to pin away on Pinterest," reported Roger Yu in a *USA Today* article highlighting how *minorities rush to Twitter, Instagram, Smartphones (G)*.

Going to the source of great information on all things social, we again turn to Altimeter's Brian Solis who compares the move to Twitter to a similar move that occurred a few years back to texting, which "became a natural form of common communication." Says Solis:

> Over the years, Twitter has become a human seismograph measuring world events, popular culture, and everyday sentiment while providing a lens into every nuance that captivates our attention. What was once a Twitter paradox is now part of our digital culture. Everyday people who are connected to Twitter become the nodes and their shared experiences form one of the most efficient information networks in the world.

That Smell of Successful Twitter Business Strategies

In our first book, we referenced two great posts from the author of *ProBlogger: Secrets of Blogging Your Way to a Six-Figure Income*, Darren Rowse. Since then, SocialMediaExaminer.com's Michael Stelzner has posted a wonderful video with Rowse in which he lays out *how bloggers should use twitter (G)*, which we think is great place to start with an exploration of developing integrated business strategies in social networking.

In his earlier articles, Rowse admitted to being slow in adopting Twitter because "I didn't think it had much to offer me." But slowly and surely, Rowse used Twitter to improve the quality of his blogs, to network, expand his subscriber base, and "grow my profile." He also used Twitter to help sell his successful book.

And as in his earlier posts, Rowse uses his Stelzner interview to give you a number of Twitter Tips and to demonstrate how committed he is to using Twitter to improve his blogging, he has developed a new blog that he will happily connect you to.

One of the best pieces of Rowse advice applies to so much more than blogging. He warns us against the kind of mission creep that can ruin almost any project.

"Stay disciplined with your objectives," he says. "If the tweet that you are about to put out there doesn't advance your business objectives for using Twitter, then don't tweet it."

That may be the best business strategy advice you can get. In other words, make sure that you "keep the main thing the main thing."

Focusing your Twitter account on one subject may be your key to success. Twitter is a popularity contest, but Twitter accounts with a large following aren't necessarily the most influential.

Among the most (how you say?) adopted posts on the subject of Twitter business is *Chris Brogan's 50 ideas on using Twitter for business (G)*. His original post on the subject dates way back to 2008, but we like the PartnerWithRichardToday.com repost from late 2011 in which he reminds us all to give due credit to Brogan.

Brogan's *50 ideas* moves through the basics to a section of ten helpful ideas on what to tweet and on to basic advice to preserve some sanity for you. It begins with point #21: "You don't have to read every tweet."

Praise the lord, and relieve me of this feeling of guilt.

Cindy King posted a wonderful article in SocialMediaExaminer.com, also in 2011, that reiterates or confirms many of the points Brogan made earlier. She emphasizes the importance of making sure your tweets are personalized:

Do your best to craft your content tweets, @replies and promotional tweets all with a seamless style that matches your personality and/or brand.

Ideally, you want people to read your tweets and feel naturally compelled to click on your links and retweet you.

You just want to add value and have no agenda or attachment to 'making the sale,' yet you're strategic and mindful about how you tweet. Then you'll see a marked improvement in your retweet and click-through rates.

Amy Gahran, writing for CNN.com, explains *how to gain influence on Twitter (G)* and what it means to be influential and successful on Twitter. She cites results of a study from the Association for the Advancement of Artificial Intelligence.

An international research team examined the metrics of about 55 million Twitter accounts. The article suggests different tactics to help point your Twitter account in the right direction and become more influential and gain attention.

Cheryl Conner introduced us to Utah's Card Access Inc.'s Kip Meacham in a Forbes.com post on *how to use Twitter chat to increase your businses (G)*.

In the social media universe, Twitter has become an increasingly strong tactic. It is a highly democratic message delivery system whose barriers to entry are simply 1) understanding the syntax, 2) understanding the players in the relevant conversations, 3) providing relevant content, and then 4) understanding how to participate and influence the conversation.

"Twitter Power" by Joel Comm inspired Dino Dogan's post in SocialMediaExaminer.com in which he identifies *seven Twitter strategies for growing a great following (G)*.

Unless you're a Kardashian cast member or what a jaundiced TV viewer might call a more a "legitimate" celebrity, generating a following on Twitter is hard work. To get on with it, Dogan encourages Twitter users to search for the people you already know. He describes a clever method for using a free Gmail account to use your existing contact list to find Twitter friends.

Integrating social networks with each other and joining in on conversations are two of the many suggestions Dogan offers to help define your Twitter account as a credible source.

Tools, Tips, Tactics, and Tricks of the Trade

The Twitter Guide Book (G) from Mashable.com could rock your world even if you're not some dictator wondering if you can keep your various exploits private in this era of tweets.

The Twitter Guide Book is the most complete all-in-one resource we have found for this amazing social network. Mashable organized the *Twitter Guide* for a simplified search system. Credible resource articles and links are divided into like-minded subjects, saving you valuable time by making search easy.

Resources are available to help anyone—from beginners to business owners to marketers—build a community through their Twitter account:

> Twitter is a social network used by millions of people, and thousands more are signing up every day to send short messages to groups of friends. But where's the user manual for Twitter? Where do new Twitter users go to learn about Tweeting, retweets, hashtags and customizing your Twitter profile? Where do you go if you want to know all about building a community on Twitter, or using Twitter for business? How can you find advanced tools for using Twitter on your phone or your desktop? To answer all these questions and more, we've assembled *The Twitter Guide Book*, a complete collection of resources for mastering Twitter. Happy Tweeting!
>
> Pete Cashmore, @Mashable

This guidebook will teach you how to develop and manage an account for a number of purposes. Reference the *Twitter Guide Book* from Mashable anytime by downloading the free PDF version.

Beginners, have no fear and prepare to jump into the Twitter game head first with confidence. The information you need to get started is everywhere online, and most of it is clear and simple. For example, we also like Bianca Boske's HuffingtonPost.com *Quick Tips: a Twitter Guide for Beginners (G)*.

Start out by learning some basic Twitter terminology and simple actions to get you engaged, like how to share pictures instantly on Twitter.

Boske also discusses options for URL shortening and how to correctly use hashtags. Create your Twitter account with the basic understanding of the differences between @replies, @mentions, and direct messaging and be on your way to becoming a Twitter star.

Google the phrase *Twitter Cheat Sheet (G)* and you'll find a virtual papal conclave of social media mavens contributing their versions. We remain partial to Aliza Sherman's version of *Tweeting 101: A Twitter Cheat Sheet (G)* and thank her again for putting it together. We love the photo of the student who has his test answers written on the inside of his wrist. Must have been a short test.

The advice in Sherman's Gigaom.com post is pretty basic, for sure, but it's also very useful. We always appreciate the step-by-step approach, and this is sure it. Step 1: "Check @ messages. First check to see who has publicly referenced you in their tweets and acknowledge, answer or respond."

There's more, but not too much. If you're looking for a cheat sheet, this one will almost fit on the inside of your wrist.

Despite the dangling preposition (does anybody really care anymore?), Lauren Fisher's Ragan.com post, *11 Twitter Tools You (Probably) Don't Know About*

(G), does exactly what it says, although any journeyperson Tweeter knows about many of these. If that's you, consider this a refresher post. Here's the kind of information Fisher catches:

> Many people use the advanced search function on Twitter, and the same search operators apply when searching on TweetDeck. TweetDeck offers a more efficient and streamlined search if, for example, you want to filter by location or exclude certain keywords from your search.

It's one thing to become a credible source on Twitter, but getting people to listen to you doesn't happen by accident. Problogger.com's list of *27 awesome ways to get people to listen to you (G)* begins with the most straightforward advice imaginable: You have to ask.

Guest poster Nick Thacker of Livehacked.com says he "can think of no better way, and no way that's led to more open doors, than simply asking people to do something. Sure, it takes guts—but that's why you're different. You have the guts. Go ask!"

Each one of Thacker's 27 ways makes sense to us—some are easier to do than others, and all require a commitment to and discipline about using Twitter to advance your business interests. This one applies a principle we call the 80/20 theory, first described by Italian economist Vilfredo Pareto.

> For many events, roughly 80% of the effects come from 20% of the causes. To use this in your own marketing, try to promote other people 80% of the time, and your own work 20%. This establishes you as a connector and sharer of helpful content—not as a spammer.

Again, returning to what some might consider the very basics, we think there's value in asking yourself *what are hashtags in twitter by Lenin's estimation? (G)*. Hash out the confusion and learn how to get the most out of #Hashtags on Twitter. The article in DailyTut.com, that's right—by "Lenin,"—will help you learn how important hashtags are on Twitter and how to use them to stay out of the Gulag (or was that Stalin?)

Lenin begins by describing the function of hashtags on Twitter as a system to organize tweets. Credibility is essential and learning the proper hashtag etiquette will contribute to credibility.

Using hashtags is a great way to create conversation via Twitter and will help build your brand on Twitter.

Stephanie Buck's post, which originally appeared on the American Express OPEN Forum with a photo, was picked up by Mashable.com. And if a picture is worth a thousand words, the one she created for her post may be worth a million.

Buck's position on *four ways to Tweet as a visual brand (G)* is quite clear.

Despite the fact that Facebook provides an easier format for picture stories, the days are long past when an effective business can bypass Twitter.

> Companies that rely on a visual or photographic web presence often find it difficult to convey their media on Twitter. Take, for instance, apparel brands that need to get social media eyes on their merchandise, or a design firm that seeks exposure. How can these types of businesses ensure that Twitter followers see their wares?
>
> Ecommerce or design companies may prefer Facebook, due to its inherently visual and expansive nature. However, businesses these days can't afford to bypass Twitter entirely—especially because many people keep their Twitter feeds open all day long.

Read on to discover four pillars of "visual tweeting," or how to make sure that your Twitter followers get the picture.

Most businesspeople want to see the numbers, whether that means the ROI, increase in sales, or whatever for a social media marketing campaign. This is sometimes hard to do and that's the reason analytics are extremely important.

Rand Fishkin, SEOmoz CEO and co-founder says, "Not many of us spend time thinking about how or taking action to improve the CTR [click- through rate] we get from the links we tweet."

Fishkin's SEOmoz.com article on *calculating and improving your Twitter click-through rate (G)* will teach you how to calculate the click- through rate for a Twitter account.

"As analytics junkies, we're well aware that we can only improve things that we measure, analyze and test," Fishkin says.

Fishkin takes you through the process, "For measuring our tweets, analyzing the data and testing our hypotheses about bettering our click-through-rates." He adds, "If we do it right, we could increase the value Twitter brings us as a marketing and traffic channel."

No doubt you are seeing how Twitter is a great tool for business. If used correctly, it can help establish your brand as an industry leader. The article *Use Twitter for Your Business the Right Way (G)*, from TwitTip lays out some proper practices for using Twitter in any business or nonprofit organization.

Twitter for Business is all about building relationships and interaction with the community. This article can teach you how to create good karma by retweeting certain posts of people you follow and how to incorporate your business/product into the conversation at the right time to be successful.

A simple tweet can skyrocket your business's success, help you land a job, and create a public image. This HudsonHorizons.com blog post by Rania Eldekki lays out the *benefits of using Twitter for your business: Infographic (G)* and delineates the magnitude of Twitter's influential place on the Web and in society.

You've set up a Twitter account and made a super-optimized bio. Now comes the hard part: tweeting—or at least posting tweets that will generate conversation and in turn grow your audience and increase your brand's presence on the Twitter channel.

Posting funny photos, blog posts, and tips are just a few of the ideas from the article *35 Conversation Starters to Share on Twitter (G)* from MarketLikeAChick.com. The article suggests combining conversation starters and to be yourself and respond to your followers.

Blogger Pam Moore put it this way in a recent blog post:

"Twitter is all about the conversation, connecting with real people. You wish you could have a conversation. You wish even one person would talk to you on a regular basis. Don't worry, you're not the only one."

You're also not the only one with a disorganized desktop and closet. Consider this: It might be time for some spring-cleaning at least as it relates to the people you follow on Twitter.

The more you use Twitter, the more people are going to follow you, and all of these people can get confusing, especially if you are following thousands of people—not to mention the stress it could bring to your psyche if out of the blue you got an email that said @MassMurderer is now following you on Twitter. Mashable.com features editor, Josh Catone, can help you find *10 Twitter tools to organize your tweeps (G)*.

Catone's post describes different tools that will help you easily manage your followers/following lists on Twitter. You'll be introduced to tools that allow you to figure out who you're following and to manage lists to help you better organize your Twitter account.

Integrating various social media platforms is key when creating your online web presence. This can be time consuming and tedious, from creating a blog post to disseminating it across all of your other platforms.

Co-editor at MediaBistro.com Lauren Dugan explains how you can easily integrate Twitter with the popular blogging and Web design platform WordPress by using what she calls the *top ten Twitter tools for WordPress Blogs (G)*:

> There are dozens of different ways you can integrate Twitter into WordPress, like showing your latest Tweets, displaying your followers, or adding a button for your readers to easily Tweet your articles.

Dugan highlights tools that will make tweeting for yourself and others easier and will ultimately increase the viewership of your web page. Learn about different Twitter widgets and comment tools that will help you communicate with readers and make tweeting and blogging easier and more beneficial.

It's quite understandable if you are struggling to comprehend just how to go about incorporating Twitter into your marketing strategy. You're not alone.

Reviewing KyleLacy.com's post listing *25 case studies using Twitter to increase business and sales (G)* can give you the confidence to start a Twitter campaign of your own. Lacy demonstrates how businesses like JetBlue and Comcast used Twitter to connect with customers about customer service issues instantly and directly.

The case studies also look at how companies like the outdoor apparel company The North Face used Twitter to extend their brand's identity by providing customers with outdoor tips that subtly promote products.

Aaron Lee lays out *three ways to get a Twitter user's attention (G)*. The post includes some more basic advice about using Retweets, for example, to get other Twitter users reading his 140s:

> I know everyone has been telling you that retweets get attention from other Twitter users. Truth is they DO get attention from them. Some of the stuff that I say to everyone is that retweet someone once, and they will notice you. Retweet them a few times and they will remember you. Why?
> This is because your avatar is appearing on their timeline more often than usual.

It doesn't get much more basic than that.

Dan Zarrella, "The Social Media Scientist," says that the best use of Twitter is as a broadcast medium. "You should be creating a ton of interesting content and sharing it with your followers. To that end," he says, "I have done a bunch of research on how to optimize the clickthrough rate (CTR) of the links you're tweeting. His *Infographic on how to get more clicks on Twitter (G)* is a must-see. Check it out and if you feel the same way we did, you might consider subscribing to his RSS feed or email newsletter. And at the bottom of the Infographic are what he calls related posts, many of them are presented in a clean graphic format.

Speaking of Zarrella, we're particularly fond of his blog.hubspot.com post that details *eight ways not to get retweeted (G)*. It's a must-read before you move on to the next section.

He's got data—lots and lots of data—and he presents it in Tweet-talk:

> There is nothing that will keep you from getting ReTweeted like talking about yourself constantly. It will probably also prevent you from getting many followers.
> Like any form of marketing, calls-to-action matter in social media. So if you don't want ReTweets, don't ask for them, and especially don't ask for them politely.

And our personal Zarrella favorite:

> If you say only the same things everyone else is saying, you'll avoid any risk of being worth ReTweeting. It's easy. Just agree with everyone around you and work hard to never bring anything original to the table.

Tweeting Your Personal Brand

What's the first thing your mother taught you? It very may well have been not to talk to strangers—or at least never get in a car with a stranger, no matter what story they may tell you.

Kyle Lacy says there are *three important rules to remember when tweeting (G)*. And as much as they may make common sense, they bear repeating. As we all know, it's usually the expert swimmers who drown trying to swim across the lake.

First, Lacy stresses, don't drive and tweet. He offers a visual reminder of the fate of the late Dr. Frank Ryan, who Lacy says "was tweeting before his fatal car crash" in August 2012. Need we say more?

You can google his other two important rules. It's worth the trip.

Here's a question everyone who is engaged in Twitter must be asking from time to time. Hello? Is anyone there? Is anyone listening? Does anyone even read my tweets?

You may be asking these questions too, or you may feel like your tweets just aren't important. Well, maybe they aren't. Or maybe they are—very important.

Neal Schaffer, a leader in helping businesses and professionals embrace and strategically leverage social media, attempts to resolve all doubts in favor of Twitter in his article on *what to tweet—twitter and your personal brand (G)*, an article he posted on WindMillNetworking.com: "In short, the world is watching you on Twitter. So what better place to share your expertise with the world?"

Neal's point is that when using Twitter, you'll learn how to leverage this media to help make your personal brand stand out.

Don't write so pretty good?

Twitter can help. Twitter supports business marketing tactics and creates more effective writers. Or, it can make your company (and you) look stupid.

Talk about counter-intuitive commentary, Jennifer Blanchard's article posted on Copyblogger.com makes the case for *how Twitter makes you a better writer (G)*.

Here's Blanchard's opinion: "A 140–character limit means every word must count, and every message must be concise. It's as simple as that."

One additional idea—businesses should demand Twitter users are also Webster users.

Lauren Dugan, posting in MediaBistro.com, reminded us that its not only product content or news that needs to be tightly written. Twitter biographies should be tight and concise also. They don't have to tell your life story. In fact, they can't. You have 160 characters to tell the world about yourself, make them count.

What do you want the world to know about you? Dugan's mission is to give you *three tips for writing a killer bio (G)*, and to do it for one purpose, and one purpose alone—to attract the followers you want.

Quality, not quantity, is the goal with Twitter followers, since these are the people who will share your content. Learn the dos and don'ts for biographies. The article will help you convey the correct image of who you are, your accomplishments, and your goals through strategic keyword choices. The objective is to help get your Twitter account found, followed, and shared by like-minded people.

We're not sure whether we should be surprised or not about the article that Jeff Dunn posted on Edudemic.com in October 2012. It's a report that, according to him, makes it *official: Using Twitter makes students more engaged (G)*: "We've covered the benefits of the social network ad nauseum for teachers and administrators over the past few years, but a new study solidifies the worth of Twitter for students."

The study, conducted by Dr. Christine Greenhow, found that students who tweet as part of their instruction are more engaged with the course content, and they end up with higher grades.

A follow-up post in that same Edudemic.com blog submitted by "volun-TEENnation" identifies four reasons *why every student should use Twitter (G)*. Here's one:

> There are loads of scholarships, essay contests, STEM competitions and grant opportunities for middle school, high school and college students posted daily on Twitter. Having a Twitter account allows you to access all that and more. Students that are interest in a writing career or journalism can easily promote their blogs and find out about writing contests, opportunities and internships.

You're caught using Twitter on the job? Busted? Well, maybe not.

Sarah Milstein, in this early Twitter-related post on a *New York Times* blog for job hunters, shares her advice on *how Twitter can help at work (G)*.

This little article might just get you out of a jam with your boss if you get caught tweeting. There is a timeless nature to this piece that comes out of Milstein's advice regarding using Twitter to share ideas, show respect for your co-workers or competitors, or build your brand.

> Zappos, the online emporium known for outstanding customer service, encourages employees to tweet and to respond to customers who also use the service—increasing the company's reputation as a friendly place to shop and work. Notably, the chief executive of Zappos, Tony Hsieh, is active on Twitter. Because the company cultivates an un-corporate image, he's the rare executive who can effectively post personal updates.

But don't despair. If the ogre in the front office shows you the door because you are tweeting on the job, maybe Twitter can score your next job for you. If you're still a skeptic about the value of Twitter, check out Lindsay Olson's advice on *how to use Twitter to land a job (G)*—an article that was posted in 2010 in Money.USANews.com.

Olson is a founding partner and recruiter with Paradigm Staffing. This is a national search firm that specializes in placing public relations practitioners. In the post, Olson shows you how to customize your profile when searching for a job. If you don't think Twitter's going to help you get back behind a desk, think again:

> Recruiters, HR representatives, hiring managers, and executives all use Twitter on a daily basis. Unlike an online job posting where you can only apply via the information provided, Twitter allows you to interact with these people directly by sending them an @ reply or a direct message.

What, you say? I landed a Twitter interview for a real job? You must be kidding. According to Cindy King, the managing editor of Social Media Examiner, Twitter interviews can be extremely valuable, and she'll show you *seven steps to successful Twitter interviews (G)* in her post on SocialMediaExaminer.com.

You can use your job search as an opportunity to "expand your Twitter business network and get to know someone before connecting with them outside of Twitter," says King.

King's post presents different kinds of Twitter interviews, the type of language to use while conducting a Twitter interview, and much more. And you'll be interested to see how this new style of interviewing can be beneficial to your personal development as well as encourage business expansion.

Monitoring, Evaluation, and Twitter Security

If you want to keep up with what's happening in the Twitter universe, you might consider signing on to a blog like TwitTip.com, which offers everything from tutorials to tools to tips on all aspects Twitter.

One recent tip that we found extremely valuable while researching our first edition on social media resulted from work done by the Internet security company BitDefender.com. They discovered that more than 250,000 user names, email addresses, and passwords for Twitter sites easily are found online. More shocking was their finding that these security wounds are largely of the self-inflicted variety.

The study revealed that *75 percent use the same password for Twitter and Email (G)*.

The sensitive user data were gathered from blogs, torrents, online collaboration services and other sources. It was found that 43 percent of the data were leaked from online collaboration tools while 21 percent of data were leaked from blog postings. Meanwhile, torrents and users of other social hubs were responsible for leaking 10 percent and 18 percent of user data respectively.

So, what to do?

BitDefender has advised users to be extra careful while creating passwords for Twitter and email accounts, and to avoid using the same password just for the sake of convenience. Considering the fact that online collaboration tools are not that adept in protecting sensitive user information, users have been told to be more careful the next time they decide to share their emails, user names and passwords with a third party website.

Spam alert! Marketing on Twitter is often mistaken for spam. There are certain things a marketer can do in order to get through the spam traps, and one of them is to develop a Twitter marketing strategy.

TwitTip.com blogger and web designer "Salwa M" explains this and other related tidbits in her TwitTip.com post, *ten tips to be effective on Twitter (G):*

Anyone who knows how to benefit from regular blogging formats can also find advantages in using Twitter, which offers the same benefits of blogging but in a quicker and more bite sized format.

Salwa explains the importance of sending the right message through Twitter, and just how to go about doing that. You'll learn how to avoid spam-like comments and, as a consequence, be more likely to mount a legitimate marketing campaign.

There's a great deal going on in the area of legal eavesdropping in social media. Social monitoring tools are plentiful and increasingly being incorporated into both marketing and public relations activities.

Begin by taking the time to read what people are posting about your organization. This means monitoring your brand, your competitors, and yourself. Cindy King posted *eight easy Twitter monitoring ideas (G)* in SocialMediaExaminer.com to help users learn the value of listening and how to do it.

Monitoring your Twitter means determining what and who to follow and the value this has for your brand. King shows us how to find the right marketing-monitoring tools to help increase the amount of information that can be monitored. She begins by reminding us to create a regular listening schedule on Twitter as a first step in an overall business intelligence strategy.

We cover this subject in a bit more detail later in this book, and our colleague

Allie Siarto of LoudPixel Inc. is collaborating with co-author Cole on a new book that will provide clear and simple approaches to listening and learning.

Security is a very real issue on all social networking sites, and we are talking more than job security here. Whether you are tweeting from a personal account or for a business, there are certain things that shouldn't be posted. If you haven't figured this out yet, well. . . .

HuffingtonPost.com post contributor Catherine Smith lays out *what not to post on Twitter: Eleven things your tweeps don't need to know (G)*. Her advice can protect (somewhat) you and family members from criminals, and in some cases, from your employer. A slideshow of photographs and real tweets illustrates the list of what not to do.

- Tweeting about your personal life issues is not advisable. That's what a diary is for.
- Listing exact locations and photos of children and their names is too inviting for criminals and child molesters.

Remember, as we've pointed out before, a misguided tweet could cost you your job or compromise your personal safety.

Extra Point—Twitter Tied to World Changers

Here is one more reason that *Time* magazine is still around and reportedly profitable. Despite their storied role in traditional media, many folks think that the only way magazines of *Time*'s stature can survive is to not only be delivered in a new media format, but also to make sure they are covering new media as the major sociological phenomena it is.

It's been more than three years now since *Time* writer Steven Johnson expressed his opinion on *how Twitter will change the way we live (G)*.

In the meantime, Twitter has played a role in riots in London and uprisings in Libya, Egypt, Bahrain, and Tunisia. Shortly before she retired as Secretary of State, Hillary Clinton held what was called a global town hall that was accompanied by official State Department Twitter feeds.

But Johnson was on top of Twitter's potential long before these world-changing events occurred, though he admitted that he was a skeptic at first:

As millions of devotees have discovered, Twitter turns out to have unsuspected depth. In part this is because hearing about what your friends had for breakfast is actually more interesting than it sounds. We don't think it at all moronic to start a phone call with a friend by asking how her day is going. Twitter gives you the same information without your even having to ask.

> The social warmth of all those stray details shouldn't be taken lightly. But I think there is something even more profound in what has happened to Twitter—something that says more about the culture that has embraced and expanded Twitter at such extraordinary speed. Yes, the breakfast-status updates turned out to be more interesting than we thought. But the key development with Twitter is how we've jury-rigged the system to do things that its creators never dreamed of.
>
> In short, the most fascinating thing about Twitter is not what it's doing to us. It's what we're doing to it.

Even more prophetic than Steven Johnson's *Time* post was a groundbreaking academic study of Twitter's media landscape that was reported in late 2009. Four scholars presented the study first at an international conference associated with the Association for the Advancement of Artificial Intelligence. They had analyzed "links and tweets of 80 popular media sources and their 14 million audience members."

This article on *media landscape in Twitter: A world of new conventions and political diversity (G)* was written and submitted for publication long before the Twitter-assisted uprisings in the Middle East in the spring of 2011.

The authors of the media landscape study have made it easier for us to comprehend the significance of Twitter in world affairs by posting a video briefing that is available by googling the title of the paper.

CHAPTER 6

Emerging Powerhouse Networks: Pinterest, Instagram, Foursquare, and YouTube

Pinterest: Holding Our Interest

Millions of people are now using Pinterest, which makes it an increasingly viable channel for business. Millions more want to know just *what is Pinterest? (G)*

The official "about Pinterest" page of the company describes it simply as a "tool for collecting and organizing things you love."

Pinterest is described in Wikipedia "as [a] pinboard-style website that allows users to create and manage theme-based image collections such as events, interests, hobbies and more. Users can browse other pinboards for inspiration, repin images to their own pinboards of like photos."

"Allison," posting in blogworld.com in her *Beginner's Guide to Pinterest Basics (G)*, encourages social media users to just give it a try:

> What I've found is that the more you use Pinterest, the more little tricks you learn. I've already posted *Seven Cool Ways to Use Pinterest (G)*, and later this week, I'll be linking to other brilliant bloggers who are also writing Pinterest posts. Today, though, I wanted to write a little beginner's guide to using this new tool, especially if you're interested in using Pinterest to drive traffic to your blog, Etsy store, or other website.
>
> For those who've not yet familiar with Pinterest, the concept is pretty simple. When you sign up, you create "boards"—as many or few boards as you want. Each board has a certain theme. When you come across something you like online and want to both remember (like a bookmark) and share with others, you can pin it to one of your boards. For example, I found this really cute costume idea and wanted to remember it for next year. So I pinned it to my "Halloween" board.

Allison's list includes a variety of uses that should have immediate interest to individuals for personal use as well as to businesses as varied as bridal boutiques and retail outlets, bookstores, and accounting firms. They include: creating a gift registry, pinning your best blog posts, starting a book club, using Pinterest for project management, creating a Pinterest test kitchen, bookmarking inspiration pieces, and pinning as an affiliate.

> This Pinterest board idea comes from James Dabbagian, who created a board called *Books on Blogging and Social Media (G)*. All the pins on that board are affiliate links, so if others check them out on his recommendation, he'll get the credit on Amazon (or wherever). You can easily disclose that your links are affiliate links in the description, which James has done, and it makes total sense, since it helps people who are interested in a specific type of product find an entire list of items to check out.

PRNewsOnline.com offers a great *infographic: How small businesses can use Pinterest (G)*. Google it. It's worth your time.

Bill Miltenberg's infographic is essentially a vertical slide show that begins by telling small businesspeople about the incredible growth of this relatively new social network and walking through relevant demographics.

Miltenberg shows us other big name brands and products capitalizing on Pinterest's growing user base, but also emphasizes that the key to Pinterest success is to share and post useful content.

> Online retailers can share 'How To' guides that go along with their business.
> If a user sells a physical product, they can post images of them on their Pinterest page.
> Users can share images of the custom services they provide . . .

If you are still interested in getting a bit more detail on Pinterest before joining in, you might google *Pinterest Tips—A Tutorial Guide for Beginners (G)* and go right to the YummyLife.com blog article posted by Monica Matheny.

Matheny walks you through a very basic explanation of the network, a useful set of unique Pinterest words direct from the company help page, and a step-by-step guide for getting started.

Tools, Tips, Tactics, and Tricks of the Trade

Inc.com's magazine tech reporter John Brandon says Pinterest may not yet be as popular as Facebook or Twitter, but "this virtual pinboard is attracting plenty of eyeballs." His post provides *nine tips to boost your business with Pinterest (G)*.

His article begins with the age-old admonition that there isn't much that can substitute for time on task:

> Like any social network . . . Pinterest.com requires an investment in time. Jason White, who owns Quality Woven Labels, says one key is to build relationships with those who are known for quality 'pins' at the site. He says once these movers and shakers get to know you and your business, they

will be more likely to post about your product. White says to focus on the users who get the most likes and repins.

'All of these repins and likes share a common interest, making it easier to take the conversation to Twitter or Facebook to nurture the relationship,' he says. 'Like everything else, be real and show your true self. Authenticity is hugely important.'

Brandon also talks about a custom T-shirt shop, Sevenly, whose owner, Justin Palmer, uses Tumblr and Facebook to point people to Pinterest:

Sevenly has created a daily pin to promote its brand. The idea is to come up with a catchy slogan that is tied to the organization's charity work and memorable enough so that the images get repinned.

Mitt Ray offers his favorite *six tips for using Pinterest for business (G)* in a post for SocialMediaExaminer.com. "Pinterest is one of the hottest social media sites at the moment," Ray says. It "was the fastest alone site ever to reach 10 million monthly unique visits."

Ray advocates using original pictures to drive traffic: "If you visit the popular section of Pinterest, you'll see that most of the popular pictures and images in this section are original and unique. The popular images are 'repinned,' 'liked,' and commented on the most number of times."

Todd Wilms's *ten things people love and hate infographic (G)* is presented in a wonderful infographic form in Forbes.com. It attempts to tackle the question of Pinterest's long-term prospects: Is the site . . . "a colossal waste of time, and only good as a platform for scrap-booking, or will its stellar design help it keep moving into the #2 social site?"

Wilms reports that he reviewed the more than five million impressions from online conversations regarding Pinterest, including 2.5 million mentions of Pinterest in blogs, news articles, and social networks. The results:

Pinterest people are passionate and positive (Passion Intensity score: 80 and overall Net Sentiment score: 74). What does all that mean? The conversation is overwhelmingly positive and people who talk about Pinterest are really excited about it. But does that mean it is all good stuff? Alas, no. There is no positive without a negative.

Google Wilms's impressive infographic and you can develop your own opinion regarding the future prospects of Pinterest. What do we hate about Pinterest? Well, 75 percent of the input concluded that Pinterest is a huge time suck and you'll never get the time back. Forewarned is forearmed.

This book is about the business applications of social media, after all, and so since time is money, we ought to get right down to the brass tacks. Beth Hayden does that by providing *56 ways to market your business on Pinterest (G)*.

Do you doubt the efficacy of using Pinterest to drive volume to your business? Writing in Copyblogger.com, Beth Hayden said this:

> Pinterest has nearly five million users, and is rapidly growing. Nearly 1.5 million unique users visit Pinterest daily, spending an average of 15 minutes a day on the site.
>
> Think those inspiring vision boards don't result in referral traffic to websites and blogs? Think again. In January 2012, Pinterest drove greater traffic to websites than LinkedIn, Google Plus, Reddit, and YouTube—combined.

John Penrod, product manager and watch collector, practices what he preaches in putting together his *Pinterest nine best practice tips for brands (G).*

Penrod is using Pinterest to collect and share the best infographics on the hot new online pinboard.

JeffBullas.com's Pinterest marketing strategist graphics walks you though profiles, pins, board, images, copyright, contests, collaborations, and research highlighting 64 separate and mostly wonderful ideas. The SocialTimes.com graphic gives their take on how Pinterest is revolutionizing the home décor industry. And the SocialMediaToday.com graphic on *five killer strategies on Pinterest and LinkedIn (G)* ties new to older in a message emphasizing synergy.

BillMcIntosh.com has a wonderful graphic that Penrod also displays on his best practice sheet that is taken from a larger piece McIntosh posted on *20 ways to drive traffic with Pinterest (G).* Here are the first three tips:

1. Use Smaller Images and Infographics for Better Click-Throughs: Infographics and small images are hard to see on the Pinterest site. If you have built up enough interest in these images with engaging headlines, you will find that more people will click through so that they can see the full-size infographic or image depicted.

2. List Your Business Name Prominently on Your Pinterest Profile: If you haven't done so already, you should change your username and profile name to be the name of your business. This will build more brand recognition for everyone who visits your profile or board.

3. Don't Skip The About Section: As it should be for all social networking profiles, never leave any spaces you're afforded blank. Your About section should be filled with interesting and engaging content that makes visitors to your profile want to learn more. When people visit your Pinterest board, your About paragraph(s) will appear directly under your photo. Your About section will be seen by other Pinterest users and it could bring more traffic to your site, blog or page. Fill it out.

We want to send you one more of the very many interesting McIntosh posts regarding Pinterest. You may also want to subscribe to his regular blog posts in which he writes on a wide variety of social subjects. But the post we're most anxious to have you read involves *how to use Pinterest legally (G)* without fear of copyright infringement:

> Some lawyers are issuing warnings about Pinterest, saying that a copyright claim is imminent if users continue to use the site as they have been. With the site being the third largest social media site behind Facebook and Twitter that could amount to a lot of lawsuits if users aren't careful.

"To keep your account from getting pinned with a copyright suit," we are strongly recommending that you google McIntosh's advice. It's clear, simple, and appears to be very well documented.

NonProfitsOrgs.wordpress.com has a list of the *10 Pinterest best practices for nonprofits (G)*. Nonprofits are always looking for a greater competitive advantage (?) for funding and volunteers and this advice is right on and very well illustrated. Take point #2, for example:

> Add quality descriptions to your pins:
> Many nonprofits are rushing through the process of adding descriptions to their pins and it shows. Your descriptions should reflect how your pins relate to your mission or be used to call the Pinterest community to action. They shouldn't be more than a sentence, but 2–3 words is usually not enough. Please also use proper punctuation and grammar in your descriptions . . . so make sure your descriptions give a good first impression.

How Pinterest Can Be Used to Develop Organizational-Public Relationships (PR)

Douglas Idugboe is a Canadian author and technology wiz who wrote about *how to use Pinterest for public relations (G)* in Smedio.com. He was responding to a flood of requests on the subject as a result of a previous Smedio.com post. One of our New Media Driver's License® students, Sanghoon Lee, put the article into context for us by sharing this:

> According to the Public Relations Society of America (PRSA), the definition of PR is 'a strategic communication process that builds mutually beneficial relationships between organizations and their publics.'
> Today, it is often said that a clear distinction between marketing/advertising and management/PR has become blurred since social networking sites appeared.
> It's important to remember that a clear distinction does exist between advertising and PR. In other words, a brand or a company tends to focus on its products' or services' features, prices, and benefits when marketing/advertising products or services to customers.
> But, when it comes to management/PR, a brand or a company more

focuses on building mutual relationships via providing potential customers with positive information of organizational resources, knowledge, ideas, and concepts.

Even though organizational-public relationship building involves much more than the publicity normally associated with PR work, media relations cannot be ignored.

One of our favorite PR sources is Ragan.com. Carrie Morgan posted her opinion as to *how Pinterest can boost your press release results (G)*. She breaks out her five favorite PR tips, one of which is something that many businesses would not think of immediately.

> **2. Create a Pinterest newsroom.** If you are pinning one press release, why not create a corporate newsroom pinboard to showcase it, along with your other media/news assets? It can mirror your website's newsroom, or enhance it with fresh material. Here is a great example from Cisco.
>
> In addition to press releases and infographics, your newsroom pinboard can include news clips, company blog posts, short pitches or expert opinion comments, video—even executive headshots and logos. Just make sure that anything pinned to your newsroom is legible enough to entice clicks, properly trademarked, and approved for public use.
>
> Another powerful media tool is an executive staff pinboard, which links headshot photos to biographies, bylined articles, and other content that demonstrates their credibility as an expert resource.
>
> When you quote them in a press release, try linking their name directly to their pinboard for added oomph.

MSU grad student Nicole Roofner told us "PR can use Pinterest, in much the same way as Instagram was used." She cited a post in GutenbergPR.com in which Veronica Olah encouraged practitioners to "*Pin it: How to effectively use Pinterest for PR*" (G).

> Social media is everywhere these days, whether we see a company's social media advertising on billboards, magazines or websites, we can't seem to miss the logos for Facebook, Twitter, LinkedIn, and Pinterest on the bottom. It's become the norm to be asked to subscribe to blogs, become fans, friends, follow, share and connect in a limitless number of ways.
>
> More and more businesses are beginning to use Pinterest as a marketing tool to connect with users and spread the word. Here are few suggestions on how you can use Pinterest as a PR tool . . .

Olah goes on to detail her list of the three most salient PR tips for Pinterest.

> Think visual and engage with customers.
> With Pinterest you must think visual—focus on pinning items that will help you create exposure for the stories you are trying to communicate. While you're pinning items to your boards, engage with your customers to

share interesting items and have them repin from your boards to increase exposure.

Ashley Shafer (with help from Ani Araya) posted in JWalcher.com's blog about *pinning down Pinterest for PR (G)*.

Pinterest has developed into a PR tool, reaching vast, pin-hungry audiences that may be relevant to appropriate (PR) clients.

Here are some helpful tips for PR professionals using Pinterest on behalf of clients:

Keep it simple and focused: Categorize pin boards to one theme and pin appropriate photos that represent the theme. The amount of photos on Pinterest can be overwhelming, so it is important to stay consistent. Don't confuse your audience by pinning unnecessary or random photos that have nothing to do with the theme of the pin board.

Shafer offers three other quite specific tips on using contests, pitching story lines, and acknowledging sources.

JeffBullas.com is a great source of new media information, and we go there quite often. Tehmina Zaman offered a very practical article on *how to schedule your pins on Pinterest (G)*, and so far well over 100 of Jeff Bullas's regulars have commented.

Up until recently your only option when embarking on your Pinterest journey was to go on a pinning rampage. I admit I've been guilty of this in the past but blasting 30 pins in one go is like gate crashing someone's party. It's an absolute no-no. You'll end up overwhelming your Pinterest feed, turn people off and most likely they'll unfollow your boards or worse, report you as a spammer.

The ideal approach is to log into your Pinterest account several times a day and drip feed pins into your stream at each sitting. But who has the time to do that? We're all busy people with businesses to run and even though Pinterest is an awesome marketing resource, you don't want it to eat into your productivity.

That's why I decided a couple of months ago to test different Pinterest tools to find out if any of them allow you to schedule pins in advance. Some resources promise to do this but in actual fact they're still in beta and this service is currently unavailable. Then I stumbled across Pingraphy and everything changed!

Pingraphy is a remarkable new tool that I've been using daily in my business and I can honestly say I'm a devotee. Besides being totally free, Pingraphy is also quite easy to use. But if you've never used it before, I'll share a few key points that will take the guess work out of the equation for you!

Extra Point—Pinterest and Personal Branding

Google "*My Personal Brand and Style (G)*" and you'll be taken to the Pinterest page of Diana YK Chan. It shouldn't take you long to figure out that Ms. Chan has a thing for pink and blue, which she describes as "my fave color."

We're not sure, but it looks as if, perhaps, she might have read the Valentine's Day column in Forbes.com about *the first step to building your personal brand (G).*

The world of personal branding has now been extended to Pinterest.

> Your first task: Developing your 'brand mantra.' Basically, this is the 'heart and soul' of your brand, according to branding expert Kevin Keller. It's the foundation of all of your branding efforts.
>
> It's not a mission statement [check out Guy Kawasaki's blog post for the difference]—rather, it's a quick, simple, and memorable statement describing who you are and what you have to offer. Ivanka Trump is 'an American wife, mother, and entrepreneur.' FedEx is 'peace of mind'. Disney is 'fun family entertainment.'

Picture This: Instagram

> It's a **fast, beautiful** and **fun** way to share your photos with friends and family. Snap a picture, choose a filter to transform its look and feel, then post to Instagram. Share to Facebook, Twitter, and Tumblr too—it's as easy as pie. It's photo sharing, reinvented. Oh yeah, did we mention it's free?"

With these words, Kevin Systrom and Mike Krieger launched their photo-sharing and social networking service in late 2010. By January 2013, the latest Internet juggernaut was reporting nearly 100 million monthly active users. Within two years, the founders and a small group of venture capitalists that put up roughly $50 million had sold Instagram to Facebook for a reported $1 billion in cash and stock, and the promise to allow its independent operation.

Ryan Northover posted his *Guide to Kick-Ass Brand Marketing on Instagram (G)* on SocialMediaToday.com. Our grad students were impressed with the degree to which Northover's post explains how a brand can build positive relatioiships with consumers simply by providing authentic and visual content.

> We must always remember in our digital marketing activities, that 90%+ of users 'trust' what their friends and other online users say about brands and Instagram represents an exceptionally unique field of social media where consumers are creating brand recommendations every day. Like it or not, users of Instagram are capturing moments associated with your brand 24/7; as a brand marketer, you have no choice but to be there. Instagram is a potential gold mine for authentic, positive brand content for you to curate

and encourage, and a place where brands can take relationships with customers to an extraordinary level.

Instagram might be a great shiny new object, but we need to remember it is still a shiny new object, and not all of its performance is likely to meet the hype it has gotten in the two years or so since it was introduced. Some of the hype may be the result of misconceptions of the new Facebook-owned app.

Thibaut Davoult wrote about the *five biggest misconceptions about using Instagram for business (G)* in the Kissmetrics.com blog:

> Instagram offers an opportunity for brands to diversify their content as a means to broaden their online reach.
>
> Yet, many still see limitations in the service and refuse to use it for their brand, missing out on a one hundred million strong user base they could potentially engage. But the 5 most commonly cited reasons to **not** consider Instagram as a social media-marketing platform are not true.

The first myth in need of debunking is that Instagram only works if you are selling "visual products."

> This might be the belief I hear the most, which doesn't make it any more real. Selling unsexy products or being a service provider isn't a reason to not share photos. Rather, it should be seen as an incentive to get even more creative. The goal for these companies is to find valuable, compelling, or entertaining images to share with their audience.
>
> Since these companies cannot show products, what *can* they show on Instagram?

Davoult advises to begin by showing off your employees at their desks. The culture of a company is one of the factors customers use to feel connected to a business. Other recommendations include showing employees generating community goodwill, volunteering or contributing to local charities, celebrating special occasions.

Other Instragram objections that the Kissmetrics's team attempts to debunk include that it only works for the big brands, its results can't be measured, and that Instagram can sell your photos.

This last objection took a turn for the worst in December 2012 when what the photo-sharing network described as "sloppy wording" in an update to its terms and conditions statement set off a firestorm of protests.

In a NYDailyNews.com report, Instagram officials told reporter Rheanna Murray, oops, *"We're not going to sell your photos to advertisers" (G)*.

So this question seems resolved, perhaps: *Is Instagram a good marketing platform for business? (G)*

Pingler.com answered that question on a 2013 post that concluded, yes, Instagram can be a great marketing platform for your business if you do it right.

Doing it right requires knowing your purpose for marketing on Instagram and creating purposeful posts.

With any social networking platform, it often matters more in regards to what you post than how often you post. Sure, proactive updates can keep a steady stream of followers coming to your page, but without substance or promotion, your marketing efforts will not be realized. As mentioned prior, be sure to use Instagram's visual prowess to showcase your business's abilities and offerings. If each of your posts offers both an aesthetic element and valuable information, tips or discounts, then your readers will be more likely to return to your profile in search of said content in the future.

Luis Sanz filed a report for BusinessInsider.com laying out *six simple steps for marketing your brand like a pro on Instagram (G).*

Within the thousands of doughnuts snapped under Brannan or painted nails shot under Hefe, lies a marketing tool many brands are ignoring.

The content that Instagram users are generating and consuming allows innovative brands and e-commerce sites a way to harness the power of photo sharing to increase customer relations and enhance the feedback loop.

Sanz's six simple steps are outlined in more detail in his post, but as he said:

If you still need some ideas to get started, here are some themes you can use to define your initial content strategy:

- Shots of your current products
- Sneak peeks of upcoming products
- Creative uses of your products
- Shots of your brand ambassadors and representatives
- Behind-the-scenes shots
- Shots of your products in the wild
- Sneak peeks of future marketing campaigns/ads
- Photos that relate to the lifestyle your brand represents

Gabrielle Karol filed a post in SmallBusiness.FoxBusiness.com that highlighted a YFEntrepreneur.com article in which *ten entrepreneurs share how to promote your business using Instagram (G).* Here's Jeffrey Tinsley's contribution. Tinsley is founder and CEO of MyLife.com.

Focus on capturing images outside of what you sell. That may sound counter-intuitive, but taking photos of people, places and things that represent your company's culture provides a deeper look into who your company actually is, and what you are all about. That's not to say you can't take photos of your products from time to time—especially if you're launching something new—but focusing on other subjects will help create a more profound connection with your customers and promote engagement.

Hartfordbusiness.com's Tyson Goodridge has his own opinion of *why Instagram makes sense for your brand (G)*, and he says a lot of it has to do with Facebook's $1 billion purchase of the popular photo-sharing app.

There's a greater emphasis on visual storytelling. Facebook's (recent) move to Timeline was no accident. They know that pictures and videos create much stronger engagement with fans and followers, and they changed your profile page, and your company's business page, to take advantage of that. The Instagram acquisition prevents Instagram from moving deeper into this space and competing directly with Facebook and its 800–million-strong user base.

Tools, Tips, Tactics, and Tricks of the Trade

"From Levi's to the local craft foods shop, businesses of all sizes are flocking to Facebooks's free photo-sharing app Instagram, hoping to get noticed by its 80 million active users and expand their reach," says Kim LaChance Shandrow, writing on *five ways Instagram can boost your marketing plan (G)* in Entrepreneur.com.

Hot tips include simply promoting your goods and services with creative snapshots, hosting photo contests, creating images that feature promotional codes, going behind the scenes and showing your customer what happens at your company and, perhaps most importantly, "making your followers stars."

Choose a follower of the day and promote him or her with an @mention. Similar to Facebook and Twitter, an @mention is how Instagram users tag each other in comments. This can fire up powerful word-of-mouth promotion and deliver more followers and potential customers. Many people—Instagram photo buffs included—like to be personally recognized by companies for their loyalty, and they're more than happy to spread the word about their special status within their Instagram network.

SocialMediaExaminer.com's Rachel Sprung provides some interesting tips in her article on *five ways marketers can use Instagram (G)*. Here's a sampler:

#1: Use Instagram profiles to reach a wider audience.
Users waited a long time for Instagram to have a web presence in addition to the mobile app. Even though Instagram is now available on both Android and iPhone devices, there are still many people who would like access to it on the Web.
The launch of Instagram profiles in November 2012 gave marketers an opportunity to market on other devices besides profile.

Instagram pictures provide a great collage and give your audience a better insight into your company.

Vanessa Au listed *10 creative ways to use Instagram for business (G)* in an important SocialMediaExaminer.com tip sheet.

Her tip#2: Show How It's Made.

The longevity of the show *How It's Made* 'is a testament to our curiosity about where our manufactured goods come from.'

Let followers in on the origins of their favorite products with snapshots taken at various points in the manufacturing process. If that process is a long one, you might consider making it a multi-part post that follows the process from planning to production to delivery.

Constance Aguilar posted a very useful warning in SocialMediaToday.com in which she talks about *effective Instagram marketing: dos and don'ts (G)*. Aguilar is a social media strategist at the Abbi Agency, and if you want to see her wonderful photo, you have to go to this resource. And when you do you'll get some useful advice like this:

Brands such as Red Bull, Southwest Air, and Audi have mastered creating communities on Instagram using hashtags and contests that get users to interact with their products and brand by connecting to their lifestyle and emotions. Southwest gave away a series of gift cards over the holidays to people who posted photos of their holiday 'photo of the day' and used a special hashtag (also had to include their account handle) to enter. The entries flooded in, and during a time when people have traveling on their minds, Southwest caught their attention in all the right ways. Smart digital communications right there!

How Instagram Can Be Used to Develop Organizational-Public Relationships (PR)

InkHouse Media + Marketing is a PR company that specializes in providing relationship-based social content for its clients.

Jen DeAngelis, writing in their house organ InkHouse.net, describes how we can use Instagram in public relations. She says "one overlooked area" for Instagram is how it can be used to promote the different types of announcements a company can make, such as these:

- A new product. Post a cool picture of the new product, screenshot, or someone using the product on Instagram. Be sure to make the photo simple. It should give off a vibe, not jam in technical details.
- A new hire. You often see headshots along with a press release for a new hire. For Instagram, make this picture a more relaxed version of the person at work or of his or her office, or use a shot of the

welcome package on the desk. Try not be literal, or the content will be viewed as too salesy, thus not interesting enough to like or share.

- An upcoming event. Consider posting an image of the venue or city it will be held in. Take advantage of Instagram's brand-new feature—a photomap that lets members plot their pictures on an interactive world map.

- A recent award. Instead of a picture of the team accepting the award, a hand gripping the trophy, or nailing a certificate to the wall could be more compelling.

Carlos Pandian uses a post in Business2Business.com to show *how to exploit the power of Instagram for PR (G).*

On the surface, Instagram simply seems like a fun app that lets you use filters to give your photos a funky vintage look and upload them to a stream. However, Instagram is much more than hipsters taking photos of their food or their skinny jeans. It's also a very useful tool that businesses can use for public relations.

Instagram provides companies with a method of conveying an idea or a message in a simple image, which can sometimes be much more engaging and effective than a blog post or a tweet. These images can help customers build a more personal and emotional connection to a brand.

Instagram also has features that allow users to interact, such as tagging each other in photos and leaving comments. This allows companies to reach out to others and make connections, which can lead to networking opportunities online.

By now you know that visual marketing is both a viable and powerful tool to sell products and services. One reason we think it works so well is because of the degree of engagement a product picture can produce. A picture is, after all, worth a hundred, if not a thousand, words.

Lots of big brands like Starbucks and Nike have already jumped on the Instagram bandwagon. But just how much of this jumping is actually producing marketing results?

Deepa Mistry, writing in OurSocialTimes.com, tells us *how to use Instagram for marketing and measure the results (G).*

The rise of management platforms that help measure Instagram activity is giving additional fuel to this already impressive adoption rate, and best practices in Instagram monitoring and analytics are arising. But why and how should businesses use Instagram?

One answer lies in making sure business leaders know, before they attempt to get engaged in Instagram, as much as they can about their Instagram followers and prospects.

> Follower's stats should be coupled with analyzing the interactions generated by the account's shared photos. With that knowledge, brands can use a trial and error approach to their sharing on Instagram, aiming to post gradually more engaging photos while avoiding posts that followers would judge to be dull.

Mistry makes a good case, and his entire article is more than worth the effort to google and read. He emphasizes how simple it is for brands "to track Instagram Hashtags, the volume of photos shared, the number of likes and comments they generated, and their overall reach."

Elise Lévêque, writing in SocialMediaToday.com, shows us a number of ways . . . *to use Instagram and boost your business (G)*, and in so doing gives us some ideas of what to expect now that Instagram is a Facebook subsidiary.

> You should think of any social media profile page like a shop window. What make's Instagram so good as a marketing tool is that you can do much more decorating. You can showcase your brand with recent images and use color to create an inviting atmosphere. Remember: Pictures are evocative so try and make sure you have some good ones!
>
> An attractive woman could be wearing your range of clothing? Using Instagram is a lot cheaper than hiring models too!

Google the phrase *five Instagram tips for PR pros (G)* and you'll find a series of articles in various online publications using the same tagline. That's because they are all the same post—written by "Dear Gracie," Grace Lavigne—and originally posted in ProfNetConnect.com.

> Each week, Dear Gracie answers questions from ProfNet Connect readers with advice from our network of nearly 50,000 ProfNet experts. Has there been a question burning in your mind lately, something you've been wondering that none of your colleagues can answer? Please send it to grace.lavigne@prnewswire.com."

One of the questions she was asked to answer was how Instagram can increase publicity for clients.

We're glad she clarified the question. It's an important one, but it only refers to the publicity aspect of organizational-public relationship building.

First things first, "Dear Gracie" sent us to Instagram's business page. "*Instagram for business (G)* provides information on how to get started," and it provides some good examples of marketing and advertising approaches and opportunities.

Lavigne went on:

> 'Instagram is a social network where users can share photos and comment or like their friends' photos,' explains Jeff Peters, social media specialist at The Halo Group.

'It offers users a simple, easy way to take and edit photographs, and then post them across all major social media portals,' says Seth Grugle, digital and social media specialist for Much and House Public Relations. 'It borrows the #hashtag concept from Twitter and aggregates friends like Facebook.'

'One of the most interesting aspects of Instagram is that it's not really a "site," but lives almost purely on mobile,' notes Peters.

Extra Point—Instagram Trending Up

Christian Adams is founder of Sigma Creative and author of "InstaBRAND, a guide to marketing with Instagram." He placed a guest post in Vocus.com that identified the *five Instagram marketing trends from Instabrand (G)*.

Ironically, Adams's first point is that Instagram signals a return to "tradition of sorts."

> This year, the visual medium will regain prominence over the written word (blogs). This is in part due to increased mobile usage, responsive design, social networks, and mobile commerce.
>
> Twitter is showing signs of age. While its 140-character limit beats blogging, it is still more difficult to use words to create the context that a photo does. Yes, Twitter has photos, but the user experience is often overly complicated when compared to Instagram's strategy to keep it simple.
>
> Apps and filters make it easy for even novice photographers, brand managers, and social media managers to quickly create touch points across multiple networks to attract, engage, and retain paying customers and brand advocates.
>
> B2B marketers will finally be less hesitant to use video as a tactic, but photography will lead the way due to its low production cost and ease of use for contextual distribution.

Adams also jumps on what seems like one of the biggest current bandwagons in social media by saying that "big data equals big opportunities."

> While there is no silver bullet for marketers with new social platforms seemingly cropping up every six months, third party enterprise platforms will help to drill down into consumer behavior for a qualitative and quantitative approach to maximizing revenue.
>
> Hashtags and GPS tagging are just the beginning of available information to advertisers. Expect Facebook to lend its Open Graph expertise to the Instagram crew for building better insights for which marketers and advertisers will be willing to pay big money. One such company already working with Instagram is social/mobile commerce startup *Chirpify.com (G)*. Social shopping from your smartphone by liking a product picture will be the next step in monetization.

Seems like everybody is a shutterbug (an old term that means avid amateur photographer) these days. We all carry cameras the way we used to wear watches, and now we have multiple channels through which to share the photos we take.

One of the principles that we believe strongly in is that the first step in innovation is imitation. We were reminded of this principle in reading the oft-reposted message Bill Miltenberg gives out in PRNewsOnline.com to *PR shutterbugs: ten must-follow brands on Instagram (G).*

> Consumer brands, nonprofits and news outlets alike are using Instagram to snap photos, apply Polaroid-like filters, captions and hashtags and posting their creations on Facebook, Twitter, Tumblr and other popular social networks.
>
> Here, we've compiled an alphabetical list of 10 must-follow Instagram brands—both for your personal enjoyment and for generating some ideas of your own on using Instagram for your own brand.

Miltenberg advises you start out by looking at @charitywater:

> Nonprofit *CharityWater.org (G)* brings clean and safe drinking water to people in developing nations, and 100% of donations go to funding water projects. The account shows its grassroots efforts around the world and beautiful imagery of water and its role in developing countries.

Alan Pearcy's PRDaily.com post about *Aldo's PR stunt that offers free shoes for Instagram photos (G)* highlights how Instagram can be used successfully for PR and marketing activities.

> I swore I'd never again let someone take pictures of my feet and post them online. That's the kind of thing you only fall for ~~once~~ twice. But if I could score a pair of new kicks from the deal, I might put my big toe and company back on display. Footwear brand Aldo did something similar as part of a recent street campaign in Israel. The shoe retailer asked pedestrians to upload photos of their shoes along with sizing information and the hashtag #aldo. In return, participants got a box containing a new pair of Aldo shoes.

YouTube determined that the video Miltenberg included on some aspect of the Aldo campaign violated its terms of service so they removed it, but the article is well worth the read. It demonstrates the degree to which one simple Instagram contest could spin off a huge amount of publicity.

Even Mickey D's has joined the Instagram bandwagon. Another PRDaily.com post, this one by Samantha Hosenkamp, called 2012 a year of the image.

> Pinterest, a virtual pinboard in which users share images, has emerged as the third most-popular social network in the U.S. Meanwhile, image-sharing

service Instagram—which Facebook bought in the spring for $1 billion—just surpassed 80 million users.

Brands are taking notice of the trend, and many of them have joined Pinterest and Instagram to reach new audiences (and old audiences on new platforms). McDonald's is among these brands.

'Social media is increasingly becoming a visual platform,' says Rick Wion, the director of social media at McDonald's. 'We are frequently seeing higher level of engagement around pictures than just text alone.'

Location, Location, Location and Foursquare

An October 2010 Mashable.com post projected *Foursquare would hit four million users (G)* that week, and that was less than two months after the August date when the fledgling location-based network hit the three million mark.

Mashable contributor Jennifer Van Grove (with an assist from Flickr photographer Mari Sheibley) attributed Foursquare's impressive growth in its first two years "most notably" to "the release of version 2.0 for iPhone and Android, a Symbian release, as well as celebrity attention from the likes of Conan O'Brien and hip-hop artist Big Boi."

She projected Foursquare additions of roughly 20,000 members per day—an annual rate of roughly 7 million. Turns out that projection was eerily accurate.

This kind of growth would have put the total number of users at nearly 10 million members by June 2011. And, guess what? Here's a mid-June 2011 Adweek.com headline: *Foursquare says 10 million members have embraced the check in (G)*. Current estimates place the membership above 25 million.

Not all the news is happy talk for Foursquare, however, as Anthony Ha, in the Adweek cover announcing Foursquare's milestone, asked the question: But how many will stick around?

"Foursquare's news doesn't really address the biggest criticism heard about the service, that most people will quickly tire of check-ins that serve very little purpose," Ha said.

"As any Foursquare fan can attest, first-time users frequently ask, 'Okay, I've checked in. Now what?'"

One thing we know for sure about any new technology. We never know it's going to catch on until it catches on, and then, we don't know for sure it's going to stay. And with Foursquare, and the other location-based networks, you can be sure that staying involved now will help you catch on faster to whatever the next big thing in this space turns out to be.

Geo-location networks involve using mobile apps for not only telling your friends what you are doing but where you are doing it. Foursquare clearly got out front first and fastest, but other geo-location services like Gowalla.com are on the list of up-and-coming companies that Sree Sreenivasan and Shane Snow explain in their MediaBistro.com tutorial on the subject of *understanding Foursquare (G)*.

The basics of Foursquare, Gowalla, and other geo-location apps are increasingly in use, but they are not for everyone. Sreenivasan makes the case that using location-based services can be a big advantage to media professionals today. On their tutorial they advise you on "what apps to use, when to use them, and simple tips and tricks for maximizing the networking capabilities of geo-location apps to expand your base and build your brand."

Dustin Kratz, posting in MojoCreator.com, describes Foursquare as a social media site that acts like a game:

> Think of a well-known application such as Facebook Places where you are able to check yourself into a venue, letting others know exactly where you are at any given point in time. The more places you check in to, the more points you receive. This is the basis of Foursquare.

So how does this service help business owners? It's all about branding, Kratz says.

> Foursquare helps business owners promote and market their company through a variety of methods. Businesses can create helpful tips, allow users to follow the company and receive special offers when they check-in at a specific location. By promoting multiple check-ins to earn a badge, Foursquare can help drive new customers to any company.

That's the theory, anyway

Foursquare, as we said, is not the only location-based social networking site, but if you want to dig deeper into the concept and potential of this kind of service, Foursquare is a good place to start.

We're partial to a Gillmour Gang Foursquare YouTube video interview with Foursquare co-founder and CEO Dennis Crowly. It appears as the second in the video stack. In it Crowly talks about the history of his new network and tries to explain its problems and potential.

Techcrunch.com's Ingrid Lunden caught up with Dennis Crowly after 2012's Mobile World Congress in Barcelona to report on *Foursquare's inflection point: People using the app, but not checking in (G)*.

Lunden believes Foursquare's growth in reputation "is matched by a growth in Foursquare's business: the company has tripled its numbers in the last year, going from 'around five million' to more than 15 million."

> People are using the app, but they're not checking in,' he (Crowly) told me. 'I asked myself: did we break something? But in fact, it's because people are using Foursquare to look for where their friends are, to find

things, and as a recommendation service. It's almost like it doesn't occur to them to check in.'

Crowley compares this to the moment on Twitter in 2009 when the service suddenly shifted gears, and it was not about the number of people tweeting but about how many are reading those tweets.

'When you start, you are so focused on engagement,' he said. 'Then you hit this point when you are big enough and say there is something awesome going on anyway. At some point you look and say, oh wow, the consumption model is actually taking off.'

If you haven't jumped on the Foursquare bandwagon yet. and if you can accept the possibility that you don't really use it because of a lack of understanding, today may be your lucky day.

Follow the simple instructions in PublicRelationsBlogger.com's *what is Foursquare introductory guide (G)* and you can do everything from creating an account to making Foursquare an instrumental aspect of your online brand identity. Anyone can learn how to upload photos of different locations, receive discounts and benefits from checking in, and find out how to get badges, points, and friends.

This post also discusses the benefits of using Foursquare to help develop a business: "For a company looking to increase their presence in the real world and the online world, monitor whether or not people are checking in at your location."

Tools, Tips, Tactics, and Tricks of the Trade

"Wish you were more aware of all the incredible things around you?" asks How-Cast.com's Foursquare tutorial on *how to unlock your world with Foursquare (G)*. HowCast.com staffer Dave Bourla created this user-friendly instructional video to show you how to "unlock your world and find happiness just around the corner." That's a big promise, and the language is somewhat metaphorical, but check it out.

The post is designed to show you how to use Foursquare without even reading—kind of like an amateur's perfect set of instructions. The only thing better is to plug it in and figure out how to play it later.

This step-by-step format is designed to remove the mystery of what Foursquare is and how to use it, but you'll still have to remember that practice makes perfect.

Using Foursquare can be fun. People seem intrigued by the idea of letting your friends know where you are and being rewarded for multiple visits there. And this is where business applications to this new social networking begin to come into play.

Scott Bishop, editor at RealTimeMarketer.com, RTM, and self-described marketing strategist, shows business owners *seven quick steps to Foursquare marketing (G)* in a post designed to demonstrate how to exploit Foursquare's built-in marketing capabilities:

> Marketing using Foursquare is beneficial because although (it currently has) a small user base, they (members of the base) are loyal. It also takes up almost no time (to set up and use), so the ROI (return-on-investment) can be high. Anyone can take advantage of Foursquare.

This post plants idea seeds about how to get involved with Foursquare and recommends tips to users, who check into their business via Foursquare, or offer special promotions. For example, Bishop demonstrates how an event built around Foursquare can boost business and build customer relationships. "Because of the little time commitment, he says, "it is my opinion that the ROI is worth it."

SocialMediaExaminer.com comes through again with a great piece by Brian Honigman on *ten ways to market your business with Foursquare (G)*.

Here's a tip to get you started:

> There are nearly 1,000,000 businesses on Foursquare currently, and it's your turn to leverage this network to build your customer base with new prospects and reward your most loyal customers all at once.
>
> Here are 10 tips to effectively market your business on Foursquare.
>
> #1: Claim Your Business's Location
>
> The very first thing any business with a physical presence should do is claim its physical locations to ensure ownership by their company on Foursquare.
>
> Your venue is your business's home base on Foursquare. To begin the process on your mobile phone, *download the Foursquare app (G)* and attempt to check in by searching for your business.

Extra Point—Foursquare Evaluation and Security

Checking in to places is a good way to network with people who are in the same area you are at the same time. It is also a good way to let everyone know where you are and when, and, theoretically at least, to come home and find someone has hauled off your plasma and laptop.

Privacy 101—Foursquare (G) is a basic class everyone should sign up for before you go sign up. Here's the word from Foursquare itself:

> We know an important concern for most anyone using location-based services is privacy. We want everyone to feel comfortable that their trust has been well placed, which is why we've written this description of our privacy

> ethos—the guiding principles that inform how we develop Foursquare and the decisions we make. Our full Privacy Policy is available . . .

Privacy controls are important (ya think?), and Foursquare Labs U.S. has put together a readable informational grid that organizes privacy and sharing options into what they describe as an easy to read and understand format. They do admit it's "detailed," however, and to some of us the word detailed seems perilously, semantically close to "complicated." You judge.

Peter Wylie, writing on *how to control your privacy with Foursquare and other geo-location services (G)* in SocialMediaExaminer.com reported that early on, more than half of the respondents to a Webroot survey said they had privacy concerns related to using these services.

> The first wave of criticism about the privacy implications of geo-location social networks followed the launch in February 2010 of *Please Rob Me*, which combined people's physical location through geo-location services with data about their residence from other public data.
>
> When people were "checked in" at other places, unscrupulous individuals could find out and take advantage through *Please Rob Me (G)*, though the site's founders said they were only trying to demonstrate the problems posed by sharing geo-location data.

You-Tubing in the Streams of Consciousness

These days more people are watching YouTube videos than watching TV. Online video has broken into our living rooms with live streaming on TV's. Videos are being archived and shown in Google and other search engine results. And YouTube is the second largest search engine, right behind Google.

So what's the lesson in all this?

You need to understand online video and how to use it to market yourself and your business.

YouTube(G) and *Vimeo (G)* are two of the leading platforms for online video.

Online video-sharing competition is fierce. YouTube is king, but there are many other video-sharing websites you might consider when uploading video.

The website TopTenReviews.com compared and contrasted the top ten video-sharing websites:

> We've scoured the Web for the very best video share websites—so after reading about the advantages and disadvantages each has, you may want to try a few sites before choosing one.

Understanding the Basics of Video Hosting

The *YouTube Handbook (G)* is a simple guide to YouTube basics that will help you view, share, and interact with other YouTube users online.

The handbook from YouTube.com instructs users on the best practices for watching videos and finding, sharing, and saving YouTube favorites: "This area of the site is all about helping you to use and enjoy all of YouTube's features, no matter what your level of interest is."

YouTube video production tips and techniques are also part of the handbook.

Vimeo is another great video-hosting service similar to YouTube.

Mark Robertson, founder and publisher of ReelSEO.com, posted an article on his website defining *Vimeo Video sharing: history and overview (G)*.

Robertson describes what he sees as the major differences between YouTube and Vimeo. He describes the types of content Vimeo generally hosts and accepts, and he gives an overview of Vimeo registration and user-video privacy controls.

A Vimeo user video describes the types of videos generally uploaded onto the website, and can help you determine what major video hosting site will be the most beneficial for your own goals.

Using video for Internet marketing can be a very smart idea. There's no doubt about it. But, which way do you go: *YouTube, Vimeo or both? (G)*

Peter Baron posted in EdSocialMedia.com as a way to "generate conversation about using video in your social media outreach." And he compares YouTube and Vimeo.

Baron's post displays two different videos—one posted on YouTube and the other on Vimeo—to show the difference in quality of the two web hosting sites.

Tools, Tips, Tactics, and Tricks of the Trade

Help Center/Vimeo Basics (G) is a great resource to teach you the basics of Vimeo. It's designed to provide a lot of helpful resources to start you off on the right online video foot.

"Simply put, Vimeo is the home for videos you create. We offer the best tools and the highest quality video in the Universe." What would you expect them to say, you ask? Well, here's a good way to hear their case.

This comprehensive site will show you how to upload, share, and connect with others. It provides links to other helpful tools like Vimeo Video School where you can learn different video production tools to help you produce and edit better videos.

YouTube users expecting an easy path to becoming the next YouTube superstar are in for a big surprise. Going viral on YouTube is possible, but it requires a lot of hard work, and a certain amount of luck learning *how to engage the YouTube community for audience growth (G)*.

Founder and publisher of *ReelSEO.com (G)* Mark Robertson says: "Content creators need to get out there and engage the public. If you build it they will come is not a valid video marketing strategy."

This Mashable.com article provides wannabe YouTube stars and online marketers important tips to increase YouTube viewership through audience engagement.

Yogi Berra might say that making a popular YouTube video is 50 percent inspiration, and the other 90 percent is perspiration. But as the worst examples of online video prove without a doubt, there's also an element of skill required for good online video production. Some basic business sense is also very important to getting the exposure your video needs.

Website101.com blogger Merle makes the case that there are some tried and true methods to successfully promoting videos using YouTube's site features. His goal: Showing you *all you need to know about YouTube's promoted videos (G)*.

"The purpose of 'Promoted Videos' is to help your videos stand out from the millions of others on the site," says Merle.

Merle shows you how to promote YouTube videos and enhance your online marketing campaign. His article walks you through the entire video promotion process to drive traffic to your video.

The little guys can now get in on the big action in business. YouTube is a great way for a small business to get big business.

A Mashable.com staff writer, Amy-Mae Elliott, posted her *Top 10 YouTube Tips for Small Businesses (G)* to help small businesses use YouTube. This resource will teach you how to leverage a small business to success on the video-sharing platform.

> Rather than video production hints or content tips (there are tons of other resources that can help you on that front) here are the dos and don'ts of using YouTube from a behind-the-scenes perspective.

Everything from creating and customizing your business's YouTube channel to promoting videos is covered in this article. Different video production techniques are examined to help your small business create quality videos.

Learn how to track YouTube analytics to manage content and continue to create web videos that customers are watching and enjoying and will help make your small business, or any business, shine.

Blogger Chinetech wants to help you do a makeover to your YouTube.com videos: "The key for YouTube to display your video the best possible way is to upload the best possible quality video that meets or exceeds their requirements."

Chinetech offers tips on *Squidoo.com's how to make YouTube videos look great (G)* and turn them into red-carpet-ready Internet videos.

It may be true that it doesn't help to put lipstick on a pig, but ugly YouTube videos are usually uploaded directly without any real preparation. This resource can help you understand how to encode, compress, and optimize YouTube videos to produce higher-quality, if not beautiful, videos.

Chinetech describes tools to match nearly any skill level of a YouTube video producer and makeover your video channel.

Armed with a webcam, wireless connection, and a YouTube account, hopeful viral "vloggers" and YouTube stars begin producing content they deem worthy of fame. Unfortunately, these hopefuls don't understand that successful YouTube personalities and videos are more often than not the result of hard work and strategic planning.

If you're interested in another perspective on how to create credible and interesting web videos, Grant Crowell's *ReelSEO.com five tips for successful and professional online video projects (G)* post can help.

Crowell, a professional consultant and developer in the online-marketing space and regular *ReelSEO (G)* blogger, describes five "Sesame Street-style" tips to help you.

> If you want an easy way for people to remember a complex subject like online video, do what I call the 'Sesame Street Rule'—include a single number and letter in your presentation.

This resource is an easy way to help you remember what to do when creating web videos.

> I came up with these five P's from my own years of professional experience in online video project management for my own business and clients, so I can testify that each one of these P's will be essential for your own professional needs.

Online Video Marketing and Advertising

"Keeping it real" on YouTube is an important marketing issue.

Joe Whyte wrote the *Guide to video marketing on YouTube (G)* to help marketers use the video hosting website to drive sales.

Effectively marketing your YouTube video means keeping the content fresh and producing viewer engagement. Creating a YouTube channel specific to your brand and submitting videos in the right category are a couple of other pointers for marketing your video.

Whyte suggests some tools and techniques to create engaging materials to gain subscribers, share content, and successfully market your video.

Understanding the value of YouTube may be difficult for some marketers to comprehend, and it can be even more difficult to convince a business to spend the money necessary to create a successful YouTube campaign. This video may help you or others answer this question: *Social media marketing with YouTube: Why? (G)*

Here's what you'll hear on this BlastMediaPR.com YouTube video:

> The social media team at BlastMedia.com has a wealth of experience creating successful YouTube marketing campaigns for our clients—from major consumer tech companies to small businesses and startups.

Social media is creeping its way into every aspect of our lives and in marketing. This video describes the reach YouTube has. The amount of viewers, videos viewed a day, and the amount of content created are examined.

Learn the social aspects of YouTube, where content can be viewed, and how marketing on YouTube will help every other aspect of a social marketing campaign and online advertising efforts as well as engaging consumers.

Hate it or love it, advertising is important for a successful business, and YouTube may be a great place to advertise your business and/or YouTube videos.

To help users understand the different types of ads and advertising approaches used on YouTube, Rick Silvestrini, product marketing manager at YouTube, asks some frequently asked questions and provides *YouTube answers: ads & advertising (G)*.

He describes what different ads formats are and where they are placed, for example, home page ads, promoted videos, banner ads, and pre-role ads.

This video will guide you to other advertising resources for webmasters who wish to use YouTube's many advertising features.

To help advertisers be successful on YouTube, SocialTimes.com blogger Megan O'Neill provides *10 tips for advertisers to go viral on YouTube (G)*.

> Advertisers need to stop thinking in the commercial mindset and start thinking about producing compelling content. An informative video that explains the benefits of your product and how it works just won't cut it anymore.

This is a great resource if you want to learn how to produce great content. O'Neill examines popular commercials from television and the Web; the article explains how web videos can advertise content without making the audience think it is being "advertised to."

The Old Spice campaign, where the commercials were popular offline and went viral online, is an example of thinking long-term and combining online and offline advertising efforts.

The post includes other great tips and examples of alternative forms of Internet-video advertising to engage consumers help your brand go viral.

Your mom isn't just using Facebook; she may be using YouTube also. It is important that marketers recognize that a diverse group of people is using the Web and social media.

A SocialMediaExaminer.com article with a supermarket aisle headline of *The Secrets of YouTube Marketing Revealed (G)*, explores how businesses can market on YouTube. "Whether you work for a high-tech company, a hardware store, or a university, you might want to learn more about using YouTube to publicize your operation," says writer Ruth M. Shipley.

Shipley's post explains exactly what YouTube marketing is and what businesses can do on YouTube.

"YouTube is all about video broadcasting. And videos are perfect for showing technical equipment, demonstrating a procedure or giving parents of prospective students a virtual tour of the campus."

You'll learn the type of reach you can expect and the market share present on YouTube that will boost marketing efforts. Different ways a business can use YouTube are suggested including introducing a new product, demonstrating a product, and publicizing news.

Extra Point—Tubing Ahead of the Game

Tutorials that help you fix a toilet, connect with education loans, and indulge in your wildest surfing dreams come from just about anywhere. YouTube marketing takes image to another level in *YouTube Brands: Five Outstanding Leaders in YouTube Marketing (G)*.

Catherine-Gail Reinhard, creative director at Videasa, reviews five companies that lead the way in YouTube marketing in this Mashable.com post.

> YouTube represents a great opportunity for marketers to reach consumers who are searching for information about a brand or related products and services.

Chicken Sandwiches and Waffle Fries, Hiding yo' Kids and yo' Wife, Choosing the Right Seat on a Friday, Charlie Biting a Finger—believe it or not, these statements describe famous YouTube sensations.

An assistant features editor for Mashable.com, Zachary Sniderman, helps decode the alchemy that produces fame and stardom by rendering his opinion on *how to become a YouTube sensation (G)*:

> Becoming a hit on YouTube is no easy task. Actually, correction: Becoming a hit on YouTube on purpose is no easy task.

The popular video platform is loaded with viral videos of people doing silly or embarrassing things.

Getting your 15 minutes of fame, even if it's on YouTube, is time consuming. Viewers are hungry for funny content they can't find on TV.

We're not sure if you can make silk purses out of sows' ears, but Sniderman's post will give you some insights into how current YouTube sensations achieved their success.

The *YouTube Blog (G)* could by your go-to website for all things YouTube. The blog keeps you updated on YouTube news, hottest trending topics, user advice, staff video picks, and more. "Each weekday, we at YouTube Trends take a look at the most interesting videos and cultural phenomena on YouTube as they develop," says the Official YouTube Blog.

MAKING YOUR PRACTICE PERFECT

Some tasks that will help you understand the ideas and concepts talked about in Part II.

Blogs

Exercise 1: Find blogs to follow. Go to Technorati.com or Google Blog Search and find some blogs that interest you. When you find a blog you like, subscribe to their RSS feed. There are several good *RSS tutorials (G)* to help you set up. Then you can read these blogs and keep up on topics that relate to your interests or industry.

Exercise 2: Start commenting. The best way to get into blogging is to comment on other people's blogs. This will give you an understanding of how the blog community works. And it will help you build some relationships with other bloggers. Comment, share your thoughts, and give praise or constructive criticism. Try it on for size. After a few weeks of commenting, you will be ready to start your own blog.

Exercise 3: Start your own blog. Now it's your turn. Pick a topic you like, and one that you can write about consistently. Choose a blogging platform such as Typepad, WordPress, Blogger or Tumblr. Think of a name for your blog. Build your blog. Add a blog roll of other blogs you like. Write your first post. Customize the look and feel of your blog. Starting a blog is not easy. You will need to decide if you want your blog to be hosted so your web address looks like this: *www.yourblog.wordpress.com*, or if you want your blog to have its own URL like this: *www.yourblog.com*. If you choose the latter. you may want to ask for some help in setting up your hosting to get your blog launched. Or you can read or watch one of the many online tutorials on starting a blog.

Exercise 4: Post once a week. Pick a day that works for you and commit to it. Sure, you can post daily to your blog, but if you commit to posting at least once a week, you will get good results. When you write your blog posts, it's always good to include some visual impact by adding a photo or video. Also, you can link from your blog to relevant outside resources that will give you credibility and show your sources, if you used any. Posting once a week will give you some content, and help your blog get going. Now it's time to take the last step.

Exercise 5: Promote your blog. Submit your blog to Technorati or other blog directories. When you comment on people's blogs, now you can leave a link to your blog, so they can find you and comment on your blog. Promote your blog on Facebook, Twitter, and LinkedIn if appropriate. You can even email a link to your blog to your friends or business colleagues and ask them to give it a read. You are now a blogger. Tell the world, and build your audience.

Social Networks

Exercise 6: Facebook—Practice, practice, practice. Add photos and videos to your Facebook profile. Tag some friends. Write a note and share it. Update your status daily and tell us something interesting. Now that you have a Facebook profile, you need to use it. So find some interesting things from your life and share with your friends. You may just like it. Make lists. Turn your Facebook friends into lists so you can follow them, and communicate with them based on the topic. Share vacation photos with all your family members. Share some business advice with your business contacts. To make lists, simply click on the Friends tab on the left side of your page, then click Manage Friends. You can then add your friends to specific lists you create.

Exercise 7: Facebook—Pull in your other social media. By integrating your blog into your Facebook through RSS (real simple syndication) you can update your page with interesting content with little effort on your part. Apps like Twitterfeed or HootSuite allow you to pull in posts, and share across multiple platforms like Facebook and Twitter.

Exercise 8: LinkedIn—Join groups! Groups are one of the best ways to meet people who can help advance your career, and who you can help too. Search groups and find 10 that will impact your business and your career. Once you join them, you can post resources, respond to conversations, and connect with members. This will be a big boost to your LinkedIn experience and help you get more qualified connections.

Exercise 9: Twitter—Now that your Twitter account is set up, join a Twitter management site such as HootSuite or CoTweet. These will allow you to set up Twitter lists and follow people based on industry or interests. You can also update multiple social media profiles from one place—a real time saver. We suggest you download the mobile version of any site you use, to make for each Twitter posting on the go.

Exercise 10: Location-Based Services—Now that you have FourSquare on your phone, it's time to make it even more fun. First, add friends to your network, so you can see where they check in as well. Then, go after some badges! Here is a list of Foursquare badges: http://thekruser.com/foursquare/badges/

You will find that checking in can be very addicting. And if you play the game, you will be ready when the marketing opportunity comes up. Have fun on the way!

PART III

SEARCH

CHAPTER 7

Google: Searching Out the Changes in Our World

You cannot even imagine the volume of hoots and howls that the opening line of the official Google overview page generated only a few years ago. An awful lot of people saw this as the ultimate overstatement:

Google's mission is to organize the world's information and make it universally accessible and usable (G).

Laugh if you will, but it's hard to argue that Google hasn't already, in the 15 short years of its existence, largely reached this goal. A great deal of the world's information has been organized, and it has been put within the reach of anyone with a hook-up to the Internet, thanks to Google. It's hard to imagine a world without Google. In fact, we think it's safe to say that if Google didn't exist, someone would have to invent it.

Take a few minutes and run through the abbreviated history of Google entitled *Our history in depth (G)*.

It begins in 1995 as 22–year-old East Lansing native with an Ann Arbor degree, Larry Page, visited Stanford to check it out as a potential place to attend graduate school. Upon his arrival, he was met by 21–year-old Moscovite-student Sergey Brin, who was assigned to show Larry around the Stanford campus. By the next year, Larry and Sergey were running a search engine they called Back-Rub, which evolved into Google.

They picked the name for their invention, Google, as "a play on the word 'googol,' a mathematical term for the number represented by the numeral 1 followed by 100 zeros. The use of the term reflects their mission to organize a seemingly infinite amount of information on the Web."

The official Google history includes gag entries for nearly each of the past ten April Fool's days. Our personal favorite: April 1, 2000, when Google announced MentalPlex: "Google's ability to read your mind as you visualize the search results you want." The question we have is this: How far from reality can MentalPlex be today?

As we said, one great way to begin to get a sense of the immensity of Google—what it is, what it does, and how totally unprecedented in so many ways the emergence of Google has been—is to click through the history. It contains hundreds of links, which in some way chronicles more than just historical facts about Google. For example, the February 2010 historical overview contains a link to the first-ever Google Superbowl ad: *"An American finds love in Paris (G).*

If you are interested in getting a summary overview of Google from the business pages of one of the world's great newspapers, *The New York Times*, here's what they had to say:

> It has built a powerful network of data centers around the globe in hopes of, among other things, connecting users instantly with high-resolution satellite pictures of every corner of the earth and sky; making the entire text of books, in and out of print, available online; and becoming the leading distributor of online video through YouTube, which it acquired in 2006.

Understanding Google

There's a reason why we refer to this collection of resources as a "sampler." Imagine, for a moment, how overwhelming the task would be to attempt to detail each and every Google tool, let alone the tools of the other "search" vehicles that exist—Bing and Yahoo—for example. The big search engines are developing new tools, most all of which are available at no cost, every day. And if you don't believe it, just go ahead and try googling the phrase "search tools."

And that brings us directly to our first point. There's no doubt Google is the undisputed king of search. After all, what other search engine is a verb?

While we were writing this book, for example, we heard one of the princes of the Roman Catholic Church, New York's Timothy Cardinal Dolan, tell CBS's Norah O'Donnell that the newly elected pope, Francis I, has a reputation for both having a great head and a heart for caring for the poor and downtrodden.

"Just Google 'Jorge Bergolio'," he said. "You'll see."

Nick Bilton, writing for NYTimes.com has said that for a start up to become a verb is "even bigger glory than cash."

"It didn't take long for Google to win this honor, as people began saying 'let me Google that' instead of using the verb 'search.' Microsoft hopes that its search engine, Bing, is on its way to this usage too."

While the list of general search engines numbers around ten, by some counts, search engines can be classified by a variety of methods ranging from content and topics to information types and models.

It should be quite obvious for anyone who is reading this book that we're focusing, primarily, on Google.

We looked at one rather comprehensive list of Google products and did a rough count of those tools that, to the best of our knowledge, are in current use. And by the way, just to feign objectivity, we went to Ask.com with the question. That search engine, of sorts, took us back to Google.com/about/products. We counted 49 separate products on that list.

Google products fall into six separate categories—web, mobile, media, geo, home & office and social—each product with its own distinct logo. In the category of social products, for example, we find Google+, Groups, Blogger (which we describe in our chapter on blogging) and Orkut.

The list of Google tools is significantly more extensive. *Kissmetrics.com (G)*, for example, recently published a list of *25 awesome free Google tools for marketers (G)*. Many of these "tools" also appear on the Google products list, but many don't.

So, we went back to *Ask.com (G)* and we asked them to explain to us a clear distinction between Google products and Google tools . . . and we stumped 'em. But we did find a list of *10 Google products you (probably) never knew existed (G)* in a column by Adam Vincenzini posted in TheNextWeb.com. Vincenzini says that these new products fall into two distinct categories: "Incredibly useful and incredibly bizarre." Here's one example, and you get to choose which category it goes into.

> While you're probably familiar with Google Earth, Google Mars is a little less well known. However, what it lacks in notoriety it makes up for in in geeky coolness. It gives you the ability to check out spacecraft landing locations, crater depth and even comes with an infrared option.

Or how about this example?

> Google Correlate—If you've been watching the new TV show starring Kiefer Sutherland called Touch, you'll appreciate this one as it allows you to find patterns within data samples. Oooh yeah, go get your geek on!

Just so you don't think that Yahoo! has been asleep at the switch, we googled the phrase *Yahoo products (G)* and that produced a list of roughly 60 separate products for which they have specific privacy practices listed.

Trying to come up with a discrete listing of Microsoft's Bing products wasn't quite as easy. So we decided to use the Boolean search skills we learned from our friends at Ithaca College in New York. Googling the phrase *Boolean logic AND Ithaca College (G)* took us right to the site we found when doing some research for the book we're co-authoring with Allie Siarto on the Social Current—Social Media Monitoring and Measurement.

Here's how Ithaca's librarians John Henderson and Jennifer Strickland describe Boolean logic in the opening paragraph of their very useful skill developer.

The principle of Boolean logic lets you organize concepts together in sets. When searching computer databases, including keyword searching of the online catalog, these sets are controlled by use of Boolean operators **OR**, **AND**, and **NOT**.

We recommend you review this site and you'll find several nearly foolproof ways to make your searches—whether you're Googling, or Binging, or Yahoodling—more meaningful.

"Google is not a conventional company. We do not intend to become one." So began the "letter from the founders" penned by Sergey Brin and Larry Page in the company's securities registration form in 2004. Despite ever-increasing commercial success since that date, Brin and Page have kept to their word according to Mashable.com's Amy-Mae Elliott writing *10 fun facts you didn't know about Google (G)*.

Here's Amy-Mae's fun fact number one.

1. The First Google Doodle

Google's famous home page Doodles (the changing Google logo graphics) are well known and enjoyed by millions around the world as a way to mark an event or anniversary. But did you know that the very first Google Doodle was designed as a kind of "out of office" message?

In 1998, Brin and Page took the weekend off to go to the Burning Man festival in Nevada. The Burning Man doodle (shown above), was designed by the Google guys and added to the home page to let their users know they were out of the office and couldn't fix technical issues, such as a server crash.

Here's another personal favorite that emphasizes Google's tremendous sense of humor from its earliest state.

4. Google's First Ever Tweet

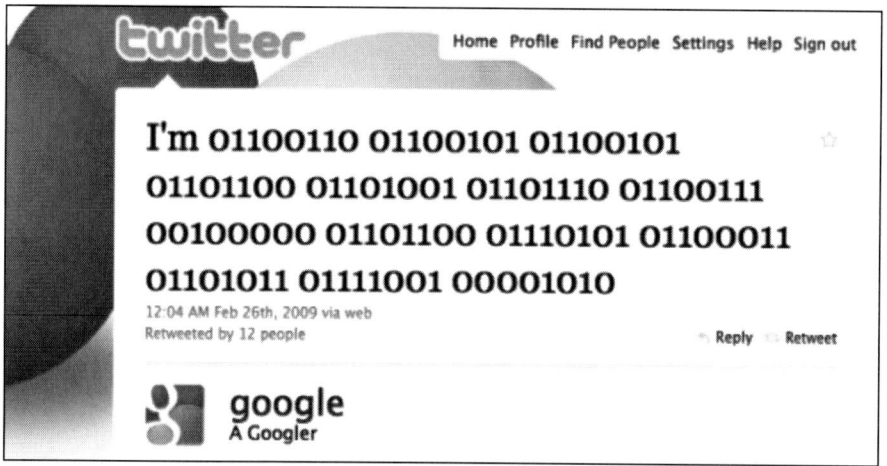

Google's first ever Twitter post was as satisfyingly geeky as you could hope for. The message, sent in February 2009, reads "I'm 01100110 01100101 01100101 01101100 01101001 01101110 01100111 00100000 01101100 01110101 01100011 01101011 01111001 00001010."

For anyone not fluent in binary, here's a hint: It's a well-known phrase from the company's home page. Got it? Yep, it reads: "I'm feeling lucky."

Which got us thinking . . . what does the *"I'm feeling lucky" button (G)* mean anyway? For the answer to this question, we went back to About.com. This time they sent us to Google.about.com's Marziah Karch who came to the rescue with this answer:

> The button may have been named as a play on the Clint Eastwood line in the movie *Dirty Harry*:
>
> 'Do you feel lucky, punk? Well, do you?'
>
> Ordinarily when you type in a key phrase in a Google search, you press the search button, (you can also just press return or enter on your keyboard), and Google returns a results page that shows multiple websites matching your search phrase. The *I'm Feeling Lucky* button skips the search results page and goes directly to the first ranked page for that search phrase.

There are a lot of different aphorisms regarding luck, and Google, through its corporate genius, and perhaps the good humor of its founders, provides a great demonstration, if not metaphor, for one of our favorites: "The harder I work, the luckier I seem to get." We think the next resource shows you how to "get luckier."

Mashable's Sam Laird told us that *Google's 'I'm Feeling Lucky' button has a cool new trick (G).*

If you go over to the Google Search home page and hover your cursor over the *I'm Feeling Lucky* button, something pretty cool happens. The button starts spinning like a slot machine before stopping at a random completion of the phrase, *I'm feeling . . .* Then, you click the button to experience some related corner of the online Google empire.

Select *I'm Feeling Wonderful*, for example, and you're whisked away to some part of Google's World Wonders Project, which highlights fascinating cultural sites from around globe. *I'm Feeling Trendy* takes you to the Hot Searches page, which shows the topics and stories that are trending online. *I'm Feeling Stellar* brings up image search results for the Orion Nebula. And so on.

"Fair warning, though," Laird says. "You might get hooked and it's a major temptation for procrastination."

Matt McGee told us a couple of years ago about *Google Instant Search (G)* that most of us didn't notice when it first appeared, and many of us take for granted today.

Google's Marissa Mayer called it a 'fundamental shift in search.' As with any big Google announcement, there are questions: Who can use Google Instant? Can I opt out or turn off Google Instant? Why am I not seeing it when I do a Google search?

Answers to those questions and more are in SearchEngineLand.com's guide.

Google Business Uses, Tools, and Apps

We use Google all the time, for example, for spell checking. Just type in the word *onomonopia (G)* and you will be taken to multiple dictionaries. Spell it *omonopia(G)* and it will correct the spelling for you faster than a train says choo choo.

Want to find out what time it is in Rome? Google: *Rome Time (G)*. It's 3:13 EST here. It's 8:13 in Rome, Italy. What about current weather is in Salt Lake City, Utah? Google: *Salt Lake City weather (G)*. But wait, you're about to go on a walk outside. What to wear? Google: *East Lansing temperature (G)*. Or, how about those 20 cashews you just snacked on? Darn—160 calories.

These search tips are right from the horse's mouth . . . from Google itself.

> The *Basic Google Search Help (G)* article covers all the most common issues, but sometimes you need a little bit more power. This document will highlight the more advanced features of Google Web Search.
>
> Have in mind though that even very advanced searchers, such as the members of the search group at Google, use these features less than 5% of the time. Basic simple search is often enough.

That having been said, we found advice in this resource to be very valuable. For example, take a look at the use of the asterisk (*), which is actually basic Boolean logic.

> Fill in the blanks (*)
> The *, or wildcard, is a little-known feature that can be very powerful. If you include * within a query, it tells Google to try to treat the asterisk as a placeholder for any unknown term(s) and then find the best matches. For example, the search [Google *] will give you results about many of Google's products. The query [Obama voted * on the * bill] will give you stories about different votes on different bills. Note that the * operator works only on whole words, not on parts of words.

If the basic training in Boolean logic made you feel a bit uneasy, check out the GoogleArticles.com lesson in *shortcuts in Google search (G)* and pretend we never said Boolean.

Here are more tips on how to make googling more effective and efficient. For example, use quotation marks around the phrase if you are searching only for results with the exact phrase.

Jonas Salk, father of the vaccine that put an end to the epidemic of polio in the 1950s, said, "In order to have a great idea, you need to have a lot of ideas." That was his way of saying that not all ideas are going to be good.

Libe Goad, writing in ZdNet.com, either wasn't a Girl Scout or was and never recovered from the experience. The New York-based Texan, an excellent video game journalist, wasn't knocked out by Google's announcement that it was climbing on the "gamification bandwagon, adding badges to its Google News service and she made that clear upon the announcement.

Here's how it works. Do you want to earn a Harry Potter badge? Spend about a week reading certain types of Harry Potter-related articles, and you'll earn a badge.

Within a couple of years of its celebrated christening, Google announced that this dog just wasn't hunting, and it mercifully killed the badge program. As TechCrunch.com's Robin Waters, among several others, said in a parody of Mel Brooks's *Blazing Saddles: We don't need no stinking badges(G)*.

In yet another Mashable.com post, by Ben Parr, we learned that Google isn't satisfied just improving the way blog posts appear on Blogger, they wanted to give *Blogger a dynamic new look (G)* and "change the typical way people consume content on the web."

Blogger product manager Aril Sabharawal described these changes as much more than cosmetic. He said the changes are "really revolutionizing the blog consumption experience."

"To that end," Parr says, "Google launched five views that harness the power of new web standards."

Within a year, blogger.com's software engineer, Maite Ubl, announced a new way to grab someone's attention by mentioning people in your posts with Google+.

> Now you can add a link to a Google+ profile or page when you want to mention someone in a post. If you then share your post from Blogger to Google+, we make it easier to notify your mentions by including them in the share box. To mention someone, just type "+" before their name while you're using the Blogger post editor.

Google Scholar (G) literature search engine has changed the way many academics and other researchers do their work. Again, we turn to Google for a brief explanation:

> Google Scholar provides a simple way to broadly search for scholarly literature. From one place, you can search across many disciplines and sources: articles, theses, books, abstracts and court opinions, from academic publishers, professional societies, online repositories, universities and other web sites. Google Scholar helps you find relevant work across the world of scholarly research.

Go to the Google Scholar home page and you can find everything from a help site to advanced search tips. Libraries and publishers also can get the scoop on how Google attempts to support them. We're particularly grateful for this Google acknowledgement:

> We recognize the debt we owe to scholars everywhere whose work has made Google itself a reality and we hope to make Google Scholar as useful to this community as possible.

Maybe the best way to get googled up is to head straight for the site called the *Google Apps Education Training Center* (G). If anyone would have told you ten years ago that a profitable company—by some measures, among the world's biggest companies—was going to offer you free computer applications and then provide content modules to train you, again for free, you would have said that's absolutely nuts. But that's the truth.

For example, if you have ever felt like you are not getting the most out of your Gmail account, take a run at *Becoming A Gmail Ninja (G)*. The training starts with a 55–minute video of a webinar run by Christopher Craft, a sixth-grade teacher. If you can't learn from him, you might consider yourself un-teachable.

If you go to Craft's video, you'll see a link to a catalog of 381 videos, most of which are considerably shorter than this video.

Again, we relied on a wide variety of resources in coming up with this resource sampler. We were intrigued by the *College@Home Blog's 57 useful Google tools scholars, students and hobbyists can use (G)*. Albeit kind of an older list now, it's still a great rundown of many useful Google tools and apps, some of which most people have never heard.

A great deal has happened since the post first went up in 2008, and some of the products are out-of-service, but this is still a great resource to get you started.

By the way, if you're interested in off-campus learning, you might consider doing what they suggest by checking out their reviews of the 100 or so online schools and correspondence college programs.

About their post, the College@Home folks say:

> If you're like most people, you use Google's products several times a day to search for information or check email.
>
> Most people don't know, however, how many useful tools Google has to make research and time management much easier. Here are just a few of the products Google offers that may be worth trying whether you're a scholar, student, or hobbyist.

Learning categories include "must haves," maps and travel, web browsing and developing, social networking and communication, custom search tools, third party tools, and miscellaneous.

We identified a great list of the *best Google tools you never use (G)* in a post from *China Daily (G)*. Since a goodly number of the students in our New Media Driver's License® program are from the People's Republic, we like to keep up to speed on what's going on in the homeland of so many of our new friends. We're hoping that those who return to China will be lifetime social media pals, and that they'll help spread some of the good ideas and goodwill they got while they were here.

Here's a highlight from the February 2, 2009 edition:

"Google's headline applications—search, Chrome, and Gmail—get all the attention. But behind the scenes, the company has released an impressive array of applications that most people have never heard of or used. As you might expect, they're all designed to make it easier for people to use today's Internet more efficiently. And they're all free." (At least those covered in this article are free.)

China Daily highlights Google Docs (Google: Google Docs), Google's Blogger tool (Google: Blogger), and Picasa.

"You can spend a lot of money on software to organize and manipulate your digital photographs. Or you can use the free Picasa," says *China Daily*, which also promotes Google's Notebook, which we are sorry to say has been closed off to new users since 2009, and Alerts, which "draws upon Google's main search engine to notify you when new entries for a particular news item, blog, Web page update, or video appears."

Source: Forbes.com (Want to Capitalize on China? You Better Have Good Guanxi (G)) and GlobalPartnersMBA

We're thrilled to share some of the things about us we learn from our Chinese friends. After all, we think that's good *guanxi (G)*.

Jake Widman, writing in InformationWeek.com, described the Google Apps marketplace as a "gold mine for businesses offering dozens, if not hundreds, of generally inexpensive, cloud-based software solutions for everything from project planning to invoicing."

You can google *Jake's top 15 Google apps for businesses (G)* and take advantage of some wonderful advice to using these tools to build your business.

First on Jake's list is *SlideRocket (G)*, which "lets you import presentations from Google or Microsoft PowerPoint or create them right within the program, and then access them from any PC, Mac, or Linux computer. You can add audio and share presentations with your Google Contacts. It also includes analytics for measuring audience engagement."

And as Jake points out, the price is right for this app—it's free.

Just about the time we were putting this new edition of our book together we picked up a story that really didn't shock us, but that disappointed us, nonetheless.

Perhaps you've heard of *Google Reader*. This is, or shall we say "was," the free Google tool that puts content into an RSS feed and makes news easy for users to read and, more importantly, much easier to keep up with.

Mathew Honan described Google Reader's demise in a Wired.com post entitled *RIP: Google Reader Meets It's Inevitable End (G)*:

> Reader gave users the ability to friend, follow and share stories with others. It let readers share stories with each other, and comment on them too. It became a place not just to read new stories, but to share and discuss them with friends. It was a discovery tool and a salon all in one.
>
> However, Google removed the ability to natively share and replaced it with a Google + sharing option in 2011. That was effectively the end of the Reader community, many members of which publicly lamented the loss.

Bottom line: Internal cannibalization. But don't despair. As Honan pointed out, Feedly.com is building a clone and will help those of us who are interested in *transitioning from Google Reader to Feedly (G)*.

Richard Lawyer, posting on the engadget.com blog, wrote that Feedly promises seamless transition after Google Reader.

> If you (like many of us at Engadget) are in a state of shock facing the end of Google Reader this summer, there may be an easy replacement. RSS app/service Feedly posts on its blog that it has been anticipating the shutdown of Google's service for some time, and invested in building its own backend. Dubbed "Normandy," it is intended to be a clone of the Google API running on Google's own App Engine, set to swap in on July 1st when the service ends.

The days of receiving your Google Alerts as feeds you can read in Google Reader may be over, but this tool remains one of the most powerful free tools available.

Jason Poulos, posting in Crttbuzzin.com, flagged *five Google Alert tips to help monitor your client's reputation (G)*. And if you're looking to strengthen the capacity of your own business, just consider yourself your best client, and follow this advice.

> At face value Google Alerts comes across as a simple single purpose tool that's only good at monitoring the Web for new content. With a little bit of tweaking you can do a lot more with Google Alerts to help monitor your client's web property, reputation and content.

Here's Poulus tip number one:

> Monitor Your Client's (or your own business) Name.
> This basic approach allows you to monitor your client's name, product or branded term. To do this, simply put your client's name into the *search*

query field, leave the result type set to *everything* and then fill out the rest of the form to create an alert. Depending on what you selected from the *how often* dropdown, this simple alert could send you an email every time Google indexes a page that contains your client's name. All in all, a pretty quick and easy way to see who's mentioning your client out there on the Web.

This is by far the most basic form of a Google Alert that most people might be familiar with. As useful and simple as this alert is, you can do much more with Google Alerts to get different and more specific results for your client.

Other ideas include: Monitoring links; monitoring for plagiarism; monitoring a specific website; and, monitoring local news.

Harvey Raybould, posting in Compila.com's blog, laid out *four Google Alert tips for business owners (G)* that are definitely worth the read.

His third tip is a feature of Google Alerts that may, to many, be hidden in plain sight: Use Google Alerts to monitor what your competitors are doing.

This simple step just doesn't occur to many business owners. You aren't restricted to tracking only your own domain name and brand. You can also track your competitors by setting up a once-a-week alert on their product titles or business names. This allows you to see what new developments they are making, the marketing strategies they are employing, and where people say they fall short or lack features.

You can also use this to target similar websites and niches, or even the same ones. If a website posts a review on a similar local restaurant to yours, you can ask if they will send a reviewer to your restaurant, too! Many website owners like being reached out to by friendly businesses.

Consider this an appetizer on the sample platter of Google AdWords. But even though we are going to devote considerably more on that subject, it's quite important that you read *how to get the most out of Google AdWords (G),* if only to whet your appetite for what's coming next.

Matt Silverman's Mashable.com article doesn't answer every question about AdWords, but as the string of comments that follow Silverman's post indicates, he's done a nice job of laying out some AdWords pros and cons.

Silverman offers up some small business Google AdWords success stories. One of his sources, for example, was "an engineering company that specializes in LED lighting and testing. Its customers are technically-trained engineers," but consumers looking for Christmas lights were clicking on their ads, and the company was wasting money on useless pay-per-click impressions.

Quoting Timothy Thomas, a small business consultant whose specialty is developing Adword campaigns, Silverman's article goes on:

The solution was eliminating 'broad matching' criteria. We put our keywords into either Phrase Match or Exact Match. Each day we would look at what the company had paid for on the previous day and just started [adding] negative keywords. Words like 'Christmas,' 'automobile,' 'rope light,' 'Playstation,' and all the variants for 'television' were identified and blocked from matching.

Let us try to put something in perspective. In September 2004, Google stock was selling for under $100 a share on the New York Stock Exchange. In March 2013, Google shares rose to more than $800, the same month that Priceline.com announced that it was boosting its annual ad spending to more than $1 billion dollars.

It would be perfectly reasonable to assume that because William Shatner's image has become inextricably intertwined with Priceline the lion's share of the annual Priceline ad spend would be going to television and radio—Shatner's venues, right?

No, that's not exactly right.

Some estimates are that more than 90 percent of this year's Priceline ad spend is going to the Internet, and 90 percent of that number will go to Google.

There's a Google ad spending war going on between Priceline, Expedia, Trip-Advisor, Orbitz, Hotels.com, and others in that niche. Google is building and selling weapons to all sides in this ad war, and as is always the case, the arms dealer profits from warfare no matter who wins. And that kind of marketing activity is getting more and more businesses, small and large, interested in Google's AdWords program.

It's not hard to find a comprehensive article with a good listing of *Google Advertising Tools (G)*. Rose Broyles, contributor to EHow.com, put together a particularly good one that, besides the list, includes useful advice on how to use the tools.

Each of the five primary advertising tools—AdSense, AdWords, Analytics, Feedburner, and Product Search—are explained in simple terms with links going to the official Google site.

Google AdSense (G) is primarily of interest to online entrepreneurs who are providing content to a solid readership base.

Google AdSense is a flexible, hassle-free way to earn revenue by showing relevant and engaging ads alongside your online content. You can easily show AdSense ads on your website, mobile sites, and site search results.

Go to the *Google AdSense (G)* website and you can see a video which, in the words of Google, will show you "why over two million publishers of all sizes worldwide are using AdSense."

Google Product Search is getting a new name—Google Shopping—and with the name is coming a new business model, where SearchEngineLand.com's contributor Danny Sullivan tells us "only merchants that pay will be listed."

> It's the first time Google will decommission a search product that previously listed companies for free. The company says the change will improve the searcher experience, but it will also likely raise new worries that Google may further cut free listings elsewhere.
>
> 'This is about delivering the best answers for people searching for products and helping connect merchants with the right customers,' said Sameer Samat, vice president of product management for Google Shopping, when explaining that by moving to an all-paid model, Google believes it will have better and more trustworthy data that will improve the shopping search experience for its users.

Sullivan reported on a panel that he moderated at the 2013 Austin South-by-Southwest (SXSW) conference. "Had a bad experience purchasing from an online merchant? Google says it wants to protect searchers from that, and it may crackdown later this year with changes intended to prevent bad merchants from ranking well."

Google Feedburner is a 2007 Google RSS acquisition that appears to be headed for the Google boneyard. Woody Leonard, writing for InfoWorld.com, has speculated that with *Google Reader gone, Feedburner can't be far behind (G)*.

Google Analytics (G) is the tool, a dashboard of sorts, that allows businesses to generate detailed stats about a website's traffic and traffic sources, sales conversion, and other measures that provide insights into your visitors and "how you can keep them coming back."

We turned to *a beginner's guide on how to install Google Analytics in Word-Press (G)* for an illustration of the utility and versatility of Analytics with basic websites or blogs, and why we might care enough to install it.

As WordPress.com says, "The best way to know your audience is through your traffic stats and this is what Google Analytics provides for FREE."

You need to examine many of the related posts to get a deeper feeling for what good, day-to-day analysis can do for you. Among the questions Google Analytics will answer is:

- Who visits your site?
- What do they do when they visit your site?
- When did they visit your website?
- Where were they immediately before arriving at your website?
- How did they interact with the content on your website?

Look, we know some of this may seem daunting at first. How about doing a little experiment?

You have a Facebook page. (We have ways of knowing these things.) Why don't you take a few minutes right now to learn *how to add Google Analytics to your Facebook Fan page? (G)*

How do you do that? We thought you'd never ask. And thanks to Miriam John's article at SocialMediaExaminer.com, it may not be as difficult as you fear.

> Facebook Insights shows some demographic information on your page, but is limited to information about interactions with your fans. The free Google Analytics tool offers more sophisticated and comprehensive data. Adding Google Analytics to your fan page can be done easily but requires some special steps.
>
> One of the limitations of Facebook fan pages is that the pages can only run limited JavaScript. Google Analytics needs JavaScript code included on a page to correctly track visitors in the traditional way. And running JavaScript won't work on your fan page. . . .
>
> However, there is a new solution. Using free and open source FBGAT *(Facebook Google Analytics Tracker (G))*, you can get Google Analytics working on your Facebook fan page. Now you can track visitor statistics, traffic sources, visitor countries, and keyword searches with all the other powerful reporting of Google Analytics.

Ms. John takes you through the entire process, step-by-step, including doing what, just a few months ago, would have been impossible: working around Facebook JavaScript's limitation by using FBGAT, the free tool that will generate the custom image code that you will need to keep tabs on all visitors to your fan page.

Get tracking now, but if you're still a little spooked by the techo-dramatics you've experienced in the past with what are allegedly simple installations, take a few more minutes and review this *Google Analytics Tutorial 1: Setup (G)*.

Setting up Google Analytics might not be quite as simple as Mark Widawer seems to say it is. But it is pretty simple.

Google the YouTube video and you'll find a number of different tutorials that should make it pretty easy for you to get started.

If Google Analytics provides the dashboard, the engine for Google-related marketing has to be *Google AdWords (G)*.

AdWords advertises that with this service, businesses "only pay for results."

> No matter what your budget, you can display your ads on Google and our advertising network. Pay only if people click on your ads and visit your website.

Rose Broyles's EHow.com article provided a good overview of key Google advertising-related product, for sure. But the thing we liked most about it is that she also has offered up several related, and sometimes contrary, resources that you should explore before you get too smitten with Google as the sole solution to all of your online advertising needs.

For example, while Broyles describes Google AdSense as a powerful Internet marketing tool, she also talks about competitors like AdBrite, Bidviser, Chitika, Clicksor, and Kontera.

One newer addition to the Google marketing family is Google AdWords Express. Michael Levanduski writes about the new offering in an article in PerformInsider.com. In it, he answers this question: *Should small businesses be excited (G) about Google AdWords Express?*

> In display advertising, it is a well-known fact that Google has provided the world of marketing with some of the most popular and most successful tools that can be found on the Web. Some time ago, Google created their own social network, allowing small businesses to access both social marketing tools and display marketing tools under the same company umbrella. Now, Google has released an addition to their marketing tools with Google + that should have small businesses excited.

Levanduski goes on to quote Google project manager Christian Oestlien, speaking on his personal blog about how small businesses can use AdWords to promote their own pages on Google+.

> They can attract new customers and followers with ads that run across Google (on Search and Maps, for instance), and across the Web (on the Google Display Network)
>
> And of course, we only show these promotions when they're appropriate—not overwhelming people with random ads when they're trying to spend time with friends.
>
> Page promotion with AdWords Express is initially available to local businesses in the U.S. . . . Eligible businesses will see an 'Advertise' link on their Google+ page.

There's a good deal more we could say about Google tools and features. But you're capable of going as deep as you want into the world of Google in particular and SEARCH writ large, in general.

We would recommend, however, that you examine the *ten features of Google Chrome (G)* that is available in a brief YouTube video. This tutorial provides quick tips on how to exploit Chrome. It's less than ten minutes long and does exactly what it promises.

And there's one more resource we debated including in this resource guide. Some might say that Karl Hodge, who wrote about *30 essential Google developer tools (G)* for TechRadar.com, went a bit too deep to be practical advice for a new media driver, but then we had a friend in high school who was racing dragsters by his seventeenth birthday, and he didn't learn this skill practicing parallel parking in an empty church lot.

Google tools for design, speed, coding, and teamwork are always a bit more complicated than they may look at first blush. But as Hodge says, "Google has an excellent repository of tools to help web developers get the most from their sites."

We'd say that Google has such an excellent repository of tools that, with a little patience and a sincere effort to experiment, even a relative novice can dress their website up so that it almost looks like it's been worked on by a real web developer, and that ought to be of interest to student and small business owner alike.

Extra Point—Google+

Maybe you're starting to get the feeling that Google is just a bit bigger than you had imagined? You're in pretty good company. No heavier media source than *The New York Times* also just figured out that Google is much more than the media company they once thought it was.

Here's *Times* reporter David Carr's take on *The Evolving Mission of Google (G)*.

> What company derives 96 percent of its revenue from advertising, has a video platform that is currently negotiating with the National Basketball Association, a movie studio and various celebrities, and is developing a subscription service that would be plug-and-play for publishers and consumers the world over.
>
> Time Warner? News Corporation? Viacom?
>
> Nope. Google . . .
>
> There have been reports that Google has set aside $100 million for incentives for well-known celebrities to program their own 'channels' on YouTube to increase the amount of high-profile content on the platform.

What's new about this, you say? Google's connection to media companies, after all, reaches into some of the oldest and most traditional publishing houses. In fact, on this next link you can see how Cambridge University Press, the "world's oldest continuously operating printer and publisher uses Google Book Search to offer its extensive booklist to more scholars more efficiently, boosting sales."

We call this kind of article "inside baseball." You really have to be in the dugout to either understand or appreciate much of what is being said, but if you want a little insight into how nervous Google is about Facebook's domination of "social," this is a great article to read.

MG Siegler, writing for TechCrunch.com, lays out Google's springtime 2011 announcement that it is tying employee bonuses to the success of their social strategy: *I'm having a party. Here's $50. Bring cool people or you owe me $100 (G).*

Siegler's reveal links you to a deeper read on the Google social strategy published in BusinessInsider.com, but you don't need to read that to get the gist of what Google is trying to do, or why Siegler seems relatively pessimistic about its likelihood of success.

Contrasting Google's strategy to rivals Facebook, Twitter, and others, Siegler says this: " . . . Google has nearly 25,000 employees. It seems that will lead to an artificially and prematurely inflated re-creation of the launch environment described above. And that may only serve to create the type of paid-for party that I talked about at the beginning. It's a party that will attract a lot of people. But it's not one that anyone will likely remember—or want to go to again."

Since Siegler wrote this somewhat prescient piece, Google brought out *Google+ (G).*

Will Google+ be the app that changes the world of social media? We don't purport to know, but in any case, the well-orchestrated build up to Google+ appears to have hit its next level.

Amir Efrati, writing in *The Wall Street Journal* (online), says *There's No Avoiding Google+ (G).*

> Both Facebook and Google make the vast bulk of their revenue from selling ads. But Facebook has something Google wants: Facebook can tie people's online activities to their real names, and it also knows who those people's friends are. Marketers say Google has told them that closer integration of Google+ across its many properties will allow Google to obtain this kind of information and target people with more relevant (and therefore, more profitable) ads.

What's the solution for Google?

> Google is challenging Facebook by using a controversial tactic: requiring people to use the Google+ social network.
> The result is that people who create an account to use Gmail, YouTube and other Google services—including the Zagat restaurant-review website— are also being set up with public Google+ pages that can be viewed by anyone online. Google+ is a Facebook rival and one of the company's most important recent initiatives as it tries to snag more online advertising dollars.

Mashable.com has published the complete guide to Google+. It walks you through how the system operates, provides a handy cheat sheet, and speculates on how Google+ might fit into, if not redefine, the future of social media.

MAKING YOUR PRACTICE PERFECT

Some tasks that will help you understand the ideas and concepts talked about in Part III.

Exercise 1: Time to get a Gmail account. It all begins on Google with a Gmail account, and now is the time to get one. Sign up and work to get the best username you can. First Name. LastName@gmail.com is often a good choice. When you sign up, you can import or invite all your contacts from your previous email. This is a good way to see who is there, and build your contact list on Gmail. Once you have an account you can chat with people and access all that Google has to offer.

Exercise 2: Build your Google+ profile. The Google+ Project is a chance for you to have an enhanced online profile that is easily found on Google and can help you make connections in the digital world. Add keywords to your profile, add your location, add photos and videos, add links to your websites, and connect your Twitter account. Go through all the steps to build a profile that represents you and tells your audience what they need to know.

Exercise 3: Set up your Docs and Calendar. These are two of the most useful Google functions. With Docs you can write and share documents easily across the Web and store them on your Google server for free. The calendar is a wonderful way to stay organized. You can import or integrate it with other calendars such as iCal or Microsoft Calendar. And you can follow other people's calendars and collaborate very easily. Set these up and you won't be sorry.

Exercise 4: Download Google Chrome. Why not use the browser from Google. Chrome will give you good insight into how Google works. It integrates easily with Google apps, and is a good browser choice. Chrome is built to load fast, and it's simple to use like Google. You can even get a Chrome Book—a laptop with a Chrome operating system, designed to give you easy web browsing using WiFi or a Verizon Wireless data plan. These new laptops are under $500 and with the Google cloud and web apps, it could be the only machine you need.

Exercise 5: Explore. Google is an ever-changing company and offering that will keep you guessing and on your toes. Go to the *Google Products page (G)* and see what you can find. With Google, you have to experiment to see what you really

like and what will be useful in your personal life and professional career. With Google, you can make free phone calls, chat with your friends, upload your entire photo albums, search online trends, build a new website, create groups for your friends, and much, much more. So learn Google and you will be on your way to greater Internet understanding.

PART IV

ONLINE ORGANIZATIONAL-PUBLIC RELATIONSHIPS (PR)

To get more detail on the resources in this book, follow our advice and Google the phrase followed by (G).

CHAPTER 8

Building and Keeping Organizational-Public Relationships (PR): The Dialogue We've Wanted All Along

Before we go forward with this discussion of the role of social media in building public relationships and the role of PR in social media—the first point that needs to be made is to dispel the notion that the primary function of PR practitioners is dealing with "the media."

PR practitioners (as opposed to publicists, one of the many roles associated with PR) are involved with a wide variety of activities that chart the course of the relationships between an organization and the broad list of individuals and groups upon which the organization depends. One of those audiences, arguably one of the most important, is "the media." But it is only one of the many audiences with which excellent PR is engaged.

Effective organizational-public relations begin with an understanding that actions speak louder than words. The PR team can play a major role in helping the organization make the necessary adjustments to get its behavior into alignment with the interests and values of the segments of society upon which it depends. If the organization is out of sync with its publics, what it says about itself will not be taken seriously.

Modern public relations practitioners have come to understand that the PR department doesn't hold the exclusive license to speak on behalf of the organization, no matter how big or small the organization is. The organization's reputation is being built or eroded by the actions—including the speech acts—of employees, customers, suppliers, old and new media, government officials, and countless other segments of the public, day in and day out. So, while we'll look at how PR practitioners use social media to implement relationship building and strengthening, it's wise to remember that social media are a long ways from being either the exclusive activity or within the exclusive domain of the PR department.

That having been said, PR practitioners are using social media in a variety of new ways every day to take the offense in building relationships between their client organizations and key constituencies. Most importantly, they use social media as a vehicle to carry the claims that are supported by the behavior of their client organizations.

PR practitioners use social media to find new groups with which to "hook up" their client organizations. They use social media as an important new vehicle for marketing communication supporting the activity that builds our brands and sells our products. They promote social causes near and dear to their organization and its management within the new social networking vehicles available.

Practitioners use these social media vehicles to keep employees and other constituencies up to date and in the know about what's going on in the organization. And, perhaps most importantly, they use new social media monitoring tools to listen in on public conversations about their organization and their products, and they feed this information back into the organization in a way that stimulates satisfaction and sustains relationships. These are just a few of the many ways social media are being used to provide offense for organizations and their relationship-building activities.

PR practitioners also need to think about social media's defensive role in public relations. Social media networks are great breeding grounds for issues that ultimately can blow up into major disasters for organizations.

PR practitioners increasingly use social media as an early warning system for impending crises. They use social media to help identify conditions that could create problems for their organization or clients. They use social media to help resolve problems before they begin to burn out of control. By the time a social media fire spreads, it may be too late to avoid major reputational damage.

And besides serving as a social media listening post to warn organizations of impending crises, PR personnel are training clients to exercise caution in the use of these new social media tools. This is the defense we are talking about.

In either case—offense or defense—it's hard to guess whether social media have had a greater impact on the practice of PR or that PR has, in fact, become the activity that is shaping social media. In either case, we believe it is important to understand several critical concepts and distinctions of PR before delving any deeper into this subject area.

The first distinction that needs to be made is the distinction between public relations and publicity. We talked about this earlier in this introduction, and we believe that this distinction is essential in getting a clear understanding of the potential impact of social media on organizational-public relationship building.

There are by the way dozens, if not hundreds, of definitions of PR. Some focus on relationship development while others focus more on persuasion. All of them extend well beyond managing relationships with representatives of the media and garnering free publicity.

It turns out a word that is often used to describe PR is "spinning." The idea is that through the clever use of language, a PR pro can make a bad situation look good. That's what we call trying to put ten pounds of crap into five-pound bags.

Good PR doesn't and can't work like that. We like to think of PR broadly as the art of adjusting the behavior of a client organization to better conform to the values and aspirations of the audiences upon which the organization depends for survival. It's a definition that is based upon the understanding that behavior is more important than words.

In a recent interview in PRSA's *Tactics* magazine, PR pro Richard Edelman emphasized the need for PR to come to grips with the tarnished image of American business. He said that requires building trust.

"We operate in a world without trust," Edelman said, talking about public perception of both the government and American business. "There's no other word than dire. . . . People see everything as spin and lies."

So here's the lesson for the person trying to build the reputation of a business, or the PR person trying to help a client accomplish this. In the end, the truth is the truth. There is not other truth than that.

Positive publicity generated through social media is very important for our organizations, but in order for it to have a lasting positive effect, the publicity must be authentic. If you are seen as a publicity hound, someone who is "seeking publicity," you won't be treated as a serious person, and your organization won't be treated seriously either.

Cheryl Gale made this observation in a post in Bulldog Reporter:

> Social media has given customers a public platform to engage directly with companies. Social media sit on the very pillars that PR is built upon: an uncontrolled medium, conversations, and engagement. PR professionals are trained in the art of two-way conversation, unlike advertisers, who are accustomed to buying time and audiences.

PR's principal objective is, simply, to build and support relationships that the organization has, and needs to have, with a wide variety of individuals and audiences.

Some of this activity may support sales. And customer satisfaction, in fact, is another function supported by PR. The dialogue occurring in social media is playing a larger role in customer satisfaction every day.

PR practitioners also use social media to help identify and hopefully avoid potential crises. And, once a crisis exists, the PR team uses social media networks as another vehicle to interact with a broad range of stakeholders—from the owners and board, to the federal, state and local government, to the suppliers, dealers and individual customers, and the media.

Another distinction that needs to be understood involves the difference between social marketing and commercial marketing.

One of the real geniuses in the world of new and social media recently came out with a brilliant book. Eric Schwartzman, with co-author Paul Gillin, has done a good job of showing how social media can facilitate business-to-business marketing. "Listen to our B2B market, generate major account leads, and build client relationships," says the headline of the cover of the book. Almost everything is right about this book. Everything, that is, except the title which is oh-so wrong. The title of the book is *Social Marketing to the Business Customer (G)*. Why is that wrong?

Social marketing is the well-established discipline in which the objective is to apply commercial marketing-like techniques to achieve socially desirable behavioral-change goals. And the target for the change in behavior is often thought of as applying to entire segments of the population—heavy drinkers, smokers, or perhaps, eaters.

If the book had been written in order to describe and refine strategies to keep your business customer from drinking and driving, that would be *social marketing (G)*.

The title of Schwartzman's book should have been *Social Media Marketing to the Business Customer*, or words to that effect. Social media doesn't have anything to do with social marketing—except this. The field of social marketing has been given a whole new set of tools to influence people to take actions that are in their interest or in the public interest, and the new tools are the tools we are looking at and learning about here.

The tools of social media are perfect for assisting social marketers in their efforts to change people's behavior, as they are proving to be equally perfect in a commercial marketing context in the sales of products. Social media provide wonderful tools for use in either a commercial or social marketing context.

Out of this kind of discussion comes a better understanding about the differences between social media and social marketing, or between social marketing and commercial marketing, or—and this is very important—between marketing and public relations.

We need to understand these distinctions and keep them in mind as we go into this chapter on online public relations.

Once you begin to get a feel for these distinctions, you can better understand how different communication theories,techniques, and principles apply to different situations, and why if your approach to public relations begins to look too much like marketing, you'll be losing the social benefit of both worlds.

Organizational-PR's Role
in Social Media and Vice Versa

How are social media changing organizational-public relations? Well, the opinions on that subject are varied. British design firm isev.co.uk says: "organizations are jumping on the social media bandwagon left, right, and center—changing the face of public relations and the way PR organizations work forever.

In its post on *how social media has changed PR (G)*, Isev puts it this way: "Customers will no longer accept being simply bombarded with information. They now expect organizations to develop relationships with them."

As we say, social media is giving public relations the dialogue it has wanted all along.

HotPotatoSocialMedia.com has a similar take on *how social media has changed PR (G)*. PR practitioners have become the direct source of information for a wide variety of audiences. And with this new responsibility for producing content comes an increasing burden for authentic communication.

> Now more than ever, practitioners should be deploying blogs, Twitter, Facebook and YouTube profiles, Wikipedia pages, bookmarking and sharing links . . . In fact, the corporate, brand, or subject matter blog can be the hub of an integrated PR program, using social media channels for distributing blog posts and other news. If the news item is big or strategic enough, [they should] consider submitting them to paid distribution services . . .

Where you stand on the question of how and how much social media are changing PR depends upon where you sit. Online marketing firm BlueFountainMedia.com looks at PR as supporting the selling function with the central strategy being persuasion according to Jon Gelberg's post on *how social media has changed the face of public relations (G)*.

> A great many PR practitioners would say the day of PR as largely an outbound communication, persuasion-based discipline were dying long before the advent of social media. But few would deny that the ability of social media to facilitate interaction has accelerated the movement away from persuasion and toward dialogue as the central mechanism through which organizational-public relationships are built and sustained.
>
> The truth is that many people don't have the slightest idea about the degree to which social media are giving PR a great many new capabilities to reach its potential as a relationship builder. That having been said, it's clear that developing effective organizational-public relationships is an activity that ought to be at the top of the agenda of everyone who is interested in using social media for more productive business.

In a PublicRelationsBlogger.com blog post, one of the most prolific and proficient PR sages with a "marketing orientation," Ashley Wirthlin, discusses *the changing world and responsibilities of PR (G)* and five ways to take advantage of the changes the Internet brings to the expanding world of PR:

> While social media have made it easier to release information, get in touch with the public, and address crises, there is an increased responsibility because the public knows how easy it is; with that ease comes a sort of expected response.
>
> If a crisis is underway, I expect a company to be responsive, available, and accountable because it is so easy to be these things online.

This much we know: Given the tremendous capability of social media to allow you to engage in dialogue with a wide variety of audiences, you need to be thinking beyond marketing products and building brands as a primary focus of your social media planning.

A great way for you to get a handle on how effective business leaders are using social media to engage with customers through PR is *to get into the PR blogosphere through Blogrank (G)*. As we were putting the guide together, we went to Blogrank to get their rank of the hottest PR blogs. Google the phrase and pick a couple of PR blogs to check out and get involved. It will definitely be worth your time.

And if you really want to get a deeper understanding of how you can use public relations to help build your business, we encourage you to go to Brian Solis's blog post on *putting the public back in public relations (G)*.

You can't overlook the fact that Solis's post is a promotion of his book by the same title. The book was co-authored with Deirdre Breakenridge, another of our favorites, and, as Frank Gruber says, the book sits at the intersection of the new and old public relations.

Of course, we also love David Meerman Scott's work—especially his newest book, *Real-Time Marketing and PR (G)*, and we have used *New Rules of Marketing and PR* for several years in several classes at MSU. But you don't have to stop there. There is a world of David Meerman Scott material available to you—much of it for free—and like we said we love it all.

David Meerman Scott also loves David Meerman Scott's work, so we shouldn't have been surprised at his list of "must reads" in online PR and digital marketing. And he must really believe in the Confucian concept that to truly possess anything, you must be willing to give it away. Because what might surprise you is that the selections he offered to include in this book are all available to you for free.

Here they are:

David Meerman Scott—Links

Real-Time: How Marketing & PR at Speed Drives Measurable Success
Are you instantly engaging with your market?
http://www.davidmeermanscott.com/documents/Real_Time.pdf

Lose Control of your Marketing! Why marketing ROI measures lead to failure
Give this one to your boss, board, or investors
http://www.davidmeermanscott.com/documents/Marketing_ROI.pdf

The New Rules of Viral Marketing: How word-of-mouse spreads your ideas for free (2008)
Downloaded over one million times
http://www.davidmeermanscott.com/documents/Viral_Marketing.pdf

David also offered a couple other free resources for us to share with you:

Scott's iPhone / iPad app is available at:
http://bit.ly/fOxFXl

And his wonderful "Marketing Strategy Planning Template is available at
http://www.webinknow.com/2010/07/free-marketing-strategy-planning-template.html

---

Amazon.com has a listing called "Amazon's Complete Selection of David Meerman Scott Books." If you follow Derek's Ingenex "Digital Bus" blog, you must know what a stark-raving *Phish* lunatic co-author Derek Mehraban is. Rick had a hard time breaking it to Derek that David Meerman Scott had a book out called *Marketing Lessons from the Grateful Dead: What Every Business Can Learn from the Most Iconic Band in History (G).*

Rick has also been a fan of Eric Schwartzman for a long time and even attended one of his PRSA's social media seminars. You should do the same if you get the chance. And, as we said earlier, if you can get over the mistitling of his book about the use of social media in business-to-business marketing—*Social Marketing to the Business Customer (G)*—you'll find the material very useful.

Aside from resembling David Meerman Scott's treatise about The Grateful Dead, Rodger Roeser's CommPro.Biz post asks you if you *want to rock in PR and marketing? (G)*

This is a useful and interesting article that points to a growing tendency—an outgrowth of how the electronic media is being used—to blend marketing with public relations. In fact, author Roeser is president of a firm he describes as "integrated buzz marketing." His technique for making his point, though not unique, uses a number of similes, metaphors, and analogies to demonstrate and highlight some important principles in the modern practice of social and commercial marketing.

We are particularly grateful for his principle number eight: "Practice":

> There is no substitute . . . amateurs practice until they get it right, but professionals practice until they get it wrong—it just becomes second nature. I can stand out on stage, play a killer bass line, belt out my song, jump up and down, press the button for the fog machine and point to a 'fan' all at the same time without even thinking about it.
>
> So, to, must business. You must work with your team over and over and over again. Rehearse your speech, your movements, your key messages, and your interviews.

Our biggest concern with Rodger Roeser is that he may leave some of our readers with the impression that we believe turning on the fog machine is a PR skill. It's not and we don't. And this is one of the reasons, perhaps the chief reason, why if the corporate social media lead sits in the PR department that person had better understand that the days of fogging and spinning are over.

Ragan's *PR Daily* shared a post from Elizabeth Sosnow who acknowledges the irony that in this era of media defined as "social" anyone would hold such a territorial position on the ownership of social media:

> Our colleagues in sales, advertising, customer service, HR and IT all want control of the digital media PR budget. I understand why they would ask for it, but I just don't think they're as well equipped to head the effort as PR pros.
>
> We are storytellers. Thought leadership is already in our DNA. We begin—not end—every project with an analysis of how to approach influencers. We are already trained to empathize and converse with different audiences (at the same time).

We think that everyone is entitled to his or her own opinion, but we all should be working from the same fact base. And we believe the fact base Sosnow presents in this post speaks volumes about the management role (as opposed to marketing role) that PR must hold in the organization to meet its promise of relationship building.

Going Social with Media Reporters and Editors

No matter how much we might believe that public relations needs to be viewed, and needs to view itself, as going far beyond the publicity function, the news release is still a staple in the PR pantry.

Mickie Kennedy put together a useful primer highlighting *five things to check before sending out your press release (G)* on his company's blog. His post is especially informative and practical for social media operatives called upon to get the word out about a new product or service, or other newsworthy event in the organization.

So what are the tips? Again, you'll have to go to the post to find out for yourself, and if you do, you'll have a shot at getting a great insight into a fairly traditional view of news releases.

Kennedy is the founder of eReleases.com, which he describes as the "online leader in affordable press release distribution." Among the things he makes available is a 160–page book of sample news releases—something we find very valuable if only as a way of comparing to our writing.

Anyone serious about understanding how the world of social media is changing the practice of public relations should consider becoming a regular reader of *Ashley Wirthlin's PublicRelationsBlogger.com (G)*. She describes her website as "a free, educational resource for public relations with hundreds of articles to browse on various PR topics including its role in social media (or social media's role in PR), PR and marketing, PR and advertising, and much more."

If you want an opportunity to read Wirthlin's take on where the industry is and where its going, go to PublicRelationsBook.com to get her free book.

We particularly liked Wirthlin's description of some of the do's and don'ts of PR in social media because it's a good characterization of the offense versus defense view that we talked about in our introduction to this chapter:

> Connect with others in the industry and collaborate with them. Not only is it important to connect with them through social networking sites, it is crucial to the growth of your blog to connect with other bloggers and exchange links.

The moral of Wirthlin's story:

> Use social media to connect, respond, and communicate with your audiences. Be personable and personal, making it more fun for your buyers to communicate with you. Moreover, measure results so you can impress upon the shareholders of your company the importance of PR, marketing, and social media. Advertising yourself is a somewhat necessary evil in PR and in social media, but do so tactfully and in moderation.

Co-author Derek Mehraban gave some free social media online PR advice to the news directors attending the Big Ten Plus News Directors Conference 2011.

We think the advice was worth reprinting:

Mehraban's Top Ten Social Media Tips for Big Ten News

1. **Optimize yourself first and foremost.** And that includes your team. As a Big Ten news director it's important to be able to find you with ease— and I mean by googling you. So be sure you have a strong profile. Be

sure you have links from your university. Take a screen shot of your search results and build from there. What happens when I search for *Derek Mehraban* on Google?

2. **Create great content.** First and foremost you need to create great content for your organizations. Interesting. Fun. Funny. Relevant. News content. Blur the lines of news and entertainment. The more interesting the information is, the better. What is the most interesting and entertaining thing you have covered? And then think where do you post that? Facebook? Twitter? Blogs? How do you disseminate your news?

3. **Lead with your best SEO terms.** Figure out what people are searching for and lead with that. Put your keywords at the front of your titles on pages, and through out your copy. Use one phrase or 3 to 5 keywords per post or news release. Use the keywords at the beginning, middle, and end. Next, link to that article from other places using those keywords. This means—don't waste your prime real estate with words that won't help you. Search the phrase "Digital Marketing Firm" on Google and see what happens.

4. **Tweet. Follow. And ReTweet.** Using Twitter to build community is a lot like being at a tailgate—everyone has fun. So put out your content. But share and promote others' content too. Use your University Twitter accounts for the greater good. And then use your personal accounts to further promote and build relationships. Be real.

5. **Know your audience.** Figure out with whom you want to communicate. Where do they spend time? What interests them? You can use analytics to help you with this. Also, you can ask them with surveys. Once you find out the "who, what, when, where, and why," you can communicate much more effectively and get more traction from your news. Can you track your audiences? Think about remote check-in services like Foursquare, Gowalla, or Facebook check in. What can you do to capitalize on this trend?

6. **Be known for the smallest things.** The beauty of SEO and the Internet is that you can create micro-content that relates to your university. You can show up in the search results for the smallest and most obscure search phrases. Whether it's a certain type of rare spider, or a micro-fusion technique that is being pioneered by your university. Why not pick three interesting keyword phrases per university department that you want to be known for and develop a content strategy to get page one Google ranking for them?

7. **Video, Photos, and Text, Oh My!** These days you need all three to be relevant. Think about events. What can you document? What is the social play? When you publish video, photos and text—you have a much better chance of showing up on people's radar.

8. **"Coopetition" as my friends Terry Bean and Charlie Wollborg like to say, is imperative.** Work together to build the reputation of the best conference in the United States—the Big Ten. Why not have cooperative competition between the Big Ten Universities. In fact, you have a great

opportunity to help one another. Why not create a #hashtag or use #BigTen and then you can promote and Tweet or share other information from your Big Ten counterparts. This type of arrangement could be really beneficial. Linking to one another's articles could really boost SEO. Ask for people to RT, Share on Facebook, or +1 your content on Google.

9. **Monitor and track your success.** Metrics like time on site, time watching videos, views of pages or releases are all very important—track them. I encourage you to share your best practices for how you do it—by commenting on this blog post so others can see it. We use Trackur or Radian6 for tracking trends and keywords. You can too. Also, simple things like Google Alerts can really help you track. In addition, use Hoot-Suite or some sort of social content producing site that allows you to track users and #hashtags.

10. **Mobile browsing and interaction is KING.** How does your university look in the mobile environment? Mobile browsing, especially for students, is going to surpass traditional Internet browsing. Be very aware of how you show up on mobile devices. Think Apps. iPhone, Android, Windows Mobile, Blackberry. Test, and refine and promote to mobile audiences. Who is doing the best job at Mobile in the Big Ten?

Don't Forget the Blogger

A blogger is a blog author—someone who keeps and maintains a blog. So, what's a blog reader?

A couple of years ago, the Pew Internet and American Life project found that about one-third of all regular Internet users (roughly a quarter of all American adults) say they read blogs, with 11 percent of all adult Internet users saying they read blogs on a typical day. We've seen estimates of blog readership even higher, and part of the problem in coming up with a clean number is that the definition of blog itself is kind of tricky.

The word "blogger" is a bit trickier. It's a place as well as word for a person who produces blog posts. *Blogger (G)* is also the name of a free blog publishing tool provided by Google for creating your own blog.

We picked a handful of our many favorite resource entries to include as we conclude this section of the book.

Thanks to Mashable.com again for making such a big contribution to our effort to make social media for business feel, perhaps, a bit less daunting. Their *PR pros guide to blogging (G)* is one such contribution.

Dana Zemack used his Mashable post as a way to promote Mynewsdesk online news bureau owned by a Norweigian company. The platform sells itself as a service that will increase engagement between companies and their most important influencers, such as journalists, bloggers, and other opinion leaders.

While the orientation is largely media relations, as opposed to organizational-public relationships writ large, the advice is spot on and should be helpful to novice and seasoned practitioner alike.

Zemack's article repeats many of the items we touched upon in the earlier blogging chapter, and adds a few more useful tidbits including the admonition that all companies need to think like a media company. Echoing David Meerman Scott's observation, Zemack points out that there are times when a company blog "can fill a pretty significant informational void." We might say the same thing in a slightly different way.

Increasingly a larger and larger percentage of buying decisions, whether they are consumer decisions or decisions between suppliers and manufacturers, occur after some kind of an Internet search. So the key is that if you don't have findable and interesting content available online, the chances are that neither your prospects nor your existing customers are going to rely on you as a source of knowledge. So, if they aren't going to you for purchasing information, where do you suppose they'll go?

Our New Media Driver's License® seminars focus to no small degree on public relations, as you must know by now. And if you have been paying attention to the evolution of public relations, you'll know that it's growing to no small degree in the direction of social media. Why is this, you say?

One simple word answers the question: DIALOGUE.

Dialogue is a key, if not the key, to relationships at every level, from the most singular, intimate, personal relationship to the relationship between an auto manufacturer and the financial analysts whose reports influence stock prices. No tool since the invention of the telephone has contributed more to dialogue—people-to- people, people-to-business, business-to-business, and even country-to-country—than has social media.

And to add further evidence to our earlier point that you don't have to be a PR practitioner to understand how to build great organizational-public relationships, computer programmer Phillip Rhodes uses a YouTube video to show us *how to do blogger outreach the human way (G)*. His PR advice is some of the best we've heard in a long time. Principally, he reminds us that blogging is all about conversations between and among people.

The way to get bloggers to have an emotional connection to your business, Rhodes says, is simple: Let your employees develop personal relationships with them. And the only way they can do that is by getting personal.

If your employee, Bob, is out there in the blogosphere making friends, answering questions, providing honest and sincere information, asking questions, perhaps, the people he connects with are going to want Bob to succeed.

Phillip's three-minute explanation of the importance of remembering "there are people behind the pixels" should be required viewing for anyone considering a formal blogger outreach program.

"Anything you do online, be it your business website or your blog, has something to do with audience, and you should learn how to know your visitors," AnaRC tells us in a PremierSocialMedia.com post describing *three ways to get to know your audience (G)*.

Start with tools.

Keep a close eye on tools analyzing traffic—From Google Analytics to StatCounter and the demographic-oriented Facebook Insights, many online analytics tools, most of which are free, can help you with a lot of information on your visitors—from the type of content or pages they like best, the time they spend on your site and the number of pages they visit, to the keywords that bring them to you, the operating system they are using and a few demographic insights, such as age and sex. There is plenty of information on your audience right at your finger tips.

Dr. Tony Karrer, CEO of TechEmpower.com, provides some important and down-to-earth tips on *how to effectively build relationships with bloggers (G)* in a post in SearchEngineJournal.com.

I've recently been finding myself building relationships with bloggers using a very different strategy that has worked very well for me. The key to this strategy is what I call topic hubs.

A topic hub aggregates a collection of information sources (web pages and RSS feeds) to form a new information hub around a particular topic—hence the name 'topic hub.' For example, the *B2B Marketing Zone (G)* is a topic hub on 'all the best info on' business-to-business marketing.

Relationships with bloggers naturally form when a topic hub is involved.

We've put a lot of focus on the dialogue that powers public relationships, but we shouldn't forget that the marketing side of the house has a big stake in effective social media, especially blogging. With all this talk about dialogue, the power and role of persuasion that drives marketing could get lost. It shouldn't.

In a post entitled *ten tips for a successful blogger outreach campaign (G)* in TheCaffinatedBlog.Typepad.com, the anonymous, obviously over-caffeinated, blogger points out that:

. . . with more than half of blog readers saying that blogs influence their purchase decisions, it's no wonder that many companies are eager to generate some buzz about their products on blogs. Unfortunately, it doesn't happen magically.

In order to get the attention of these influential bloggers, companies have to reach out to them and make themselves known—but in a meaningful way.

The Importance of CONTENT

There seems to be an increasing feeling among those in the public relations business that their jobs are morphing into an interesting form of something that in another age might be called *journalism*. And they are right.

Everyone is a journalist (G) is the point of an important post written by Peter Auditore of Asterias Research that appeared not long ago in SocialMedia-Today.com.

> The social media tsunami is the game changer that is significantly impacting our world of communications and challenging the current models of engagement with journalists and influencers. This change mandates that we reassess our current engagement models and the importance of individual and organizational influence. Social media is more than a phenomenon. It will not go away. And it has created new and viral forms of influence that are changing the way purchasing decisions are made in nearly all industries.

It's not only PR practitioners that are required to spend an increasing amount of time writing. Almost everyone who wants their products and brands known has to spend more time writing.

So, what's the secret to good writing for social media? Well, as we said earlier, the secret to good writing is: "Writers write."

It's almost that simple. You can't expect to be a successful business leader, let alone a PR practitioner, in this day of instant opinions delivered through the Internet without being a decent writer.

"Writers write." And that's why this next resource—from EcoConsultancy.com—resonated so clearly with us.

We are tipping our hat to Chris Lake for showing us *how to write for the web: 23 useful rules (G)*. We especially liked his advice on how to break writer's block.

> Pour your thoughts out first, edit later. Write the opening paragraph last or, said another way, write the closing paragraph first. Begin with the end in mind, is how some might say it. Exercise the one-comma rule. More than one comma may mean the sentence is too long. And make sure you keep your sentences short.

If we tried to identify any more of the great rules that Lake lays out in this article, we'd violate his rule on brevity. Google Lake's post and read it yourself.

Matt Petronzio polled six well-known writers for a post in Mashable.com in which he laid out his favorite *ten pro tips for writers using social media (G)*.

His tip number one: Sign up for the big networks.

> It can be difficult to sift through all of the available social platforms and decide which ones to focus on; it helps if you think about what it is you want to achieve. If you're looking to get your name as a writer out there, it

makes sense to use the networks with the most users to boost your presence. That means Twitter and Facebook, for sure, but Tumblr and Google+ are also rising in popularity for writers.

Susan Orlean, *New Yorker* journalist and author of *The Orchid Thief (G)*, looks at each platform as a different kind of party. 'Twitter is a noisy cocktail party, with lots of chatting and quick interactions, a kind of casual free-for-all,' she says. 'Facebook is a combination high school and college reunion and therapy group. Google+ I haven't figured out yet.'

Twitter certainly seems to be the top go-to network for writers, and it's incredibly useful. Meredith Hindley, historian and writer for various publications like *The New York Times* and *Humanities*, says, 'It's both social and a big RSS feed, which makes my information junkie heart happy.'

Cindy Kim describes social media as *moving beyond the wire to real-time PR* in a post in her blog, CindyKimBlog.wordpress.com. Quoting liberally from David Meerman Scott, she demonstrates how the traditional lines between the management function of PR and marketing functions like advertising are blurring as a result of the emergence of social media.

For many, PR is still about how to provide content for reporters to repost or write a story based around a good pitch. Today, however, there is much more to it than that.

PR professionals whose job functions involve media relations must learn the rules of real-time PR. The new face of media relations requires even more speed and agility to seize market opportunities, real-time engagement and creative out-of-the-box approaches to become the first market mover.

Jaci Clement's goal of helping FreeEnterprise.com keep the wheels of industry moving is advanced in conveying her *six steps to the perfect PR pitch (G)*. And like the old axiom that if you don't know where you are going, any road will get you there, Clement insists that every good PR pitch must begin with a clear goal.

Why do you want news coverage? What is it you want people to know, buy, or believe about your company? The more definitive you can be, the more you'll be able to target the proper audience. The more you know about whom you're trying to reach, the better. Then you can determine the right media outlets to contact.

Understanding what news means—"something out of the ordinary"—is point number two. Clement, who is executive director of the Fair Media Council, wraps up her list with the importance of keeping the pitch simple, clear, and above all brief. "If you can pitch your story in 85 words or fewer, you have a greater chance of capturing the reporter's attention."

Tools, Tips, Tactics, and Tricks of the Trade

When you look at the Mashable.com post by Sara Evans on *ten of the best social media tools for PR professionals and journalists (G)*, the first thing that might impress you is how often this post has been re-posted, and where, over the past five years or so.

The first resource that Evans detailed when she originally wrote this article remains a great lead for content providers and content consumers alike—Help a Reporter Out (HARO)—her favorite tool:

> The brainchild of Peter Shankman, this is the only free resource I am aware of where reporters submit questions directly to PR professionals—no strings attached. Subscribers to the list-serve received up to three daily emails, with anywhere from 15–30 queries per email each.

We're glad that Evans listed this as her favorite tool, since it helps us emphasize the "relationship-management" nature of the business of PR, rather than reinforcing its stereotype as a propaganda mill.

On press releases, Evans says: "The emergence of the social media release (SMR) will soon dominate interactions between journalists and PR people." Her favorite tool to help on this aspect of her work is *PitchEngine (G)*.

You'll have to read the wonderful post to get the rest of Evans's top 10 list—a very good one, indeed. She talks about ReportingOn, Journalisted, Wikis, Twitter and how it is being used by media people, Twello.com, BeatBlogging.org, WiredJournalists.com and, my personal favorite, *YourPitchSucks.com (G)*, which allows you to submit your draft pitch to PR experts for a serious review.

Ian Cleary identified his fab *five social media tools to save time and boost efficiency (G)* in a post in PRDaily.com. He identified these as tools that the readers of PR Daily can use to "improve our marketing efforts online."

> It's easy to get caught up with the number of fans you have on Facebook, but we're in the business of selling our products and services. Your time spent on Facebook needs to be rewarded.
>
> If you're on Facebook and you want to take it to the next level, invest in a Facebook marketing platform that will help.
>
> Agorapulse is one such platform that contains a broad range of functionality, including page management, 14 applications, and the facility for building a profile of your fans to help turn them into leads and, ultimately, sales.

Samantha Hosenkamp also used PRDaily.com to identify *ten (mostly) free social media tools you can't live without (G)*, in a live conference blog. Her tips cover her favorite tools to monitor your brand, do SEO, track tweets, Facebook, Pinterest, and video.

Borderline overboard, Liliana Dumitru-Steffens's list of *100 media monitoring tools for PR (G)* is the most comprehensive list of media monitoring tools we, or our students in our New Media Driver's License® courses, could find.

Dumitru-Steffens, writing an "Everything PR" column for PamilVisions.net, has the waterfront covered. If you want to get a sense of the value of this post to the industry, read the comments that follow her post.

Besides expressing gratitude to Liliana for this great work, some of the comments include some links to additional resources.

You can be as skeptical as you want about what's driving the growing number of press release submission sites. But SEODiscovery.org's Ben Sibley swears he tested each of the *70 free press release sites (G)* he lists in what he calls the only up-to-date list of working sites of its kind.

If you have any doubt about the power of these sites, listen to this. In one of our first New Media Driver's License® courses, we had a student who experimented with one of these websites to put out a "hypothetical" news release he had written. The release was about a major donation to a New York hospital that had been (hypothetically) made by an executive with the New York Giants football team.

When this practice release hit the free services, it went global, generating considerable attention in the Giants's team offices and requiring the personal intervention of Hall of Fame great, former Giants defensive back, now broadcaster, Carl Banks (an MSU alumnus) to get us, and our student, off the hook.

Tom Johansmeyer, writing in Ragan's PRDaily.com provides some pretty basic and very useful information that reminds us that we need to consider *using email and analytics to track actions and score coverage (G)*.

Look at reporters, editors, and increasingly bloggers, he says, as discrete audiences that can be researched in essentially the same way a marketing department researches customers or prospects.

> You can use the same systems deployed elsewhere in the marketing department for customer intelligence to learn from the actions of your top media outlets. Use information from email marketing platforms, Web analytics, and other tools to refine your press releases, pitch smarter, and generate measurable results.

These four questions need to be asked to remove some of the guesswork about pitching articles to reporters:

- What gets the reporter's attention?
- What motivates a reporter or editor to move?
- What keeps them involved to continue on your corporate blog or in your media room?
- What keeps them coming back for more?

"Web jockeys like repeat visitors. Publishers crave repeat readers. Businesses live for repeat customers. PR is no different," Johansmeyer says.

Johansmeyer's fifth question is the kicker: "What keeps *you* from getting ahead?" He put the special emphasis on the word *you.* You have to quit making assumptions about your target markets, including editors and reporters and bloggers, and you have to do some research to find out what it is they want, and then give it to them.

You know, from the introduction to this section of the book, that we feel that a good definition of PR involves adjusting organizational behavior to conform to the expectations of key audiences and then letting the audiences know about it. That's certainly one common concept of PR, but there are others.

A great way for you to get a fix on how you want to define PR is by getting active in the PR blogosphere. And a great place to start is with the *top 100 PR blogs (G).*

As we were putting the guide together, we went to Blogrank to get their rank of the hottest PR blogs.

Number one on their list is *TheFutureBuzz.com (G).* As we went to a timely post, what social media guru should show up in the lead article other than David Meerman Scott?

> From 100 things a year to 10,000, marketing has fundamentally shifted. Rather than doing a hundred really big projects, today's marketers need to do tens of thousands of tiny things each year to be successful. It's not about the campaign. It's about engagement.

Scott's thoughts also sync well with a previous post we shared on why inch-by-inch now destroys the "big idea."

Adam Singer wrote, "In a world with infinite choice where people's attention continues to shift to stream-based platforms on web and micro interactions on mobile, this makes sense. You need to show up and show up consistently.

Number two on the list is *PR-Squared.com (G).* Today's lead post sent us over to the *SHIFT blog (G),* where the team at PRSquared.com was engaged with a psychologist looking at the principles of influence—"the psychological phenomenon, not the social media metric—and how public relations can be used to grow your influence." We were able to click through to the first three of a six-part series, this one on "PR and scarcity."

There's a composite post we want to send you to on the subject of *digital marketing and PR posts (G)* from the same Adam Singer, one of the most active PR bloggers. If you become a regular follower of TheFutureBuzz.com, you'll see more and more of these kinds of pieces. These are posts that Singer calls "some of my latest ideas published external to The Future Buzz."

This post contains a TopRankBlog.com post on thought leadership on social media strategy that includes thinking from some of the top marketing and PR leaders in cyberspace. Another of the articles describes how to develop great content, laying out *10 tips from Byron White, Chief Idea Officer of Idea Launch.com (G)*.

FlackMe.com (G) is one of many very interesting PR-related blogs we look at. Recently, we were able to find a great PR case about Sears dropping another PR ball. Doug Bedell, one of the most prolific PR writers in cyberspace, wrote this post. More than 400 of Bedell's articles are available in the blog's user-friendly archives.

One other thing we like about *FlackMe.com (G)* is its affiliation with *Talent-Zoo.com (G)*, which posts some cool PR, marketing, advertising, and media-related job openings.

Today, we were able to "social-eyes" an amazing PR director job in the Big Apple with a boutique communications firm.

We've said this before and we'll say it again: Differentiate or die. We've also said that Ashley Wirthlin is one of our favorite PR sources. Posting in PublicRelationsBlogger.com, Wirthlin wrote about *PR strategies: Three ways to differentiate yourself (G)*.

The title is somewhat misleading—the post, in our opinion, really doesn't give you three discrete activities or actions that will differentiate you in your marketplace. But it does give you some solid advice on standing out from the crowd. And it gives you a good method to figure out what your best potential points of differentiation are.

Her second point—"Analyze the situation"—is a great example of the line that PR often crosses into marketing. The line is pretty thin here, at best.

But Wirthlin does give an example of the importance of honesty as part of the differentiation equation.

Two stores, side by side, tried to differentiate themselves by outdoing one another on the markdowns it was offering. One had a 75 percent off sale. The store next door had an 80 percent off sale. It was a good example of how not to differentiate a business.

Wirthlin's example reminded us of the story of the Chicago butcher who "differentiated" his store from the other butcher shops in the neighborhood. "Best Butcher Shop in Chicago," his sign proclaimed. The shop next door immediately put up a sign that said, "Best Butcher Shop in Cook County." Not to be outdone, a couple of days later and couple of doors down the street came this sign: "Best Butcher Shop on the Block."

"On an average business day, more than 2,000 press releases are distributed by the five leading wire services in the United States—Business Wire, Marketwire, PrimeNewswire, PR Newswire, and PRWeb," says Sarah Evans in this

Mashable.com post. The key to getting through the rubble is to make your releases findable to those who might benefit from finding them.

Focus on search engine optimization (SEO). Effective SEO helps you in other ways also, and there are some keys to being able to deliver better results. (We get into SEO and search engine marketing in the Internet Marketing chapter of this book.)

Evans has *ten ways to make press releases more SEO friendly (G)*. Evans's point is quite simple here. In order for releases to be findable to potential customers you have to make sure you'll show up at the top of the search results.

We're fascinated with graphics, so when we saw the plastic safety goggles next to the opening paragraph of a posting from Adam Vincenzini in SocialMediaToday.com's post about *ten free social media tools every PR pro should master (G)*, we figured this must be for real.

Everyone who has ever done PR work knows the importance of having safety glasses at the ready. When you are standing in front of the fan and your client throws the excrement into it, you might get hit, but at least you won't go blind.

Vincenzini's column doesn't go into this "hitting the fan" aspect of PR, but it does deliver on its promise reminding us of the importance of AllTop (we've talked about this resource in a couple of places in the book), Social Mention, Bing real-time Twitter search, Klout, Backtweets, Wordle, Google Trends, BlogPulse, Alexa, and SWiX.

This is a powerful column with clear and common sense recommendations. For example, about SWiX, Vincenzini says: "If you only use one tool a day, try and make it this one. It is a really (really!) simple way of tracking activity across all of your social networks/platforms."

He describes its PR value succinctly: "At-a-glance intelligence, lovely."

Post author Mickie Kennedy, founder of eReleases.com, should be on any list of PR experts. So should Mark Ragan, CEO of Ragan's *PR Daily*.

If you haven't discovered it yet, *Quora.com (G)* defines itself as a "continually improving collection of questions and answers created, edited and organized by everyone who uses it."

So who, in Kennedy's opinion, are the *20 top PR experts that one should "follow" on Quora (G)*? It's an interesting list that not only names the names, but also offers brief biographies that, in total, looks like a "Who's Who" of modern PR. Many of these experts have gained their status in PR by virtue of their acumen in handling PR crises.

In social media public relations, as in life, it's not a bad idea to hope for the best, but you have to plan for the worst, because sometimes Murphy's law just takes over: if something can go wrong, it probably will. Andrew Gothelf summarized a South by Southwest session on just that subject in his *ten social media lessons about crisis communications (G)*.

As many brands have learned since plunging into social media, it is critical to have a plan to respond to crises that relate to your business. When issues arise, both big and small, having a chain of command and response matrix available can help thwart an issue before it gets worse.

The academic research reminds us that in any crisis we have to begin with the instructing information. Make sure that the first thing you do is warn everyone who is in the path of an impending disaster regardless of who's at fault.

Gothelf begins his list with getting the information to the people within your organization in such a way that they will all have a consistent way of sharing information and speaking in one voice.

His second point is one that cannot be said often enough. Crises are almost always situational-specific events. Contingency theory would tell us that key to responding is to be very flexible. Gothelf quotes Anastacia Visneski:

The ultimate key is flexibility. There is no longer the perfect news cycle, and people won't wait for you to create the perfect press release. It's about maximum exposure with minimum delay.

If you are really into understanding crisis management, you've probably already figured out that the most important thing you can do in a crisis is avoid it.

Gerald Baron's *Crisisblogger.com (G)* is a great place for you to get great advice on every aspect of crisis communication. Baron passed along a great list of the *worst social media reputation disasters (G)*. The list originally appeared in a *SimplyZesty.com (G)* post and begins with the now-famous photo of the FedEx deliveryman throwing a television over a gate. This video went hyper viral before anyone pointed out that a television is probably far too heavy for anybody to have thrown with such ease. Was it an empty box that FedEx was delivering so that a customer could return a defective product?

Around these parts, a tweet involving Chrysler Corporation took on a life of its own and taught an important lesson to an employee of a PR consulting firm.

Following the trend of employees posting stupid things, Chrysler found itself in crisis after a tweet outraged both consumers and Chrysler. The tweet read:
'I find it ironic that Detroit is known as #motorcity and yet no one here knows how to f#*!ing drive.'

What eventually happened was Chrysler deleted the tweet, didn't renew its contract with New Media Strategies, and the employee who wrote the tweet was fired.

Social media is fluttering with advice on various aspects of PR, and no shortage of this advice involves *how to handle a PR crisis (G)*.

Crises are when the PR consultant gets his or her chops, as they say. That's when everyone turns to the PR expert (unless the PR expert caused the crisis) and asks the following question: "Well, what do we do now?" We like Ronn Torossian's advice from a post in Entrepreneur.com. Simply spoken: Drop everything and deal with it.

There is a tremendous amount written about crisis management and reputation restoration. One of our favorite authors on the subject is Dr. Timothy Coombs. He's won national prizes from the Public Relations Society of America for his work in what he calls *Situational Crisis Communication Theory (G)*, which actually provides recommendations for what to do in various kinds of crises. Much of his research is based in attribution theory, which means when something goes wrong everybody looks for someone to blame. Try not to be that someone.

Torossian's crisis advice is more "street level." It's aimed at mostly small businesses facing big problems. He uses a variety of real-world examples that reinforce the importance of what we said earlier—plan for the worst, even if you are hoping for the best. (By the way, unlike Torossian, Coombs believes there are times when a quick apology for a crisis may not be the best action to take.)

The single truth about all crises is this: The most important work that PR people do isn't handing the crises that arise. That's important, for sure, but the most important crisis work PR people do is advising management on how to keep crises from happening in the first place. That advice begins from an orientation that PR is about adjusting organizational behavior first, and talking about it later. Unfortunately, most PR counselors never get any credit for that.

What better way to end this section than with some generic advice that will help any public relations practitioner—no, it will help anyone—who is interested in using social or any other media to build relationships.

Arik Hanson has a wonderful blog entitled "Communications Conversations," and it's a blog you might consider making part of your regular social media fare. He said a friend of his stopped him dead in his tracks with this question about *PR advice: What's the best tips you've ever received? (G)*. So he thought about it and put down a few tips of his own.

"Never burn a bridge" is Hanson's tip number one.

"Work smarter, not harder" is his second one. We always liked the story of the guy who submitted a bill to a client for some advice he'd given. The bill seemed a bit higher than the client anticipated. "How much time could it have taken you to come up with the solution?" the client asked. The PR guy responded by saying that he doesn't get paid for pushing buttons, he gets paid for knowing which buttons to push.

Hanson went to several of his friends, at least a couple of whom ought to be familiar names to our readers.

Deirdre Breakenridge told Hanson her best advice involved becoming a better listener. Many of the female PR executives echoed this kind of line—a particularly important thing for men in the PR business to hear, if you ask us.

Mark Ragan's advice was a bit more basic: "Learn how to write better than anyone else in your organization or market," advice that echoes the results of the study we talked about earlier. PR supervisors are very unhappy about the writing skills of entry-level professionals.

As *Weber Shandwick Worldwide PR (G)* social media expert Jud Branam told one of our classes: "If you can write, you can work."

Extra Point—Keeping up to Speed

Apparently there was some chatter over the past few years that social media would be the death of PR. We're not sure who actually believed that, but we sure didn't. Andy Beaupre posted on Sys-Con.com his list of *six reasons why social media didn't kill PR (G)*, and why it is actually a good thing:

> Specialized social media experts (who were ahead of the curve in the early days) understandably trumpeted this view (that social media would kill PR), leveraging the opportunity to directly or indirectly de-position PR agencies and professionals. Similarly, some journalists said PR's traditional media-relations centricity was a model for extinction.

This is one time that, had some of the prognosticators been reading the academic literature of public relations, they likely would have come to just the opposite conclusion. Over the past decade, more and more scholarship has supported the notion that PR was moving away from the "persuasion model" and into a "dialogic model." The recognition of this movement helped illustrate how the PR practice was moving from a publicity orientation to one focused on developing and maintaining organizational-public relationships. The thing that makes the media social, after all, is the dialogue they support.

Given this expanded capacity for organizations to interact directly through the Internet with the audiences they depend upon, why would we expect social media to somehow damage the efficacy of PR? That is, why would we have expected the social media to have somehow damaged PR unless our perception of the practice was framed by a shallow, journalistic, publicity-oriented view?

Beaupre concludes his post with a graph showing "The Stakeholder Ecosystem," fifteen or so separate audiences that generally constitute key stakeholders of any business organization.

Beaupre says:

> True public relations practice isn't publicity. It's much broader, taking into account every stakeholder (or 'public') with which an organization interacts.
> Strategically practiced, PR takes on a wide-ranging role, focused on earning a trusted reputation by acting in the best interests of these publics—not the organization's own myopic agenda.

We tell our advertising or public relations students to take full advantage of the broad education experience a university provides and not to get mesmerized by the shiny objects that they'll find in the world of social media. Resist the temptation to become a "social media tactician" at the expense of understanding the underlying theory that supports the marketing discipline of advertising, or the management discipline of organizational-public relations. Regardless of whatever your interests or expertise, we say, don't study social media for social media's sake. Focus on how to use social media as another tool to help you with whatever it is you want to do with your life.

Many of our students want to be PR practitioners. They need to understand social media, to be able to use it, and to know how to track what's going on with it. Increasingly they need to know how social media effects are measured. They must become experts in how to use the social media, not to become social media experts, but in their case, to have a chance at becoming expert in PR.

How could someone become an expert in modern organizational-public relationships if he or she doesn't understand the most powerful tools ever invented to create dialogue with diverse and important audiences?

We can give you many reasons to be careful about social media. But Tom Pick, posting on the B2C.com blog, has done that better than we could in providing *six reasons why social media sucks, but you need to use it anyway (G)*. Each and every one of the objections he raises in this important post should be understood and reckoned with—from the inherent loss of privacy in social media to the tendency for it to drag otherwise talented people into an endless rabbit-hole time suck.

The Future Buzz is, by its own account, "a digital marketing and social media blog." Adam Singer, a communications practitioner, runs the blog.

Singer is no withering flower. In a recent post he admonished fellow practitioners that *PR needs to shift from reactive to proactive (G)*, and it needs to make that shift right now.

We agree, and we don't want our readers to miss this very important point. Singer calls upon the PR industry to "flip" their current thinking. By inference he seems to suggest that most practitioners are too tactical. They act as if they perceive their primary role as simply fulfilling the wishes of the organizations for which they work. That sort of reminds us of the "we need a press release . . ." model.

Singer says PR needs to begin to see itself as more like media companies, which are far more proactive in their approach.

PR companies would be well served by defining "proactivity" as their ability to help their clients make news, rather than spending their time making news releases.

David Meerman Scott has observed that every organization—no matter what it does, makes, or sells—must begin to see itself as a media company, and that every executive must become a publisher of exciting and interesting content. In fact, some might say that is exactly what has happened the past few years, and as a result, a good many media middlemen (read: newspapers) have fallen by the wayside.

Others have said that in the old economy the big devoured the small. Today, however, it is the fast that are devouring the slow. How anyone, in any business, let alone PR, could make the case that they can afford to be reactive is a bit beyond us.

Co-author Derek Mehraban has posted some of his best digital PR advice on the New Media Driver's License® website for several semesters. Here's a sampler.

> The great thing about new media is it allows you to tap into a massive resource of unsolicited comments and market intelligence. If you are a savvy marketer, you are constantly monitoring these sites to listen to the buzz going on about and around your product/company/brand.

Media Monitoring

There are many sites that offer a one-stop solution for monitoring:

- Tracku.com,
- Twendz.waggenerdstrom.com,
- Monitter.com,
- Technorati.com,
- Google.com/alerts,
- Search.Twitter.com

I also suggest opening an account using either HootSuite.com or CoTweet.com and setting up some monitoring on those sites. You simply create some columns and you can track key terms, and #hashtags or @usernames. (And don't forget that Allie Siarto and Richard Cole will have a book in publication soon on the exciting topic of the social current and how you can monitor and analyze conversations in the social media.)

Blogger Outreach

Bloggers are always looking for new topics to write about. If you can get another blog to write about you, that is very valuable for both SEO links and because that blogger's readers can learn about your product from an objective outside source they trust. That's much more powerful than if you are writing about your own product or service.

Before you can pitch a blogger, you need to get to know them. Visit their blog, comment on their blog, build a relationship, and take an active interest in the topics that blogger writes about. After you've done the legwork, you can pitch your own material for publication on his/her blog.

Blogger outreach is not easy. It takes time and effort. I suggest reading more on the topic, and starting off slow. If you are good at this, then you may have a future at a digital PR agency.

Check out the resource below for a good article on how to pitch to bloggers.

News Releases

News releases are no longer strictly for newspapers, television, or radio. Online news has opened up publicity going directly to the public, so you want to be in front of users. Digital PR combines social media monitoring and blogger outreach. These days you don't have to beg for attention from the media. You can simply publish it yourself.

Some favorite places to submit digital publicity includes PRLog.com (free), PR.com, PRLeap.com and PRWeb.com. You also often can submit your digital publicity to news outlets and they will publish it for you, or you can publish it yourself on their page. Poke around on their site to see if they have a "Submit your news" link.

Five Things You Need to Know about Digital Publicity

- Don't be shy. If your company did it, write a press release.
- Monitor and engage with your peers online—it could pay big dividends. Great places to engage or for forums or groups, LinkedIn and Facebook.
- «Repeat it. If someone else says it about your business—the value goes up!
- Be interesting and bloggers (after you've done your blogger outreach) may pick up your story.
- Digital publicity is an SEO Booster, so write optimized content.

Heather Yaxley posted in PRConversations.com on one of the most important subjects for young PR practitioners—even for college students who think they may have a chance to make it in PR: *Future leaders need much more than digital PR (G)*.

Everywhere you look, those starting out on a career in public relations are urged to focus on developing skills in Digital PR.

But as such competencies shortly will be little more than a commodity possessed by most young graduates and practitioners in the field (as well as many with years of experience), future leaders will need much more than an ability to craft a Tweet or build a network of Facebook friends.

Among the tips Yaxley provides those who don't want to get sucked into what Edelman's Nick Lucido once described as the "black hole of social media":

Look to gain a wider experience than simply communications.

For an individual to have a hope of rising into a high-level job in PR— in other words, to get a seat at the table with the dominant coalition that runs the operation—you simply have to understand the business. You have to be able to speak the language of the industry you are in in order to be able to do the essential translation job of PR. You must have the capability of being creative, proactive and strategic.

"If an ability to write—or use social media—is the primary skill we can offer to organizations, PR will never be respected as a strategic function," Yaxley says.

We agree.

MAKING YOUR PRACTICE PERFECT

Some tasks that will help you understand the ideas and concepts talked about in Part IV.

Concept: *PR practitioners use PR for offensive and defensive purposes. Go to a major online news site (or otherwise search out) and identify three stories about organizations or individuals (celebrities) in crisis that are currently generating major interest by news organizations.*

Exercise 1: Relying on the framework provided in the "concept paragraph" above, identify three ways that social media either were or could have been used, prior to the crisis, to have advanced the interests of the organization in the news. Give examples of how social media were used and/or examples of how other organizations facing similar situations have used social media once the crisis begins.

Exercise 2: Relying on the framework provided in the "concept paragraph" above, identify three ways PR practitioners were or could have been monitoring social media to recognize a potential crisis and how that alone might have defended the organizational reputation against the impact of the crisis. Provide examples of "listening post" applications or technology, describing how it works to monitor and track key issues.

Exercise 3: Relying on the framework provided "concept paragraph" above, identify three ways social media could be employed once the crisis has subsided to restore the organization's reputation. Image restoration involves a complicated set of strategies. Use your search skills to identify articles and posts describing how companies have employed image restoration strategies to regain public confidence after a crisis.

Exercise 4: Go to the *Edelman Trust Barometer 2013 (G)* and download and review the results of Edelman's study. The data presented are showing a disappointing and declining trust in U.S. business institutions. Provide three examples of how social media may be contributing to a decline in trust in U.S. businesses. Also provide three examples of how U.S. companies may be standing out as trustworthy as a result, to some degree, of corporate behavior that is being validated through social media policies and accounts.

Exercise 5: Social marketing is often described as the application of tested commercial marketing tactics and techniques to behavior-change objectives that are in the public interest. Examine the wide variety of social marketing campaigns and activities that are being directed at reducing childhood obesity. Turn the tables. Highlight three unique ways that social media have supported any of these social marketing campaigns, and speculate on how these kinds of social media tactics might be applicable to a commercial marketing campaign.

PART V

INTERNET MARKETING

CHAPTER 9

Internet Marketing through Customer Conversations

> When it comes to online marketing (and information in general), we just need the truth about what works and what doesn't. And the truth is there is no miracle product for our business, meaning that while there are great things on the market, nothing eliminates the strategy work that the small business owner is responsible for.

These are the words of Jamillah Warner, reminding us that there aren't any miracle solutions or tactics when it comes to online marketing, in her SmallBizTrends.com post describing *how to think about Internet marketing (G)*. The post reveals an overwhelming and confusing mix of Internet marketing strategies, tips, and tactics that cloud our vision of what should really be important in business.

Warner examines the theory on web presence posed by Mike Blumenthal (aka *Professor Maps*—the man behind understanding Google Maps).

> Mike believes in building your core marketing first. He teaches small business owners via *GetListed.org (G)* to focus first on the marketing elements that you can control and then build from there.

Google executive and instructor in MSU's New Media Driver's License® sequence, Michal Lorenc, reminded us to let our readers know that one of his colleagues at Google has written an E-book on Internet marketing. Jim Lecinski titled his book *Zero Moment of Truth (G)*. The book walks the reader through what Lecinski calls a "fundamental shift" in the nature of marketing.

A major theme of the book, which you can google (no dah) to obtain a free copy, is that a significant change has occurred in marketing, and if you don't understand this changed paradigm, you will pay (and your customers won't).

Similar to what we have already said about the changed nature of PR, dialogue is rapidly replacing persuasion as the central modality of marketers. Google calls this change the "Zero Moment of Truth":

> The way we shop is changing and marketing strategies are simply not keeping pace . . . the Internet has changed how we decide what to buy.
> Today we're all digital explorers, seeking out online ratings, social media-based peer reviews, videos, and in-depth product details as we move down the path to purchase.

As Rishad Tobaccowala, chief strategist at VivaKi says: "When consumers hear about a product today, their first reaction is 'Let me search online for it.' "

The change is occurring in the way we select the products and services we want to buy. And it's occurring in the vehicles we use to buy them. Ethan Bloch wrote about this aspect of marketing through social media in a Flowtown.com post he titled "*Social Media Demographics: Who's Using Which Sites?*"(G)

You'll have to spend a few minutes with this post. It has an "eye chart" effect in the beginning that's a bit tough to wrap your head around. But you ought to get the point as you look at social media sites like Digg, StumbleUpon (personalized recommendations), Reddit (what's new online), Facebook, LinkedIn, Twitter, MySpace, and Ning.

You can get top-line views of which "demos" are populating the sites by age, income, gender, and educational levels.

Surprisingly, many businesses and entrepreneurs are under the impression that using social media is an easy and relatively inexpensive way to reach customers to generate brand awareness and increase profits. But it ain't necessarily so.

SocialMediaExaminer.com injects a dose of reality into the discussion when *Clement Yeung tells you how to get the M.O.S.T. from your social media marketing (G)*. "Many small businesses and solo entrepreneurs dive into social media marketing strategies without visualizing a bigger plan." Approaching social media marketing in this fashion can be lethal. Social media marketing is serious business and deserves serious attention.

Yeung stresses the "importance of developing a **M**arketing plan and identifying detailed **O**bjectives, **S**trategies and **T**actics."

Social media platforms, the importance of blogging for business, and tips for developing a successful sales funnel round off the insightful social media marketing guide.

This part of the book attempts to provide a deep dive into what we consider major aspects of understanding and using Internet marketing to its fullest advantage. Thus, the resources we present reflect a bias for information that is both understandable and (almost immediately) usable.

But before we start, there's the question about how exactly we decided to classify what is Internet marketing (as distinct from the stuff we talked about in the social media, Google, blogging, and other sections).

As a couple of the resources we have included in the book make clear, the lines between many of the subject areas within this book are blurry, at best, and blurring more and more every day. We decided to have a broad chapter on Internet marketing that includes trends, tips, techniques, tactics and tricks of the trade, and other broad categories of Internet marketing.

And so as not to discriminate between the world of commercial marketing through social media and the use of social media to aid social marketing (behavior-change related pro-social), we're carrying Search Engine Marketing, Search Engine Optimization, Pay-Per-Click, and Social Bookmarking as major discussions in the chapters that follow.

Ross Kimbarovsky posted a great article in Mashable.com that we missed in our first edition, but want to make sure we include here. He talks about his piece as *ten small business social media marketing tips (G)*, which may be why we passed on it first time through. What it really does is clarify the key networks and a handful of important strategies for getting you off on the right foot.

Trends and Concepts in Internet Marketing

To all of the people who thought Twitter, Facebook, and YouTube were fads, Cheers! Social media is here to stay, and so is Internet marketing. In fact, there's mounting evidence that new Internet marketing is rapidly replacing stuffy old business models.

Despite this mounting evidence to the contrary, some business owners are acting as if they still believe that the Internet isn't important. President of TwistImage.com, Mitch Joel, explains why, in his opinion, they are dead wrong, and he lays out what, in his opinion, are *four current trends that will change marketing forever (G).*

Emphasizing the impact of the Web on individuals and businesses Joel says, "The Internet and social media have changed everything. They are not fads. They are a new way for people to connect, gather information, share, collaborate and build their business."

Revealing the very trends that have evolved and continue to shape the marketplace, the post describes how touch screen technology—one of Joel's four key trends changing marketing—is shaping the way children learn.

"Some are saying that kids today will learn to type on glass, others (my hand is raised) think that kids will soon be learning to type on air. . . ."

There's more good news for online advertisers. According Katie Deatsch, associate editor of InternetRetailer.com, *online ads and search results leave lasting impressions (G)*—this stuff really matters. "A new study released today finds online ads and search results can stick—even if the consumer doesn't click," according to Deatsch.

Deatsch's post reports on a comScore Inc. poll that examined how consumers react to content after performing an organic search and viewing paid search results and online display advertising.

"When it comes to brand favorability, paid search listings have the most impact. . . ."

Robert Murray, CEO of iProspect, told Deatsch: "This study demonstrates that there is a lot more value to digital media than just direct conversions."

As far as social media is concerned, is it possible that we have had too much of a good thing? Steve Rubel (see the end of this chapter for a list of Rubel's favorite resources), in an AdAge.com post, tells marketers to *get ready for the validation era (G)*. He says there are "early signs that the social-media boom is fraying at the edges and that we are entering a new age of intimacy."

> Don't just take it from me. If you dig into media-consumption patterns and, in particular, who the public considers an authority, you can see the signs.
>
> Now, however, we have a new challenge: people overload. The public—brands included—has been engaging in a 'friends' arms race. But there are signs that we know we overdid it and we are longing for quality over quantity. The result is that we are now entering a new age—the Validation Era.
>
> According to a study conducted by *GoodMobilePhones.co.uk (G)*, people don't know 20% of their Facebook friends. And *USA Today* recently reported that social-media users are 'grappling with overload.'
>
> In the Validation Era, intimacy is in and 'public' may be out—or at least on the decline. What this means is that both individuals and businesses will need to increasingly work harder to earn their way in and remain in our stakeholders' circle of trust.

Including Internet Marketing in a Business Strategy

Stephen C. Campbell gives some great general tips in HowToDoThings.com's *How to Use Internet Marketing within your Marketing Strategy (G)*. Be prepared to say "I knew that" once you read his tightly written four-step model for building your Internet strategy.

One piece of advice drawn right from Campbell's playbook almost seems, on its face, unnecessary at this point in history. But it too often turns out to be a very important part of the conversation about business and marketing:

> Think of yourself as living in a global marketplace. Consider your customers to be people on the other side of the world as well as individuals in your neighborhood.

So do we.

The digital marketing life cycle begins with set up and ends with viral growth, and it takes much longer than most clients expect to get traction. Dealing with these expectations honestly is a major point in Ira Kaufman's SocialMediaToday.com article on his *five stages of the integrated digital marketing life cycle (G)*. He explains the role each step plays in the process of integrated digital marketing:

During an Integrated Digital Marketing campaign, the campaign will experience five stages in the life cycle. During each time period the number of touch points, client-marketing efforts that touch the customer, are expanded.

The insightful article provides a detailed time line analysis of how "touch points" develop for every stage of a digital marketing campaign.

And if you are interested in knowing if, let alone how, your digital campaign worked, consider consulting Kaufman and writing partner Bob Bengen's compelling post, and the accompanying chatter, on their *BeyondSocialMedia Marketing.com blog (G)*.

Going Global? Mashable.com can help your brand's Internet marketing campaign be a success across borders with some interesting advice from Erica Swallow including her best *five tips for marketing online to an international audience (G)*:

Expanding your marketing efforts to an international audience can be a great opportunity to grow your company and reach potential customers that may not otherwise discover your brand, products or service.

That may be so, but the key question is: "How do you even prepare and strategize the implementation of a business's marketing campaign on the Internet global marketing landscape?"

Start with cross-cultural competency.
Having your site translated into other languages is a huge advantage to marketing to an international audience, but having a deep understanding of your own and others' cultures is also important.

We might say, "All so important."

Beyond some basic no brainers, Swallow's post provides tips on how to personalize the marketing campaign for a brand according to a specific country's preferences: "Learning about and respecting other cultures will help you localize your brand's message," says Swallow.

Search, display, and email marketing are considered traditional forms of online marketing. Can traditional online marketing and social media marketing work together? Bill Flitter thinks they can and he says so in his article advocating creating a three-month plan for adding social to your marketing mix (G) and posted in IMediaConnection.com.

Beyond his opinion, Flitter provides an outline infographics for integrating traditional, online, and social media marketing in the form of a three-month action plan.

Learning this month-by-month plan can help you properly segment an audience and craft targeted unique campaigns and advertisements.

Tools, Tips, Tactics, and Tricks of the Trade

We found a slow but dependable upload that's worth the wait. Roy H. Williams, posting in Entrepreneur.com, advocates doing an advertising experiment. *"Target your market with appropriate ad copy" (G)*, he says. "In your next advertising experiment, why not try targeting through the content of your message rather than through demographic profiles."

Williams slips in a really cool example of what he means. Click on the word "message," and you'll see this is a guy who practices what he preaches. He uses a "sharply targeted message" he designed for the Canon PowerShot S500 camera to make his point.

And it should not be surprising in the genre of the social-media post: Williams has a "four-step" plan for deciding who you can attract into your advertisement, and who you should lose. And his copy is among the best we've seen:

> That's why no one ever replaces his or her PowerShot S500. Go to your local pawnshop and see if you can find one. We're betting you can't. But you will see several of those 'prettier' cameras available cheaper than dirt. So if you're looking for a great price on a sleek-looking camera, that's probably where you should go.

Suppose you get stuck on coming up with the creative idea you need to keep your clients happy? Listen to Todd Wasserman's Mashable.com advice:

> We've all been there: You've had a raucous weekend, and now it's Monday morning, time to drag yourself into work. If you have a certain kind of job, it's no big deal. You can coast a bit, maybe surf the web and take a few extra trips to the water cooler until you feel up to *really* working.
>
> But if your job requires you to be creative—and perhaps you're getting paid a decent amount to come up with ideas—then you don't have that option. In that case, you have to start coming up with ideas even though you'd rather be lying on your couch eating Cheez Doodles.

This is how Wasserman opened a very helpful piece on *digital marketing: seven tips for generating fresh ideas (G)*. He said he got the best advice from some of his digital innovator and professor friends who study creativity to help you get started when you are stuck. Wasserman's piece comes in the form of a wonderful slide show complete with beautiful Flickr photos.

Kristi Bergeron's guest post in SocialMouths.com's blog gives us *three lessons we can learn from big brands in social media (G)*.

As is the case with all of the resources we've selected for you, it pays to google the source document. In Bergeron's case, she highlights Tide, Orangina and M&Ms in giving us important advice about simplicity, good action-oriented content, and the importance of highlighting your brand's history.

Team members at IDEO, the global design firm, identified *five companies that mastered social media's branding potential (G)* in a post in fastcodesign.com.

> Social networks can breathe new life into old brands by enabling companies to build collaborative relationships with consumers like never before. But what's a corporate giant to do when no one wants to follow it on Twitter or be its friend on Facebook?

Their first piece of advice reminded us famous criminal Willie Sutton's response to why he chose to rob banks for a living. "That's where they keep the money," he said.

The IDEO team says rule one when choosing a new media outlet for a business is to: "Go where the people are."

> Don't try to build a community out of thin air. Tap in to existing communities, compliment, and contribute. If you are not a customer magnet, identify nodes in the network where people are, and draw them toward you. Let individuals take center stage. Focus on people over brand or offerings. Empower both your employees and the public to speak their minds, without dictating how.

There is one related danger that Kaleel Sakakeeny wanted to remind us of in a lifestyle post Technorati.com picked up—don't emphasize branding at the expense of developing organizational-public relationships as in customer service. He said that *companies use social media to stress brands, not customer service (G)*, and that's a problem.

In spite of all the brouhaha that suggested social media is the way to connect with and service customers, the facts speak differently, according to Hotelmarketing.com.

They report that 62 percent of customers are looking for more support through social media. But, brand reputation and promotions still top the list of how companies use social media.

Not many destinations or destination-management organizations (DMOs) seem to use their online presence to support the needs of their customers, or would-be customers. They're too busy promoting the virtues of their properties to actually ask what their customers want—more importantly, to answer questions and provide quality, individualized advice.

Extra Point—New Four P's of Marketing

The four P's of Internet marketing are permission, participation, profile, and personalization.

Sound different? That's because it is, at least according to Prapasri Vasuhirun, writing about the *new "4P" rules needed (G)* in the Bangkok (Thailand) Post. He says that the traditional 4P's of marketing—product, price, promotion, and place (location)—don't apply in a digital market.

"A social network is like a party. Marketers have to fit in it with the right mood. Brands must place themselves as a guest, rather than a host of a conversation, as they have done in traditional media," said Dr. Ian Fenwick, who also writes for the Post.

Vasuhirun says:

> Digital marketing can influence consumers to become aware of brands and products with less spending than traditional media. Many brands have realized the importance of social networks but they still do not know where to start.

Matthew Ellis makes his point pretty clearly in a Ragan.com post about avoiding social media mistakes: *Stop making mistakes that are fatal to your marketing objectives (G)*.

He lists six errors that might make your otherwise good effort DOA (dead-on-arrival.) We'll cite his first one and let you google the rest.

> 1. Not displaying your corporate branding.
> You would think that most marketing professionals understand the need to use corporate branding on social media. Yet, far too many businesses forget to do just that.
> Before you start using social media for your marketing, be sure to brand it carefully across all social media channels. Use your corporate colors, logo, tagline, and vision statement as your guide. To make your social media pages stand out, come up with themes that relate well to your corporate image.

We believe strongly in the separation of church and state, but that's not going to stop us from passing on the seven deadly sins of social media marketing as professed by Piedro Cardoso in Business2Community.com's newsletter.

Imagine "sloth"—going nowhere fast; "gluttony"—too much, too soon; greed—well, you get the point. And so does Cardoso, whose content is great and whose graphics are even "greater."

Jim Belsovic has this advice. Once you decide that your business needs to start building your brand and/or selling your products online, you may need to hire an employee or consultant to help you build a consistent and effective brand strategy. He offers *eight tips for training social media marketers (G)* in an important post in SocialMediaExaminer.com.

According to Belsovic, you'd be wise to begin, before you jump in headfirst, by creating a social style guide.

Agreeing on a style for outward-facing content helps solidify your company's identity and character, and is the starting point of good social media employee training, because it puts all agents on the same page. Perhaps the biggest hurdle in creating a style guide is to define your company's voice.

If you are concerned as Jim Belsovic is about consistency, you might also want to check out Cornia Mackay's post in WejungoNetwork.com in which she reveals her opinion on *how to achieve consistency with social media profiles (G)*.

Developing a social media presence for your business doesn't have to be a complicated process. Simplicity and consistency in the way you promote your brand will not only make the process easy for you, but also offer clear, uniform branding for your customers to engage with.

For social media profiles, there are three main areas where consistency comes into play: design, content, and character.

Consistency is important, but up to a point. Before you obsess, however, remember the words of Ralph Waldo Emerson: "*A foolish consistency is the hobgoblin of little minds . . . *" *(G)*.

Internet Marketing: Steve Rubel's Favorite Resources

Steve Rubel is SVP, Director of Insights for Edelman Digital, a division of Edelman, one of the world's largest public relations firms.

In his role, Rubel maintains a focus on the long view. He studies trends and innovations in media, technology, and digital culture and fuses these into actionable insights that help Edelman and its clients remain at the forefront.

We asked him to give us some insights into some resources he just couldn't live without. Here's his list:

Techmeme

http://www.techmeme.com

"Techmeme tracks the zeitgeist of the technology news media, including traditional sources and upstarts. It's my first visit to catch up on the world of technology."

Mediagazer

http://www.mediagazer.com

"Mediagazer is Techmeme's sister site. It's the best resource for all the twists and turns from the media world."

Term.ly

http://www.term.ly

"Term.ly is a simple dictionary and thesaurus that's ad free and just works."

Instapaper

http://www.instapaper.com

"This site helps me capture all the articles I want to read later, but for which I don't have time to do now."

CHAPTER 10

Buying Your Position with Search Engine Marketing (SEM) and Pay-Per-Click (PPC) Advertising

Search Engine Marketing (SEM) is the process of using the Internet and search engines to drive traffic to your website through paid search advertising. This may mean using banner ads on websites, or it could mean the text ads you see on the side of a Google search result.

Companies are spending increasing percentages of their advertising budgets on SEM because it works. But SEM doesn't work the same for every business, or for any business under every circumstance. Figuring out how to make it work best for you will take some time, effort, and practice. Let's get started.

There are a lot of different ways of differentiating between Search Engine Marketing, Search Engine Optimization, and Pay-Per-Click, but we are choosing to follow the description provided by Elmer Cagape, posting in his blog, *SEO-HongKong.com (G)*, in which he lays out the differences he sees between *SEO vs SEM vs PPC: Understanding Search Marketing Terms (G)*.

> When someone says 'we do both SEO and SEM,' he or she actually means 'we do (organic search marketing) and (organic + pay-per-click search marketing)' . . . this sounds all right, except that when you mention SEM, it's enough to cover both organic and pay-per-click search marketing.
>
> Search Engine Marketing should be the parent category whose subsets include both SEO and Pay-Per-Click and should not refer only to the latter.

Here's a brief overview of how this works.

When people want to buy a product, schedule a vacation, or find a new service, they use Google, Bing, or Yahoo to search for what they want. A Google search generally returns ten results per page. So millions of results from a search would result in hundreds of thousands of pages to review. And there are only ten spots on page one of a Google search.

You and your company are competing with millions of other websites that want to be on page one? The function of Search Engine Marketing is to move you to page one and keep you there. Here are some specific ways to accomplish that.

As a company or brand you can purchase keywords that will give you placement on the top of the Paid Search area of search results. That's SEM. And even though your intuition might lead you to believe that most prospects would prefer natural search results over paid "advertisements," that's not necessarily true.

Paid results often produce more relevant and accurate information. And they should. After all, someone is paying the search engine—Google or Yahoo, for example—so they'll show up for that search phrase. And the companies that are producing the ad campaigns for paid results should be making sure they are not paying for erroneous search results.

While there are companies that will do almost all the heavy lifting of SEM for you, you can learn to do some of it on your own, and you can become very good at it. In fact, at some point you may *become Google Certified (G).* This badge states that you are Google AdWords proficient, and if you are an IM consultant, that designation can be displayed on your website to advertise your expertise and help you win new customers.

Here are some important elements we propose that you consider:

1. Your landing page should be simple and have a clearly defined goal and action. Do you want someone to purchase a product, join your email list, or to download your white paper or any number of things? Your landing page should be written clearly. It should be obvious what you want the visitor to do. And the page should be very specific to the ad that drove the traffic.

2. You need to think value. What is a new customer worth to you? How much does the average existing customer purchase in a year? What is the cost to get that customer? Think value in your transactions. The reason is because SEM costs money, but you can quantify the costs to win a new customer, and to show the value of that customer over time. If they match up, then SEM could be a good investment for you. Essentially, the key question is did the customer deliver more in profits to your company than the cost you spent to get that customer?

3. Relevance and targeting are important. SEM allows you to segment your audience and reach them where they are on search engines attempting to find products and services to buy. You can write an ad for each search term, and each audience member. You can have a landing page for each search term too. You want to be very specific and clear in your ads, and on the corresponding landing page. Then you can drive qualified traffic, and get them to take the desired action on your site.

4. With SEM, you can track and test every concept, ad, and landing page. Split testing works. Take your two ads and figure out which one performs better. Then drop the one that didn't work and write a new ad. Track and test and you can improve results over time. It's much easier to test Google ads than to test magazine or TV ads. So businesses are wise to conduct their research in the hand-to-hand combat that is SEM.

The SEM resources listed below will give you a great start in becoming an experienced search-marketing practitioner. And even though SEM favors those who are good with numbers, it can be done by anyone. It just takes a little time, effort, and tenacity.

So, let's start with a basic refresher on how some people differentiate SEO and SEM. Not everyone agrees, but we like to think of it as a bit like some people characterize the difference between the publicity functions of PR and advertising—as "earned" versus "paid" media.

Understanding the Basics

SEO, SEM, PPC . . . confused? It's okay. Many online marketers like the umbrella concept of SEM. Abby Klaassen provides a somewhat different take on the subject of *what's the difference between SEO and SEM? (G)*

Search engine optimization and search engine marketing are as similar as they are different. If you don't understand the difference between the two, don't worry about it. You'll *get it* soon.

Klaassen asks that you think of SEM as "paid search" and SEO as natural or "organic search"—think "free listings." Regardless of whatever definition makes you most comfortable, you'll be interested to see how different search engines compare to each other.

Klaassen's AdAge.com post will help you grasp basic search concepts and learn about the benefits of paid search and how it is done, and see the impact it can have on a real business.

"Google leads the (search engine) category in the U.S.—but what's surprising is the giant continues to gain or maintain share, even off such a high base," Klaassen states.

If you aren't a SEO wizard, here's a resource that can help you bluff your way through almost any meeting on the subject. With the *Search Engine Marketing Glossary (G)*, you can reference search-marketing terms from A to Z.

The *Search Engine Marketing Resources Library (G)* is another quick way to reference a variety of marketing resources. More than ten years' worth of resources have been contributed from across the web universe and compiled in this SEM database. Users can look up search engine optimization (SEO) links to search engine marketing articles, popular blogs, SEM tools, and more, and it's all in one central location.

The SEM Resources Library eliminates searching through pages and pages of highly optimized search engine resources and compiles relevant and useful information into one place. This is a great resource for beginners as well as for industry practitioners.

Of special note is the ongoing push to get the library to articulate the subtle distinctions some people see between Search Engine Marketing (SEM) and Pay-Per-Click (PPC) Advertising.

> *Search Engine Marketing (SEM)*: Marketing and advertising via search engines that can include Search Engine (SEO), Pay-Per-Click (PPC) Advertising and Return on Investment (ROI) analysis. Activities can include Keyword Research, Link-Building Campaigns, Web Site (both for readability leading to conversions and for optimizing content for search engine results) and Web Site Usability studies (to aid in assuring that site traffic is able to achieve the desired outcome, be it sales, newsletter signups, etc.) and Log File Analysis of results of SEM campaigns (also known as Web Site Metrics or Web Site Analytics). Ideally these SEM efforts will be cyclical and the results of initial efforts will be analyzed and insights used to further improve SEM campaigns.
>
> Here's Search Engine Wiki's definition of *Pay-Per-Click*: Also known as PayPerClickAdvertising or PPC, PayPerClick is an advertising model utilized in online marketing campaigns, in which advertisers pay for ads based on the number of times the ad is ;clicked,' after which action the person clicking is taken to the web page of the advertiser's choice. There are a number of search engines offering PPC advertising, with the largest including Google AdWords, Yahoo Search Marketing and Microsoft Ad Center.

The Search Engine Wiki people choose to characterize the phrase Search Engine Marketing as the umbrella term that covers both Search Engine Optimization and Pay-Per-Click Advertising. An alternative is to use the phrase Internet Marketing as the umbrella phrase to cover paid and earned find-ability. So we lump Search Engine Marketing in with Pay-Per-Click Advertising and keep earned Search Engine Optimization as a separate category.

In contrast to the hard work and creativity that accompanies building your position through organic searches, all advertising takes is money. And the money you pay (if you spend it right) is directly tied to producing viable clicks.

"Pay per click (PPC) advertising may be one of the easiest ways to generate traffic to your website and score some decent profits from your search engine marketing campaign," says Randy Duermyer in this posting in the home business section of About.com.

Duermyer's article is a great resource and starting point to learn about doing *PPC, using Google AdWords (G)*.

WordStream.com is straight to the point. Larry Kim's post highlights different tools that can help you track and perfect PPC advertisements and *learn effective pay per click optimization (G)*.

But caveat emptor (buyer beware): this site is set up—and very openly so—to sell you PPC software that accomplishes a couple of functions according to this article—automation and PPC management.

We're not endorsing the product, nor suggesting that there are not other products out there that you could use, but we think reading the Word Stream copy is a pretty effective way to understand some of the ins and outs, and complexities and idiosyncrasies, of the PPC world.

One of the things we like about this Word Stream Internet Marketing Software site is that each pertinent phrase from "pay-per-click" to "PPC search engine" is linked to a relevant definition within the Word Stream domain.

Google isn't the only search engine option to consider when advertising. Paying attention to PPC advertising on other search engines can also help expand a business.

Take a break from your reading, mute Pandora, and sit back and watch *Pay Per Click 101—YouTube (G)*. The visuals won't knock you out, but the tutorial could get your PPC campaign started in the right direction.

The video shows viewers how to use different tools for finding keywords and what to do once you have the keyword information.

We found this posting from Internet Marketing Online by Andrei Girbea in Mikes.Quarters.com.

Girbea's article on *SEO Vs PPC—the pros and cons (G)* is quite instructive in that it lists both the positive and negative aspects of using PPC and SEO techniques. You might not agree with every one of the opinions on the subject, but then again, if you only listened to people you already agree with, you'd never learn another thing, would you?

The *PPC Hero (G)* website is a resource for all things PPC, and one that has intrigued us from the minute we found it.

PPCHero.com was established in 2007 to "educate the world on the finer skills and basic techniques of successful pay per click management," according to their "about" section. You'll find PPC case studies and review strategies developed from the PPC Hero team that will help advance your PPC efforts.

PPC Hero may not be faster than a speeding bullet and more powerful than a locomotive, but it has a great deal of information that can give a business's Internet advertising campaign quite a boost.

Here's a great question: *"When is PPC better than SEO for public relations?"* *(G)*. We thought you'd never ask.

One of the things that people often forget is a great deal of public relations work may involve developing and directing paid advertising. Advertising, it turns out, besides sales or brand building can be a great way to get a relationship-supporting message to key constituents quickly and in a way that guarantees it will go out in the language you write.

Here's a parallel situation—a case for using search engine marketing, specifically pay-per-click tactics, as a way "to attract visitors to news-related content."

Lee Odden, posting for TopRankBlog.com, makes a great case for this technique and uses examples of The New York Times "*using AdWords to promote a story about Twitter*" *(G):*

> PR professionals can do the same with brand names, company names or executive names that often get searched on. PPC can be used to attract attention to specific news items, stories and content that is likely to be passed along once people get a chance to see it.

This is another one of the posts that needs to be explored in further detail. Odden is a straight shooter and his graphics are very helpful.

Creating a "Find-ability" Strategy

The PPC Heroes are working overtime to help advertisers and marketers in the process of *developing a pay-per-click strategy (G)*. Amy Hoffman is one of those heroes.

What's in it for PPC Hero to give away all this free information? Well, they have advertisers too. So they sort of practice what they preach. And we're happy to help.

Developing a great PPC strategy can make or break your Internet marketing campaign. In fact, everyone from *Sun Tzu (G)*—if he were still among the living—to Detroit's Kid Rock will tell you that without a good strategy, you are . . . well, without a good strategy you don't have much of a chance. You see, strategy is a word that was taken from the Greeks. The word *strategos (G)* means "general," as in the guy in charge of the battle plan. Where would any army be without a general?

Hoffman's wonderful little post not only talks about how to develop a good PPC strategy, but, more than that, it helps give you an understanding of what a strategy is and how to differentiate it from a goal or from the tactics that are used to put the strategy into play.

> This article is aimed at helping you to understand and devise a strategy for your pay per click accounts. The best strategy development practices are clearly and concisely outlined, making PPC development easier.

People who call themselves "the creatives" in the advertising business often bristle at the thought of seeing their precious creative talents harnessed by a client's clear strategy. They may call themselves the creatives. But when they have an attitude like that, we sometimes call them former employees.

The real creative wizards in advertising—whether they are the wordsmiths, the commercial artists, or the planners, traffickers, account executives, or media buyers—understand what Norman Berry, a former director at Olgivy Advertising, once said: "Give me the freedom of tightly defined strategy."

We found an interesting case study about a brand without a tightly defined strategy. You might think of it as a brand obituary because it's about a once-strong retail brand that died.

David Dalka, a specialist in SEM strategies, writes in his SearchEngine Watch.com post that *effective search marketing strategy determines the fate of organization (G)*. You might think he'll try to sell you on the position that you're either into Internet marketing all the way or you're dead. Quite the contrary, Dalka is an advocate for integrated marketing, and he promotes SEM as part of a strong, "balanced, multi-channel marketing strategy."

In his post, Dalka stresses that most everyone knows "that executing an effective search marketing strategy is important to a business. However, have you ever stopped to wonder how businesses that aren't adapting to a search marketing-centered business world are faring?"

To answer this question, Dalka describes how a 150–year-old, high-prestige Wisconsin furniture store was wiped out, in part, due to a relative upstart's multichannel campaign that included a strong dose of SEM:

> Search marketing is rapidly becoming the lead strategic marketing process as brand creative diminishes in importance in a content-driven world. We must demonstrate to business leaders across the globe that this is the current reality.

If you're still unsure about the subject, buckle up and get ready to take a SEM crash course. An *OpenForum.com (G)* post by Ben Parr will quickly inform you on what steps you need to take for *optimizing your site for search engine marketing (G)*.

Parr, a respected tech writer and editor at Mashable.com, said, "I'm going to focus on some of the key issues and best practices for optimizing your site for search." And he did just that.

Parr's OpenForum.com post is it short and sweet, providing a definition of SEM, helping you quickly learn the tools to maximize the impact of your Web pages. Learn what keyword research is, how to do link building and some pay-per-click techniques to increase the rank of a Web site.

As an aside, Parr helps explain some of the confusion or ambiguity involving the very phrase SEM in this newly developing discipline.

> Essentially, there are two ways of defining SEM: either it's an umbrella term that encompasses SEO, paid search, contextualized advertisements, and paid inclusions, or it only covers paid advertising, inclusions, and search and is separate from SEO.

As we have pointed out before, the second form is the preference we have expressed in this book.

Some people see social media (and free search engine optimization) and search engine marketing (and pay-per-click advertising) as being somehow pitted against one another in a struggle for marketing dominance. Some of us never saw SEM and SEO as anything other than somewhat separate components of the rapidly evolving world of Internet marketing.

We want to tell you about another site about which we are crazy. You can find it by googling this phrase: *pay-per-click advertising and how it fits into your Internet marketing strategy (G)*.

One of the reasons we like this advice so much is that it shows you the good, the bad, and the not-so-ugly side of PPC advertising. Many facets of PPC are explained on the Portent Interactive site, for sure, though we can't vouch for the site's objectivity. Another reason we like it is that the post has been updated twice since its original publication nearly eight years ago.

Looking for a deeper understanding of PPC? "This article will provide you with a high-level view of pay per click advertising, provide some general strategies and provide an example of what to do, and what not to do," says Seattle's Ian Lurie of Portent Interactive.

As so many others, this article provided a general definition of what PPC is and how it is used, but then it went way beyond that. You can learn how PPC can be costly, but you can also learn how to use PPC efficiently to avoid cost by understanding the role PPC plays in an advertising campaign and how you can use it at its best.

"Millennials (16–30 year olds) eschew [which means they deliberately avoid] produced, trite, dumbed-down marketing in favor of efforts that are creative, true to their brands, able to connect in a way that feels authentic," something Mike Kraus says he has been talking about for years.

We read Kraus's article in AllBusiness.com about *three ways to market your retail business to Millennials (G)*.

Now we know more about Millennials than we did before thanks to "*The Truth about Youth*" *(G)*, a McCann Worldgroup (Advertising) survey.

Kraus, whose career spans general management, says: "Inform, inspire and educate your audience," to help you connect with Millennials and attract them as customers in the new social media world.

Here's a question you have to ask regularly. What keywords are you using? Have you done your keyword research?

Pete Codella, who conducts a popular PR Daily.com webinar series on social media tools for PR professionals, has these questions and more as he talks about *a PR pro's guide to choosing keywords for your web content (G)*.

"Sure, some of you may have a set of keywords you use in news release titles and blog headlines, but do you have a strategically crafted keyword list that's vetted against actual online searches?" Codella asks.

Take Codella's advice and you may be surprised at how easy it is to formulate your own list of keywords. But his post doesn't stop there. If you'll focus on this post, you'll see that he'll tell you when, where, how, and how often to use these keyword search terms.

Starting and Running a Google Ad Campaign

British accents (in our Midwest-biased opinion) make almost everything seem more serious and credible. See what you think about this *introduction to Google AdWords (G)*.

This quick (3:39) video provides an overview of how Google search results work and what influences them. You can't be an expert by watching a three-minute video, but it's amazing how easy it is to understand how to designate target audiences and when and where AdWords ad will show up.

For a bit more detail, Ben Hart provides a great *Google AdWords marketing tutorial (G)* that quite makes the case that AdWords is an essential search engine-marketing component that "allows you to target precisely and exactly your most likely buyers."

Hart wants to help you make money, not waste it. His stated goal is to help you cheaply achieve top paid search results.

The *Google Display Network (G)* should probably be your first stop in the search for how to create your own Google ad campaigns, and this advice is straight from the horse's mouth.

Google Display Network's step-by-step guide walks you through the process of creating a new campaign, creating ad groups, the targeting and bidding process, creating display ads, and measuring your performance.

> Under the Networks tab, you can easily see a performance report for all of the Display Network sites on which your ads have appeared. Coupled with Conversion Tracking, you can quickly understand which sites are resulting in

sales, leads or registrations and which aren't, and make decisions based on this information.

> For example, you can use this information to: Monitor site-level performance for each of your ad groups, seeing which sites are meeting your performance goals. You can even view page-level performance within specific sites.

And, as this resource points out, you can take several other important steps toward running a successful campaign.

Check out WebmasterWorld.com's *15 tips for AdWords beginners (G)* post to get high-quality pointers for using Google AdWords effectively. This modestly written, but very useful, post offers suggestions and detail like "Don't use broad matching . . . "

> . . . at least not to start off with. What's broad matching? From the horse's mouth:
>
> 'If you include general keyword or keyword phrases, such as 'tennis shoes,' in your keyword list, your ads will appear when users search for tennis and shoes, in any order, and possibly along with other terms.'
>
> With expanded matching it becomes even harder to know when your keywords will show, because Google will pick them algorithmically.

The comments on this are nearly as interesting and useful as the post itself—often true in *blogosphere*. Here comment #1 from Bufferzone:

> What took you so long? I have been looking for this for ages, not wanting to go into AdWords before I was pretty sure about getting it right the first time. . . .

SEM and PPC Mistakes and Miscalculation

Google the *top ten SEO mistakes (G)* and you'll get a sense of how obsessed the experts in search engine optimization are with DEFENSE. Each one of the six or eight entries you'll find stresses the importance of keyword research and how NOT to do it.

Webconfs.com's list starts with targeting the wrong keywords.

> This is a mistake many people make and what is worse—even experienced SEO experts make it. People choose keywords that in their mind are descriptive of their website but the average users just may not search them. For instance, if you have a relationship site, you might discover that 'relationship guide' does not work for you, even though it has the 'relationship' keyword, while 'dating advice' works like a charm.
>
> Choosing the right keywords can make or break your SEO campaign.

ahead of your hungriest PPC competitors (G). When the bear comes into the village, you don't have to run faster than the bear to get away. You just have to run faster than the other guy on the street.

His point in this post is that both the bear and your competition are getting faster, and it isn't getting any easier to keep ahead in PPC. It's the slower runner that gets eaten by the bear, or so goes the metaphor.

In the post you may learn how to create a better process for PPC advertising, including what might just be the most important point of all—setting aside time for learning and discovering new PPC tactics and tools.

We found another great PPCHero.com post—this one about *how to use Google Insights for search to improve your PPC management (G).* In it, John (no last name provided) lays out an effective and efficient, step-by-step way to use Google Insights for Search tool to promote digital marketing and PPC marketing.

He likes the SearchEngineLand.com description of the tool: "The tool offers a comprehensive set of statistics based on search volume and patterns. You can compare seasonal trends, geographic distributions, and category-specific searches, and you can group all these variables together to get extremely specific."

We're not alone in liking John's PPCHero.com description. Commentator Sim Garner told John that "the information you are sharing on the use of Google trends and PPC keyword research can be the catalyst to help a sharp-minded person increase their profits and expand their resources."

In fall 2012, Google announced that it had combined its very popular Insights tool with Google Trends. Elyse Betters, writing in 9to5Google.com, quoted Google Support in an article entitled *Google merges Trends with Insights for Search to create 'single powerful tool (G).*

> We have launched a new version of *Google Trends*, bringing the great functionality of both Google Insights and Google Trends into one . . .
>   . . . this release should make it even easier for you to tell stories about search and explore what people are interested in around the world.

CHAPTER 11

Earning Your Position with Search Engine Optimization

We've said it before, and we don't want to belabor the point. But just in case you skipped ahead to this chapter before fully understanding the difference between search engine marketing (and its sibling pay-per-click advertising), we'll say this once more.

Think about this. Marketers pay to improve their client's position in the marketplace by buying space on television, radio, magazines, billboards—the list goes on and includes the Internet. Paying for space assures that the message the marketer is sending will appear as planned. And while no assurances can be made—and, by the way, some classic screw-ups have happened—the idea that the message appears as it was designed increases the likelihood that the consumer will interpret it in the manner the marketer desires. We call this advertising.

When marketers elevate the find-ability of their client's brand, products, services—whatever—by paying for their search position, we call this search engine marketing, and the ads are called pay-per-click advertising.

There are many reasons why individuals and organizations are turning to a more "organic" process to optimize their find-ability in search engines like Google.

Marketers increasingly are turning to the management field of public relations for the model on how their clients can earn, rather than or as well as buy, their position in the minds of their consumers through the process called search engine optimization (SEO).

MarketingTerms.com (G) offers a simple definition of SEO as the "process of choosing targeted keyword phrases related to a site, and ensuring that the site places well when those keyword phrases are part of a Web search."

This definition goes on to emphasize the difference between the SEO process and spamming.

"Generally, legitimate search engine optimization adds to the user experience, while search engine spamming takes away from the user experience . . . "

There's obviously a good deal more behind fully understanding the role of SEO in a comprehensive campaign—whether it's a pure marketing campaign or one designed to enhance a corporate reputation or build support for a nonprofit cause.

Understanding the Basics

You can participate in *SEO training—the basics of search engine optimization (G)* in a ten-minute YouTube presentation uploaded by NextLevelProfits.com. This video will refresh your memory or introduce you to the most basic, but important search engine optimization concepts.

The video covers search engine terms and how relevant and important they are to optimization.

There's another resource to help you called *The Visual Guide to SEO (G)*. This slick infographic provides a visual conceptualization of what SEO is, how it works, and where it fits in the marketing mix.

The creative souls from InfographicLabs.com collaborated to create their graphic to communicate complicated concepts, and data. The Visual Guide defines and describes basic SEO terms and procedures, including keyword search, page optimization, and link building.

Google won't tell you all of their SEO secrets, but this is pretty close—straight from the source.

Google Webmaster Central wanted to help other Webmasters "improve their sites' interaction with both users and search engines," and we think this resource does just that.

The Google.com *SEO Starter Guide (G)* was updated in late 2010 to provide tools to "make it easier for search engines to crawl, index and understand your content."

The delightful document is complete with links and specific examples to help you create SEO websites and documents, and rise to the top of search rankings.

Here's the kind of simple tip you can uncover with a little searching. *Singular and plural keywords are not always the same for SEO (G)*, and Mike Moran demonstrates how knowing this simple fact could make a big difference in search results.

In his post in SearchEngineGuide.com, Moran advises readers to be cautious when picking a keyword and do your research to determine whether or not search results are different based on a singular or plural ending.

If you have any interest in mastering SEO, you might want to take a look at "teacher" Moran's many other articles on related subjects. He has a convenient link from this resource to an index of related articles.

If you want to understand *search engine optimization (G)* as defined by the people who know best, go to Google. Google Webmasters supplement the definition of SEO with a healthy pool of basic information. Links connect readers to more in-depth SEO knowledge and tips and tricks for the best SEO practices on Google on how to find outside help.

CHAPTER 12

Social Bookmarking—What's That? And Who Cares?

There are more than 15 billion web pages, so how do we save the web pages we like? That's the question Seattle Internet wizard Lee LeFever at commoncraft.com answers in this tutorial. Shut off your iTunes now, and you'll learn more about *social bookmarking in plain English (G)* in three minutes than we could tell you in an hour.

LeFever explains, better than we ever could, what social bookmarking is, why it's social, and how to use the free public tools at *Del.icio.us (G)* to save your favorite sites, index them according to purpose or whatever, and classify the indexed sites so you can retrieve them with ease.

> Delicious is a social bookmarking service that allows you to tag, save, manage and share Web pages all in one place. With emphasis on the power of the community, Delicious greatly improves how people discover, remember and share on the Internet.

Besides being an excellent tutorial, this saves us a great deal of time by showing how a steady stream of interesting and useful websites is available, right now, for your disposal. That's what makes this bookmarking process "social" and a thousand—perhaps a million—times more robust than the bookmarking tool embedded in your computer.

Understanding the Basics

Maybe you're still wondering: *"Can social bookmarking help me?" (G)*. You'll find a current response to that in an EmpowerNetwork.com post by Carol Douthitt:

> It's a public list of your favorites. Not all of your favorites, just the favorites you want to share with others. You can add any website to your public list and retrieve it from any computer. (This is done on someone else's server, not your computer.)
>
> When you list a site in your bookmark list, anyone looking for that same type information can do a search at the bookmark site and find the bookmarked sites. It's like a search engine without all the trash.

Here's another often overlooked perhaps, but certainly not to be underestimated, attribute of social bookmarking:

> The more people who mark a site, the more popular it becomes . . . It's kind of like a voting system. If your site is good enough to bookmark, other people will want to see what all the fuss is about.

Loren Baker is the editor in chief of *SearchEngineJournal*.com and has been involved in SEO for more than a decade. He has developed an extremely comprehensive list that demonstrates *the importance of user-generated tags, votes and links (G)*.

> To help share the wealth of social bookmarking, I've put together a list of 125 social bookmarking sites, some of which are very popular and others that are newer or somewhat unheard of.
> Baker uses Del.icio.us, StumbleUpon and Ma.gnolia—three social bookmarking services—as examples to show how search engines use them to aid them in finding relevant information for you. The list includes faster and deeper indexing of sites, as well as providing an initial measure of quality.

Baker says he put together his list to "help share the wealth of social bookmarking." We thank him for the help.

All the bases—who, what, when, where, how, and the why of social bookmarking—seem to be covered in one article on *how social bookmarking works (G)*.

The blog post on PortalTechnologiesPark-LearnSEO.Blogspot.com is designed to provide the fundamental facts.

> Not many exactly know what this process is, how it works, or what its intended purpose is. In fact, you already may be doing social bookmarking on the Internet without knowing that you are actually using it.

Tools, Tips, Tactics, and Tricks of the Trade

We're not pushing any particular brand of anything, let alone free social bookmarking services, but if a prestigious outlet like Social Media Examiner describes your service as *The King of Social Bookmarking (G)*, as it did *Delicious (G)* in a recent post by Kristi Hines, you simply have to give it a little extra attention.

Hines describes Delicious as giving you the capacity to, kind of, create your own personal Google "push" service.

> It's hard to read every great blog post that's shared with you through other social networks such as Twitter and Facebook. Why not bookmark them for

later so whenever you're looking for information on a particular topic, you have a great compilation of favorite articles and pages to choose from?

Besides organizing your resources, Hines lists creating action plans (with action tags), sharing important links company wide, and backlink recording.

With Delicious, you can simply bookmark a page you requested a link from and tag it by topic, quality or type for future reference. So if you are making a comment on an .edu blog about pets, your tag would be edu pets blogcomment, and the next time you need to look for one of those three elements for another link, they would be right in your Delicious bookmarks.

Just to prove its objectivity, perhaps, or to feature a service with a slightly different twist, Kristi Hines also wrote about *How to Use StumbleUpon: Your Comprehensive Guide (G)* in SocialMediaExaminer.com.

StumbleUpon.com is famous—or notorious if you can't tolerate any more distractions—for keeping Internet users entertained for hours as they randomly browse web pages and share content with friends and comment on what they are viewing.

StumbleUpon is a social bookmarking and rating site, where people who literally 'stumble upon' cool web pages can write reviews and share their discoveries with their followers. The network is like Delicious, but with a more enhanced social platform and sharing system.

Hines created a comprehensive guide to prevent you from having to "stumble" through StumbleUpon. So why do you care?

According to Hines, "StumbleUpon can be a great site to organize your favorite bookmarks, although it isn't quite as advanced as Delicious in organization." But, Hines says, as a user you "can easily save items by giving them the thumbs-up using the 'I like it' buttons on the StumbleUpon toolbars for Firefox or Chrome."

The SocialMediaExaminer.com StumbleUpon guide directs you through different processes on the social bookmarking website. Hines's post will help you find friends, share items, join groups, set preferences, and learn proper sharing etiquette.

Despite the fact that a picture is worth a thousand words, everyone is invited to read *social bookmarking for pictures on VisualizeUS (G)*.

See something you like and easily bookmark it. Super simple design, *vi.sual-ize.us (G)* is Firefox's extension tool that makes bookmarking as easy as right clicking or using a browser button. At least, that's how they put it.

We have to disclose right here and right now, however, that most of these "easy tools" take a certain amount of concentrated effort to install and use. And, we don't think that just because it's not as easy as the promotional material suggests that there's something wrong with you. But having said that, it's clear *vi.sualize.us (G)* can help give important marketing exposure to an artist or author.

Here's the deal: Vi.sualize.us allows you to view feeds and even embed a badge onto your own website to make bookmarking for others increasingly simple. You can share detailed images with a simple click, increasing potential viewership and traffic, or simply showing off your own talents, inspiring photographers, artists, and photographers—and possibly creating some copycats. Forewarned is forearmed.

Want to really make it big on the Web? In one way, we wish there was a single definite way to make this happen. But then, if there were one best way, what would you need this book for?

We can tell you this right off. Simply because something is referred to as the result of organic, rather than paid, search marketing, does not mean it just "comes naturally." In fact, the real truth is quite the contrary.

We like the WebConfs.com post on *how to get traffic from social media sites (G)*. It gives you 20 steps you can take to increase the likelihood that you'll generate traffic from the social bookmarking sites, and this ability will make it easier for digg.com, reddit.com, or stumbleupon.com to bring traffic to your website.

"How about getting 20,000 or more visitors a day when your listing hits the front page?" the post asks.

So, what's the catch to increasing traffic to your website by this much? How about beginning with paying attention to your headlines?

> Many great articles go unnoticed on social bookmarking sites because their headline is not catchy enough. Your headline is the first (and very often the only) thing users will see from your article, so if you don't make the effort to provide a catchy headline, your chances of getting to the front page are small.
>
> Here are some examples to start with:
>
> Original headline : The Two Types of Cognition
>
> Modified Headline : Learn to Understand Your Own Intelligence
>
> Original headline: Neat way to organize and find anything in your purse instantly!
>
> Modified Headline : How to Instantly Find Anything in Your Purse

WebConfs.com explains that, "getting to the front page of these sites is not as difficult as it seems"—once you are committed to the concept, that is.

"Are you simply using the standard sharing options—Twitter, Facebook, etc.—or are you thinking of ways you can be a little creative when it comes to sharing your blog socially?" asks Danny Brown.

Brown is co-founder and partner at Bonsai Interactive Marketing, advertised as offering integrated marketing, social media, and digital and mobile marketing solutions and applications.

Brown's blogs have been featured on the AdAge Power 150 list. But that didn't happen by accident as his post on *BestBloggingTipsOnline.com (G)* demonstrates with suggestions to create social-sharing groups with online friends and how to promote your own content. Brown says:

> The most oft-used method of sharing a blog post is via social sharing buttons on the post itself.
>
> These are either located at the top and/or bottom of the post, or to the side. I use a mix of both Digg.com to offer the floating share bar to the left of this post, and ShareThis.com at the bottom.
>
> But why not take this a little further, and create a social sharing group?

Using WordPress for blogging is relatively inexpensive. But a great many people are blogging, and there is a ton of content. So the competition for "eyes" is getting more intense by the minute.

Siva Kumar, a Web designer and blogger explains this web market fact. "Today, without a good amount of social marketing effort, chances are people will not come across your website because you are basically free from acknowledgment."

In a Hongkiat.com post, Kumar lists what he believes are *the top social bookmarking Wordpress plugins (G).* "Not everyone is a social media genius, but there are definitely tips and tricks to utilize social marketing tool on your website and blog to increase attention for your articles." Kumar suggests using WordPress plugins.

The post examines a variety of different WordPress plugins to help with social bookmarking for your blog.

Extra Point—Social Bookmarking for Business

I'll show you the *Helium.com best social bookmarketing websites for businesses (G),* promises Murray Lunn:

> Social bookmarking is not only a tool to help others find content on the Web without having to hunt it down; it can be a powerful way for business owners to build backlinks and traffic to their websites.
>
> Using social bookmarking sites not only help you gain backlinks, but it can be a powerful way to send waves of traffic if you reach enough influence.

And ultimately, he says, this will help your business to be more successful.

Lunn says social bookmarking sites allow businesses to make a profile, share their own content, share other content, and build friends within the community.

His favorites for business include: Digg.com; Reddit.com; Delicious; Yahoo Buzz; StumbleUpon; Mixx ("Mixx doesn't get a lot of light, but it's still a great site to submit your content, engage the community and send visitors your way); Slashdot, and Newsvine.

MAKING YOUR PRACTICE PERFECT

Some tasks that will help you understand the ideas and concepts talked about in Part V.

Exercise 1: Try out the Google AdWords Tool. Load it up with keywords related to your business and see what you can learn. What are the most competitive keywords? What do you have the best chance of ranking for? Test different keyword phrases, short tail vs. long tail, and see what you come up with. The AdWords Tool is a free way to determine search traffic and figure out what keywords you should target for your SEO and SEM efforts.

Exercise 2: Write a search engine optimized paragraph (minimum 75 words) and body content for a web page. You can never get enough practice because each one is different. Choose two short-tail phrases (1 to 3 words) and three long-tail phrases (more than 3 words). The most important thing to remember is that you're writing for humans AND search engines. You need to get your key phrases as close to the front or top of the content as possible, while making the sentences flow well for the people reading it.

Exercise 3: Write four search engine-optimized H1 Tags or Title Tags (maximum 70 characters). This is the text you see at the top of your browser window, above the URL. Every page of a website has its own H1 Tag, so try to optimize each one for different one- or two-word key phrases. You want to lead with the most important targeted keywords up front, these should not be complete sentences. See: *Seomoz.org/learn-seo/title-tag (G)*.

Exercise 4: Write two meta descriptions (about 150 to 160 characters). A Meta Description is a short summary of what an individual web page is about. Search engines use these to determine what that page is about, and often display them in search results. While you do want to use key phrases again, these are more advertising messages to users; you're trying to draw them in and convince them your page has what they want. See: *Seomoz.org/learn-seo/meta-description (G)*.

Exercise 5: Take your original search engine optimized paragraph from #1 above and apply internal linking for SEO purposes. Find your five key phrases (the short-tail and long-tail) and link each one to another page within the same website. Every page of your website should use keyword links to point to other pages within the site. This is the making of a good internal link structure.

Exercise 6: Join some social bookmarking sites. Try at least surfing around on Delicious, Digg, and StumbleUpon. Save some articles and give others a thumb's up for vote or comment. See how this works. You will be amazed at how sites like StumbleUpon can drive traffic to your websites. In fact, we find that Stumble is a main traffic driver to websites after social media sites like Facebook, LinkedIn, and Twitter. Make social bookmarking part of your SEO and traffic-driving efforts and you could reap the rewards.

POST SCRIPT

The resources cited in this book can be found on the publicly accessible websites we have identified. We've written the Google search lines in a way that normally will allow you to find the referenced resource at the top of the list.

Googling directly to these resources will help you get maximum value out of this book. And once you google the phrase, don't just settle for the resource we are providing. Do some of your own digging.

We owe a great debt of gratitude to the various individuals, publishers, and other companies that have made their resources freely available, and we encourage you to appreciate, comment on, and patronize, where appropriate, the writers and online publications that offer your favorite resource online.

We owe a special debt of gratitude to all the students who have participated in our *New Media Driver's License*® Courses and Seminars at Michigan State University. Our students first identified several of the resources we have included in this book.

ABOUT THE AUTHORS

 **Dr. *Richard T. Cole*** *(G)* (http://en.wikipedia.org/wiki/ Richard_T._Cole) is a recognized expert in PR— "organizational-public relationships." He has owned a PR company and other Michigan-based businesses, and served as the press secretary and chief of staff to Michigan Governor James J. Blanchard. He also headed up, at various times, public relations, marketing, strategy and other functions for America's largest nonprofit health plan, and completed his career in health care as chief administrative officer of a nine-hospital academic system in Detroit.

Cole is full professor of public relations at Michigan State University, East Lansing. He recently completed an assignment as a member of the national Knowledge-to-Action Task Force on Child Maltreatment Prevention of the Centers for Disease Control and Prevention, Atlanta.

One constant in Cole's career is that he has always encouraged people—his bosses and employees, his clients, his colleagues, and his students—to understand that organizational-public relationship building and maintaining, and the discipline of marketing, though often compatible, are two separate and distinct disciplines—a theme that he repeats often in this book.

Cole sees the power of social media from the perspective of the great capacity it has to create open dialogue between the management of any organization and its various stakeholders. And in that sense, he sees social media as a route to public relations reaching its potential by helping practitioners adjust organizational behavior to better conform to the values and aspirations of the public upon which the organization depends for survival.

While serving as chairperson of MSU's Department of Advertising & Public Relations, Cole brought Derek Mehraban to MSU to help him develop and teach the New Media Driver's License® Course that provided the inspiration, and much of the material, for this book, and for a course sequence that is distinguishing MSU as a leader in teaching how social media can be used to advance the interests of business and nonprofit organizations.

Cole lives in Haslett, Michigan, with his wife Deborah, a sculptor.

You can stay in touch with Rick at:

http://www.facebook.com/DrRichardCole

http://www.linkedin.com/pub/richard-t-cole/5/30b/a28

Email: DrRichardCole@gmail.com

Derek Mehraban *(G)* is a graduate of Michigan State University and owner of Ingenex Digital Marketing, a full-service digital agency located in Ann Arbor, Michigan. Mehraban is co-creator of the New Media Driver's License® Course and teacher of the course since its inception at MSU in January 2009.

A Crain's (Detroit Business) "40 under 40" award winner, Mehraban is passionate about marketing education. He founded Lunch Ann Arbor Marketing (LA2M), a 501c3 nonprofit, in 2008, and has organized hundreds of programs on a variety of digital marketing topics. Archived presentations are available at http://la2m.org/live.

Mehraban is married to University of Michigan professor Amy Pienta Mehraban, and has "two amazing daughters, Abigail (age 9) and Lucy (age 7), who are both great kids and fabulous swimmers." As those who know him would say, Mehraban is a father first and a businessman and educator second.

Mehraban owes a big debt of thanks to social media for making it easier than ever to stay connected and help others through new media. "And to Dr. Richard Cole, who asked me to help him start the New Media Driver's License® Course and co-author this book you are reading:, Thanks, Rick."

You can stay in touch with Derek on Facebook, LinkedIn, and Twitter, or by reading his blog http://thedigitalbus.com

http://facebook.com/derek.mehraban
http://linkedin.com/in/mehraban
http://twitter.com/mehraban

INDEX

acom **Communications** Order Form

TITLE	PRICE	AMOUNT
_____ *The Social Current,* **Allie Siarto/Richard T. Cole**	$24.95	_____
_____ *Contemporary Direct & Interactive Marketing, 3rd Ed,* **Lisa Spiller/Martin Baier**	$69.95	_____
_____ *Google This: The New Media Driver's License®* **Richard Cole/Derek Mehraban**	$24.95	_____
_____ *Aligned,* **Maurice Parisien**	$19.95	_____
_____ *How to Jump-Start Your Career,* **Robert L. Hemmings**	$19.95	_____
_____ *This Year a Pogo Stick . . . Next Year a Unicycle,* **Jim Kobs**	$19.95	_____
_____ *Professional Selling,* **Bill Jones**	$59.95	_____
_____ *Follow That Customer,* **Egbert Jan van Bel/Ed Sander/Alan Weber**	$39.95	_____
_____ *Internet Marketing,* **Herschell Gordon Lewis**	$19.95	_____
_____ *Reliability Rules,* **Don Schultz/Reg Price**	$34.95	_____
_____ *The Marketing Performance Measurement Toolkit,* **David M. Raab**	$39.95	_____
_____ *Successful E-Mail Marketing Strategies,* **Arthur M. Hughes/Arthur Sweetser**	$49.95	_____
_____ *Managing Your Business Data,* **Theresa Kushner/Maria Villar**	$32.95	_____
_____ *Media Strategy and Planning Workbook,* **DL Dickinson**	$64.95	_____
_____ *Marketing Metrics in Action,* **Laura Patterson**	$24.95	_____
_____ *The IMC Handbook 3rd Edition,* **J. Stephen Kelly/Susan K. Jones**	$49.95	_____
_____ *Print Matters,* **Randall Hines/Robert Lauterborn**	$27.95	_____
_____ *The Business of Database Marketing,* **Richard N. Tooker**	$49.95	_____
_____ *Customer Churn, Retention, and Profitability,* **Arthur Middleton Hughes**	$59.95	_____
_____ *Data-Driven Business Models,* **Alan Weber**	$49.95	_____
_____ *Creative Strategy in Direct & Interactive Marketing, 4th Edition,* **Susan K. Jones**	$49.95	_____
_____ *Branding Iron,* **Charlie Hughes and William Jeanes**	$27.95	_____
_____ *Managing Sales Leads,* **James Obermayer**	$39.95	_____
_____ *Creating the Marketing Experience,* **Joe Marconi**	$49.95	_____
_____ *Brand Babble: Sense & Nonsense about Branding,* **Don E. Schultz/Heidi F. Schultz**	$24.95	_____
_____ *The New Marketing Conversation,* **Donna Baier Stein/Alexandra MacAaron**	$34.95	_____
_____ *Trade Show and Event Marketing,* **Ruth Stevens**	$59.95	_____
_____ *Sales & Marketing 365,* **James Obermayer**	$17.95	_____
_____ *Accountable Marketing,* **Peter J. Rosenwald**	$59.95	_____
_____ *Contemporary Database Marketing, Second Edition* **Lisa Spiller/Kurtis Ruf**	$89.95	_____
_____ *Catalog Strategist's Toolkit,* **Katie Muldoon**	$59.95	_____
_____ *Marketing Convergence,* **Susan K. Jones/Ted Spiegel**	$34.95	_____
_____ *High-Performance Interactive Marketing,* **Christopher Ryan**	$39.95	_____
_____ *The White Paper Marketing Handbook,* **Robert W. Bly**	$39.95	_____
_____ *Business-to-Business Marketing Research,* **Martin Block/Tamara Block**	$69.95	_____
_____ *Hot Appeals or Burnt Offerings,* **Herschell Gordon Lewis**	$24.95	_____
_____ *On the Art of Writing Copy, 4th Edition,* **Herschell Gordon Lewis**	$34.95	_____
_____ *Open Me Now,* **Herschell Gordon Lewis**	$21.95	_____
_____ *Marketing Mayhem,* **Herschell Gordon Lewis**	$39.95	_____
_____ *Asinine Advertising,* **Herschell Gordon Lewis**	$22.95	_____

Name/Title_____

Company _____

Street Address _____

City/State/Zip _____

Email _____ Phone _____

Credit Card: ☐ VISA ☐ MasterCard
☐ American Express ☐ Discover

☐ Check or money order enclosed (payable to Racom
Communications in US dollars drawn on a US bank)

Subtotal	_____
Subtotal from other side	_____
8.65% Tax	_____
Shipping & Handling	_____
$7.00 for first book; $1.00 for each additional book.	
TOTAL	_____

Number _____ Exp. Date _____

Signature _____

Racom Communications, 150 N. Michigan Ave, Suite 2800, Chicago, IL 60601
312-494-0100, 800-247-6553, www. Racombooks.com